Emerging Real-World Applications of Internet of Things

The Internet of things (IoT) is a network of connected physical objects or things that are working along with sensors, wireless transceiver modules, processors, and software required for connecting, processing, and exchanging data among the other devices over the Internet. These objects or things are devices ranging from simple handheld devices to complex industrial heavy machines. A thing in IoT can be any living or non-living object that can be provided capabilities to sense, process, and exchange data over a network. The IoT provides people with the ability to handle their household works to industrial tasks smartly and efficiently without the intervention of another human. The IoT provides smart devices for home automation as well as business solutions for delivering insights into everything from real-time monitoring of working systems to supply chain and logistics operations. The IoT has become one of the most prominent technological inventions of the 21st century.

Due to the versatility of IoT devices, there are numerous real-world applications of the IoT in various domains such as smart home, smart city, health care, agriculture, industry, and transportation. The IoT has emerged as a paradigm-shifting technology that is influencing various industries. Many companies, governments, and civic bodies are shifting to IoT applications to improve their works and to become more efficient. The world is slowly transforming toward a "smart world" with smart devices. As a consequence, it shows many new opportunities coming up in the near "smart" future for IoT professionals. Therefore, there is a need to keep track of advancements related to IoT applications and further investigate several research challenges related to the applicability of IoT in different domains to make it more adaptable for practical and industrial use. With this goal, this book provides the most recent and prominent applications of IoT in different domains as well as issues and challenges in developing IoT applications for various new domains.

Emerging Real-World Applications of Internet of Things

Edited by
Anshul Verma
Pradeepika Verma
Yousef Farhaoui
Zhihan Lv

CRC Press
Taylor & Francis Group
Boca Raton London New York

CRC Press is an imprint of the
Taylor & Francis Group, an **informa** business

First edition published 2023
by CRC Press
6000 Broken Sound Parkway NW, Suite 300, Boca Raton, FL 33487-2742

and by CRC Press
4 Park Square, Milton Park, Abingdon, Oxon, OX14 4RN

ISBN: 978-1-032-30260-7 (hbk)
ISBN: 978-1-032-30261-4 (pbk)
ISBN: 978-1-003-30420-3 (ebk)

DOI: 10.1201/9781003304203

Typeset in Sabon
by codeMantra

Contents

Preface

OVERVIEW AND GOALS

The Internet of things (IoT) is a network of connected physical objects or things that are working along with sensors, wireless transceiver modules, processors, and software required for connecting, processing, and exchanging data among the other devices over the Internet. The name "Internet of things" was given by the British visionary Kevin Ashton, in 1999. These objects or things are devices ranging from simple handheld devices to complex industrial heavy machines. A thing in IoT can be a person with a hand watch having heart beats monitoring capability, a dog with a collar transponder for location monitoring, a car with sensors to activate automatic brake when car is about to hit some objects, or any living and non-living object that can be provided capabilities to process and exchange data over a network. The IoT provides people with the ability to handle their household works to industrial tasks smartly and efficiently without the intervention of human. The IoT provides smart devices for home automation as well as business solutions for delivering insights into everything from real-time monitoring of the working system to supply chain and logistics operations. The IoT has become one of the most prominent technological inventions of the 21st century. The total number of installed IoT devices is nearly 13.8 billion in 2021, and it is expected that the number of IoT devices will reach 30.9 billion by 2025.

Due to the versatility of IoT devices, there are numerous real-world applications of the IoT in various domains such as smart home, smart city, health care, agriculture, industry, and transportation. For example, smart homes have smart thermostats, smart appliances, and connected heating, lighting, and electronic devices that can be controlled remotely by computers and smartphones at the ease of owner. In health care, the IoT offers many applications, including monitoring patients more closely by analyzing the data gathered by wearable devices. The IoT has emerged as a paradigm-shifting technology that is influencing various industries. Many companies, governments, and civic bodies are shifting to IoT applications to improve their works and to become more efficient. The world is slowly transforming toward a "smart world" with smart devices. As a consequence, it shows many new opportunities coming up in the near "smart" future for IoT professionals. Therefore, there is a need to keep track of advancements related to IoT applications and further investigate several research challenges related to applicability of IoT in different domains, to make it more adaptable for practical and industrial use. With this goal, the book will provide most recent and prominent applications of IoT in different domains as well as issues and challenges in developing IoT applications for various new domains.

Below are some of the important features of this book, which, we believe, would make it a valuable resource for our readers:

- This book is designed, in structure and content, with the intention of making the book useful at all learning levels.
- Most of the chapters of the book are authored by prominent academicians, researchers, and practitioners, with solid experience and exposure to research in the IoT. These contributors have been working in this area for many years and have a thorough understanding of the concepts and practical applications.
- The authors of chapters of this book are distributed in a large number of countries, and most of them are affiliated with institutions of worldwide reputation. This gives this book an international flavor.
- The authors of each chapter have attempted to provide a comprehensive bibliography section, which should greatly help the readers interested in further digging into the aforementioned research area.
- Throughout the chapters of this book, most of the core research topics have been covered, making the book particularly useful for industry practitioners working directly with the practical aspects behind enabling the technologies in the field.

We have attempted to make the different chapters of the book look as much coherent and synchronized as possible.

TARGET AUDIENCE

This book will be beneficial for academicians, researchers, developers, engineers, and practitioners working in or interested in the fields related to IoT, wireless sensor networks, mobile ad hoc networks, and ubiquitous computing. This book is expected to serve as a reference book for developers and engineers working in the IoT domain and for a graduate/postgraduate course in computer science and engineering/information technology/electronics and communication engineering.

Acknowledgments

We are extremely thankful to the authors of the 12 chapters of this book, who have worked very hard to bring this unique resource forward for helping the students, researchers, and community practitioners. We feel that it is contextual to mention that as the individual chapters of this book are written by different authors, the responsibility of the contents of each of the chapters lies with the concerned authors.

We like to thank Randi Cohen, Publisher, Computer Science and IT, and Gabriella Williams, Editor, IT – Security, Networking and Communication, CRC Press, Taylor & Francis Group, who worked with us on the project from the beginning, for their professionalism. We also thank Daniel Kershaw, Senior Editorial Assistant, CRC Press, Taylor & Francis Group, and his team members who tirelessly worked with us and helped us in the publication process.

This book is a part of the research work funded by "Seed Grant to Faculty Members under IoE Scheme (under Dev. Scheme No. 6031)" awarded to Anshul Verma at Banaras Hindu University, Varanasi, India, and "DST-Science and Engineering Research Board (SERB), Government of India (File no. PDF/2020/001646)" awarded to Pradeepika Verma at Indian Institute of Technology (BHU), Varanasi, India.

Editors

Anshul Verma, PhD, earned MTech and PhD degrees in computer science and engineering from ABV-Indian Institute of Information Technology and Management Gwalior, India, in 2011 and 2016, respectively. He has done postdoctorate in Computer Science and Engineering from Indian Institute of Technology Kharagpur, India, in 2017. Currently, he is an Assistant Professor in the Department of Computer Science, Institute of Science, Banaras Hindu University, Varanasi, India. He has also served as a faculty in Computer Science and Engineering at Motilal Nehru National Institute of Technology (MNNIT) Allahabad and National Institute of Technology (NIT) Jamshedpur, India, from 2015 to 2017. His research interests include mobile ad hoc networks, Internet of things, distributed systems, and formal methods. He has participated as an advisory board member, session chair, and program committee member in many conferences, and he is serving as an editorial board member in many journals. He is serving as the Editor of *Journal of Scientific Research of the Banaras Hindu University* Varanasi, India.

Pradeepika Verma, PhD, earned a PhD degree in computer science and engineering from Indian Institute of Technology (ISM) Dhanbad, India, in 2020. She earned an MTech in computer science and engineering from Banasthali University, Rajasthan, India, in 2013. She has done post-doctorate in Computer Science and Engineering from Indian Institute of Technology (BHU), Varanasi, India in 2022.

Currently, she is working as a Faculty Fellow at Technology Innovation Hub, Indian Institute of Technology, Patna, India. She is also an Associate Professor in the Department of Computer Science at K L Deemed to Be University, Andhra Pradesh, India. Prior to this, she was an Assistant Professor in the Department of Computer Science and Engineering at Pranveer Singh Institute of Technology, Kanpur, India, and a Faculty member in the Department of Computer Application at the Institute of Engineering and Technology, Lucknow, India. Her research interests include Internet of things, natural language processing, optimization approaches, and information retrieval.

Yousef Farhaoui, PhD, is an Associate Professor at Moulay Ismail University, Faculty of Sciences and Techniques, Morocco. He is also a Chair of the IDMS Team, Director of STI Laboratory, Local Publishing and Research Coordinator, Cambridge International Academics in the UK. He earned a PhD in computer security from Ibn Zohr University of Science. His research interests include Internet of things, e-learning, computer security, big data analytics, and business intelligence. Dr. Farhaoui has three books in computer science. He is a coordinator and member of the organizing committee and also a member of the scientific committee of several international congresses and is a member of various international associations. He has authored six books and many book chapters with reputed publishers, such as Springer and IGI. He has served as a Reviewer for IEEE, IET, Springer, Inderscience, and Elsevier journals. He is also the Guest Editor of many journals with Wiley, Springer, Inderscience, etc. He has been the General Chair, Session Chair, and Panelist at several conferences. He is a Senior Member of IEEE, IET, ACM, and EAI Research Group.

Zhihan Lv, PhD, is an Associate Professor at Uppsala University in Sweden. From 2017 to 2021, he was an Associate Professor at Qingdao University in Qingdao of China. From 2012 to 2016, he was an Adjunct Assistant Professor at Shenzhen Institutes of Advanced Technology, Chinese Academy of Science in Shenzhen of China. He earned a PhD in computer applied technology from Ocean University of China in Qingdao of China, supervised by Prof. Ge Chen. Before that, he enjoyed sixteen months full-time research experience at the French National Centre for Scientific Research (CNRS)-UPR9080 in Paris, supervised by Dr. Marc Baaden, while he was a visiting PhD student at the University of Paris. He has fulfilled a two-year postdoc research experience at Umea University and has a short invited teaching experience at KTH Royal Institute of Technology in Stockholm, Sweden, supervised by Prof. Haibo Li. From 2014 to 2015, he was a Marie Curie Experienced Researcher in the European Union's Seventh Framework Lanpercept, at clinical section Fundación FIVAN in Valencia of Spain. From 2015 to 2017, he was a Research Associate at Virtual Environments and Computer Graphics (VECG) group at University College London (UCL), supervised by Prof. Anthony Steed. In 2018, he joined Event Lab at the University of Barcelona, supervised by Prof. Mel Slater. He is an IEEE Senior Member, BCS Fellow, and ACM Distinguished Speaker.

Contributors

Younes Abrouki
Laboratory of Spectroscopy,
    Molecular Modeling, Materials,
    Nanomaterials, Water and
    Environment (CERNE2D)
Faculty of Science
Mohammed V University in Rabat
Rabat, Morocco

Abdullah Alsalemi
Institute of Artificial Intelligence
De Montfort University
Leicester, United Kingdom

Abbes Amira
Department of Computer Science
University of Sharjah
Sharjah, United Arab Emirates
and
Institute of Artificial Intelligence
De Montfort University
Leicester, United Kingdom

Mourade Azrour
Faculty of Sciences and Techniques
Department of Computer Science
Moulay Ismail University
Errachidia, Morocco

Faycal Bensaali
Department of Electrical
    Engineering
Qatar University
Doha, Qatar

Aishwarya Dhatrak
School of Computer Science
University of Auckland
Auckland, New Zealand

Yassine Himeur
Department of Electrical
    Engineering
Qatar University
Doha, Qatar

Ramón O. Jiménez Betancourt
University of Colima
Colima, Mexico

Kegong Diao
Institute of Energy and Sustainable
    Development
De Montfort University
Leicester, United Kingdom

Nathan Eggers
East Tennessee State University
Johnson City, Tennessee, USA

Ghizlane Fattah
Water Treatment and Reuse
   Structure, Civil Hydraulic and
   Environmental Engineering
   Laboratory
Mohammadia School of Engineers
Mohammed V University in Rabat
Rabat, Morocco

Ramachandra Reddy Gadi
Ensar Solutions
Hyderabad, India

Mingwei Gong
Department of Mathematics and
   Computing
Mount Royal University
Calgary, Canada

Souad El Hajjaji
Laboratory of Spectroscopy,
   Molecular Modeling, Materials,
   Nanomaterials, Water and
   Environment (CERNE2D)
Faculty of Science
Mohammed V University in Rabat
Rabat, Morocco

Juan M. González López
University of Colima
Colima, Mexico

Pushpika Aroshana Hettiarachchi
School of Engineering
Deakin University
Geelong, Victoria, Australia

Shama Naz Islam
School of Engineering
Deakin University
Geelong, Victoria, Australia

Mohammad S. Khan
East Tennessee State University
Johnson City, Tennessee, USA

Siham Kherraf
Laboratory of Spectroscopy,
   Molecular Modeling, Materials,
   Nanomaterials, Water and
   Environment (CERNE2D)
Faculty of Science
Mohammed V University in Rabat
Rabat, Morocco

Efrain Villalvazo Laureano
University of Colima
Colima, Mexico

Jamal Mabrouki
Laboratory of Spectroscopy,
   Molecular Modeling, Materials,
   Nanomaterials, Water and
   Environment (CERNE2D)
Faculty of Science
Mohammed V University in Rabat
Rabat, Morocco

Aniket Mahanti
School of Computer Science
University of Auckland
Auckland, New Zealand
and
Faculty of Computer Science
University of New Brunswick
Saint John, New Brunswick,
   Canada

Hossein Malekmohamadi
Institute of Artificial Intelligence
De Montfort University
Leicester, United Kingdom

Anmar S. Mora Martínez
University of Colima
Colima, Mexico

Ashish Kumar Mishra
Department of Information
   Technology
Rajkiya Engineering College
Ambedkar Nagar, India

Ranesh Naha
School of Computer Science
University of Adelaide
Adelaide, South Australia,
    Australia

Quoc-Dung Ngo
Faculty of Information Technology
Posts and Telecommunications
Institute of Technology
Hanoi, Vietnam

Huy-Trung Nguyen
Department of Cyber Security
Vietnam Ministry of Public
    Security
and
Faculty of Information Security
People's Security Academy
Hanoi, Vietnam

Brijesh Pandey
Computer Science and Engineering
    Department
Goel Institute of Technology and
    Management
Dr. A.P.J. Abdul Kalam Technical
    University
Lucknow, India

Mahima Shanker Pandey
Computer Science and Engineering
    Department
Institute of Engineering and
    Technology (IET)
Lucknow, India

Joshua D. Reichard
American Centre for Religion/
    Society Studies (ACRSS)
Omega Graduate School
Dayton, Tennessee, USA

Shivam Sakshi
Vellore Institute of Technology
Vellore, India

Aya Sayed
Department of Electrical
    Engineering
Qatar University
Doha, Qatar

Durgesh Tiwari
Computer Science and Engineering
    Department
Goel Institute of Technology and
    Management
Dr. A.P.J. Abdul Kalam Technical
    University
Lucknow, India

Daniel A. Verde Romero
University of Colima
Colima, Mexico

Arun Yadav
Goel Institute of Higher Studies
    Mahavidyalaya
Ajgain, India

Kei Au Yeung
School of Computer Science
University of Auckland
Auckland, New Zealand

Sherali Zeadally
University of Kentucky
Lexington, Kentucky, USA

Chapter 1

Secure IoT data using blockchain

Aishwarya Dhatrak
University of Auckland

Mingwei Gong
Mount Royal University

Ranesh Naha
University of Adelaide

Aniket Mahanti
University of Auckland

University of New Brunswick

CONTENTS

DOI: 10.1201/9781003304203-1

1

ABSTRACT

Internet of things (IoT) is a network of physical objects with embedded systems that are able to communicate with each other via the Internet. It leads to a distributed network of devices that can communicate with humans and objects. The implementation of IoT will provide benefits, but it also raises security issues that affect data integrity and privacy of the companies. In order to overcome security issues, blockchain technology is used. This chapter is based on up-to-date research on the blockchain as well as IoT with the purpose of studying the blockchain as potential solutions to secure IoT data. Both blockchain and IoT are new research areas into existing research, which support the use of a qualitative research method. The results indicate that blockchain is used to secure data management, but it is not a complete solution. Most of the security issues are related to devices, and blockchain technology handles information and secures identities, stock traceability and transactions, which are made without human interaction and with automated storage management. There are still some barriers to creating benefits work into reality. This chapter is focused on investigating the integration of IoT and blockchain to analyze and improve security issues.

1.1 INTRODUCTION

The blockchain is a distributed ledger technology gaining attention in areas beyond cryptocurrency roots since more or less 2014. In this chapter, the main focus should be on security on IoT and how blockchain can be the solution to it. In IoT context, security is a primary challenge and blockchain is a way to secure IoT. Park et al. [24] defined that IoT is the interconnection via the Internet of the computing devices embedded into objects, which enables them to send as well as receive data. Malviya [19] stated that blockchain is an encrypted and distributed filing system designed to permit the creation of real-time records. The security issues are the most compelling reasons for using blockchain technology in organization. At present, failure to IoT system exposed to various devices, amount of highly personal data and supply chain partners. The security flaws revolve around three areas such as authentication, transaction and connection. By use of the blockchain technology, it is required to manage access to the data from the IoT devices.

Hassan, Aslam and Jang [14] analyzed and reported that IoT adoption continues to increase, with analysts forecasting nearly $15 trillion investment in IoT by the year 2025. Seventy-four percent of the respondents have adopted these technologies and claimed that digital transformation is not possible without it. The blockchain model is based on cryptographically protected; furthermore, distributed ledger technology could improve IoT frameworks with automatic optimization of resources in addition to safety. The blockchain-enabled IoT deployment improves the overall data integrity by allowing the IoT devices to validate themselves against the network. Novo [22] concluded that applying blockchain model to IoT could solve the real-world digital business-related challenges. A new type of blockchain platform that can be involved in IoT deployment is required, with capabilities that can extend beyond the conventional models.

The IoT and blockchain are two topics that caused a great deal of excitement in the field of technology and the wider business world. This topic has been selected to gain more knowledge and skills related to blockchain technology. Various benefits can be attributed to the idea of building smart machines that are able to interact and function via blockchain technology. With the use of encryption, the data can be trusted by the parties involving in the supply chain [22]. This topic is selected for the research as blockchain is offering prospects of improving the overall security of IoT environment. The data that are generated by IoT are personal, as the smart devices have access to important details about the daily life of users. Allowing access to the data from the IoT devices to manage throughout blockchain would need an additional layer of security. It is sometimes possible that blockchain, as well as IoT convergence, would become necessity at some point. Both blockchain and IoT technologies have become a promise to be kept in the existing world [13]. A combination of both the technologies would minimize security risks that are caused due to technological changes.

1.2 RESEARCH MOTIVATION

The information system's trustworthiness problem is critical when there is no tracking of data alteration and an audit mechanism is applied to deal with sensitive transaction information in financial institutions. As a solution to security challenges, this paper evaluates the concept of Bitcoin as virtual cryptocurrency sustains value without maintaining by the financial entity [23]. The blockchain is such a mechanism that allows the transactions to verify a group of unreliable actors. Operational issues are also considered when the blockchain solution is taken as part of an existing business. The securities, as well as privacy policies, are based on encryption, which is difficult to implement into IoT environment. Even though the blockchain technology can solve those problems, it also faces critical challenges for application into IoT environment. IoT networks are predicted to include a more substantial number of nodes as well as a rapidly increasing rate such that blockchain technology scales poorly as there is an increase in the number of nodes into network [24]. These technology protocols create network traffic flow that is becoming a disaster for communication in IoT devices. The main role of this paper is to suggest blockchain technology for IoT entities. The performance of this method is adequately analyzed.

1.3 RELATED WORK

Zhang and Jiangtao Wen [32] stated that blockchain technology is a revolution into the system for records. This technology is still quite early in development, and use cases are hypothetical. The most important application of blockchain technology is Bitcoin; it is a virtual currency implemented in the year 2009 that introduced blockchain technology. Novo [22] argued that blockchain is a data structure. This term is used to refer to a social phenomenon. The other names that is suggested to blockchain is digital ledger system. The technology uses a database structure that can be modified by various parties at the same time and corrects state. While there are challenges in blockchain technology, still it is introduced as a solution to problems. It is required to understand the type of blockchain applications, but it is not the scope of the study.

This section is focused on security on IoT and how blockchain can be the solution to it. The study describes the characteristics and features of blockchain technology. It identifies different ways to integrate IoT with blockchain technology. There are various benefits in the financial service industry due to the adoption of blockchain in IoT. Mainly, there are security challenges in the industry, and therefore, blockchain can be a solution to that problem. Blockchain-IoT applications are reviewed in this chapter.

Blockchain can be described as a decentralized technology that makes use of a worldwide network of computers for the supervision of the database of records. According to Zheng et al. [33], blockchain has excellent credibility for the construction of prospect Internet system. The blockchain is a decentralized technology by nature. It stores a growing list of records, which are termed as blocks. These blocks of data are linked together to form a chain of records, which is termed as blockchain. The blocks of data are linked together with the help of cryptography to ensure secure data connection. Blockchain enables entry of a record of information in the blockchain network, which is controlled by a community of users [9]. The blockchain is, therefore, an undeniably ingenious invention. A closer look at the architecture of blockchain reveals that a blockchain network consists of a constant sequence of blocks that are linked together.

Each block in a blockchain network has a parent block with which it is linked. The first block of the blockchain network is called a genesis block as it does not comprise any parent block. A block header in a blockchain possesses block version, Merkle tree, timestamp, nBits and nonce in addition to parent block. The block body of blockchain is composed of a transaction counter along with a number of contacts [4]. The blocks in a blockchain network are linked together with asymmetric cryptography, and each transaction in a blockchain is validated by asymmetric cryptography. The transactions in an untrustworthy environment are validated by the use of the digital signature.

Decentralization is one of the key characteristics of blockchain technology [33]. Unlike conventional and centralized transaction system, where each transaction is required to be authenticated by an expected agency, there is no need of a third party in the blockchain.

Persistency is another feature of a blockchain network. Transactions can be validated quickly in blockchain as it is basically impractical to roll back a transaction in blockchain [30]. The data persistence feature of the blockchain, therefore, enables rapid identification of an unacceptable transaction.

Immutability is of the best features of the blockchain. Blockchains are designed to be immutable. A block, once written to a blockchain, cannot be changed. One cannot add, edit or delete the block once entered in a blockchain.

The above-discussed points represent the main features of blockchain technology. There are a number of applications of blockchain technology, which include Bitcoin and smart contract Ethereum and so on. The technology of blockchain can be integrated with IoT to increase the security of the same [20]. There are a number of ways for the integration of IoT and blockchain, which are needed to be identified.

1.4 BLOCKCHAIN AND IoT

1.4.1 Integration of IoT and blockchain

Internet of things or IoT is a network of physical devices or home appliances that are embedded with electronics enabling appropriate data exchange. The applications of IoT are distributed in nature similar to the blockchain technology, and therefore, it can be integrated with blockchain to achieve better security [34] (Figure 1.1).

This is possible since blockchain is designed on the basis of the applications that are associated with transactions and interactions. Interaction is essential for IoT devices, and therefore, the possibility of integration of blockchain with IoT should be evaluated. This is needed since the technology of blockchain is able to improve the security, cost efficiency and

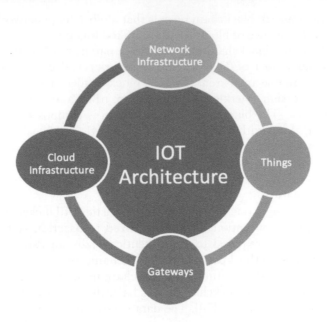

Figure 1.1 IoT architecture.

features of the blockchain. IBM has already been implementing this technology, and it has extended its private blockchain network into its cognitive IoT. Thus, it is possible that the integration of IoT with blockchain will prove beneficial across the industries. There are a number of reasons for the need for the addition of IoT with blockchain. One of the main reasons for the need for the integration of IoT with blockchain is that the use of IoT has been increasing in recent years [31]. According to the research report of Gartner, there have been around 8 billion connected devices across the world. Majority of the devices include consumer-grade electronics, including smart home technology. However, ensuring security in the IoT devices is necessary as one of the main concerns associated with the blockchain technology is its security. The urgency of finding a viable solution to ensuring security in IoT gives rise to the need for a combination of IoT and blockchain. The architecture of blockchain is the main reason behind its security. Each blockchain wallet is ruled by the use of private and public keys, and every message in the transaction is encrypted. This increases the security of blockchain. There is an increasing need to secure IoT devices since IoT defines the infrastructure of the organization [1]. The fundamental flaws of unsecured IoT devices can be eliminated with its integration with blockchain, which is a distributed digital ledger and is secure as well. The need for security of the IoT devices resides in the fact that IoT has been converting more and more offline assets online (Figure 1.2).

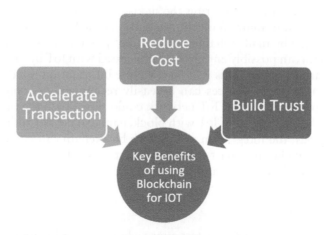

Figure 1.2 Benefits of integrating IoT and blockchain.

Another reason behind the need for the integration of IoT with blockchain lies in the fact that IoT is needed to be fast and reliable [10]. For that, the IoT needs to expand its capabilities for ensuring fast and reliable connection all the times. This can easily be achieved by integrating the same with the blockchain platform. Thus, in a number of ways, the blockchain and IoT are found to be perfect. Two of the most widely used applications of blockchain include a transaction of cryptocurrency and smart contract. The embedded smart contract and its decentralization nature can be a solution to the security problems associated with the use of IoT. Furthermore, the use of blockchain can undoubtedly ensure continual connectivity that is needed for providing the services. Currently, the technology of blockchain is segregated among a number of companies and platforms. Developing a connection between the blockchain and IoT will allow efficient use of IoT devices. IoT and blockchain are growing together, and therefore, the collaboration of IoT and blockchain will be advantageous. IoT mostly needs the features of blockchain so that the IoT services can be improved. There are a number of ways by which the technology of blockchain can be integrated with IoT.

1.4.2 Ways of integration of IoT with blockchain

The integration of IoT with the cloud has been proven to be priceless. However, the integration of blockchain and IoT can provide a number of advantages apart from security. Dorri [11] argued that these advantages or benefits include decentralization and scalability. This is removing the central points, failures and bottlenecks. The integration of IoT with blockchain will further help the participants of the IoT in easy identification of the different devices in the blockchain. The use of blockchain in IoT will furthermore help in empowering the next-generation application features in IoT, such as autonomy. With the integration of IoT and blockchain, each transaction can be made reliable, which is not possible as of now.

Blockchain can possibly enrich or be integrated with IoT by making use of trusted sharing service. This will increase the information reliability. With this integration, data sources can be easily recognized at some instance. Data leak in any part of an IoT network could slow down the process, and therefore, the integration of IoT with blockchain can help in addressing this problem. Thus, the integration of IoT with blockchain can be beneficial in certain areas including smart cities and smart cars. The three ways of integrating IoT and blockchain are as follows.

1.4.2.1 IoT-IoT

This approach is one of the fastest approaches of a combination of IoT and blockchain. This will make the IoT devices able to communicate with each other. In this approach, only the elements of the chosen IoT data are accumulated in the blockchain, while the interactions between the different devices of the blockchain network can take place without making use of blockchain technology [26]. This approach of integration of IoT with blockchain can only work in case of presence of reliable IoT data. Furthermore, to ensure that this interaction works, the IoT interaction should take place with low latency.

1.4.2.2 IoT-blockchain

Swan [28] stated that in this approach of integration of IoT and blockchain, all interactions associated with blockchain network can go through blockchain that will enable a permanent record of interactions. This can be considered as the most viable option for the integration of IoT and blockchain. This is possible because this approach of integration will rightly ensure that all the interactions in IoT are traceable. However, there are definite issues connected with the recording of all the interactions in the blockchain as it will need an increase in the bandwidth with increasing data. If this approach of combining IoT and blockchain is chosen, the transaction data are needed to be stocked up in the blockchain network.

1.4.2.3 Hybrid approach

This is another approach for the integration of IoT and blockchain. In this approach, only a part of the interactions between IoT devices will take place via blockchain, while the rest can directly happen between the IoT devices present in the network. One of the issues related to the choice of this approach for the amalgamation of IoT with blockchain is that it is difficult to choose which transactions should go to blockchain and which transaction should not [5]. However, making use of this approach is considered the best for the integration of both of the technologies since it allows leveraging of the blockchain technology along with the use of real-time IoT interactions. In this approach of combination of IoT and blockchain, the employment of fog computing can certainly help in addressing the limitations associated with blockchain and IoT.

However, in a typical IoT deployment, incomplete resource devices are used to send notes. Ouaddah et al. [13] expressed that endnotes are used to converse with a gateway accountable for forwarding the messages. If IoT can be integrated with blockchain, the endnotes will have to communicate with blockchain. This will help in integrating the cryptographic functionalities with IoT, thus achieving the desired results. Thus, these three approaches can be used for the integration of IoT with blockchain. However, there are certain challenges associated with the integration of IoT and blockchain, which is needed to be addressed.

1.4.3 Challenges in blockchain-IoT integration

The main challenges that are associated with IoT-blockchain integration must be addressed for secure deployment. The integration of blockchain with IoT is not trivial. Since the blockchain transactions are digitally signed, there are not many issues associated with the technology [15]. However, the integration of IoT with blockchain is challenging. Certain challenges that can possibly affect the integration of IoT with blockchain are as follows.

1.4.3.1 Storage capacity and scalability

The storage capacity of a blockchain network is under debate. The limitation of capacity and scalability can make the technology of blockchain unsuitable for IoT applications. However, there are certain processes by which these limits can be eliminated. The blockchain is not designed for storing a large amount of data. The integration of IoT with blockchain might require extra storage space. Thus, the integration of blockchain with IoT should deal with these challenges.

1.4.3.2 Security

The applications in IoT might need to deal with specific security problems at different levels. Liao et al. [14] discussed that the integration of IoT with blockchain, therefore, might result in an increase in risks in the blockchain. With the increase in the number of attacks in the IoT network, blockchain can be an explanation to the problems. One of the processes that increase data security in blockchain is that the data quality is checked before a transaction is entered into blockchain [8]. However, the reliability of the data gained from IoT cannot be guaranteed. It is the capability of blockchain to identify the immutable data. In case of corrupted data entering into the blockchain system, the data will remain corrupted throughout. Thus, it is a significant issue associated with the integration of IoT with blockchain, and thus, it needs to be addressed.

1.4.3.3 Anonymity and data privacy

IoT applications mainly work with private data, and therefore, the integration should also tackle the problem associated with data privacy and anonymity [5]. The problem associated with the preservation of privacy is that the data privacy in public blockchain is needed to be analyzed. The problems associated with ensuring the privacy of data in the blockchain make it more challenging to integrate IoT and blockchain.

1.4.3.4 Legal issues

Unregulated blockchain gives rise to specific legal issues. Thus, the integration of IoT with blockchain can involve specific legal issues as well. With most of the existing laws becoming obsolete, the lack of regulation can act as a significant disadvantage of integration of IoT and blockchain [17]. The legal regulations are therefore expected to have an authority on the integration of blockchain and IoT, and therefore, this challenge needs to be addressed as well.

However, the integration of IoT and blockchain can offer a number of benefits [7]. One of them is the increased security and speed of IoT devices. The interactions between the IoT devices will be improved by following these processes, which is a significant advantage of this process.

1.4.4 Benefits of Integration of blockchain with IoT

The reason behind the need for the integration of IoT with blockchain needs to be evaluated. There are a number of reasons behind the anticipation of integration of the technology of blockchain with IoT.

Decentralization is one of the significant benefits of integration of IoT with blockchain. With the integration of IoT and blockchain, a bulk of the participants in IoT must verify the transactions. In blockchain, a single authority cannot approve the transactions. The integration of IoT and blockchain will help in achieving decentralization.

The integration of the blockchain technology with IoT will ensure faster processing power and less time consumption. In an IoT network, a number of devices with different computing capabilities are present. The integration of all the IoT devices with blockchain will enable easier data processing, thereby reducing the computational time [9]. However, many of the IoT devices may not work according to the computational power of blockchain, which might be an issue. The integration of IoT with blockchain is expected to improve the reliability of the data that are being stored or processed in an IoT network. This can be achieved mainly because of the fact that blockchain ensures data quality check before storing data in a network. This is an advantage as it will help in evaluating the data authenticity.

With the integration of IoT and blockchain, it is possible to deploy the IoT network securely. This can be achieved by making use of the secure and immutable storage offered by the blockchain network [17]. The increase in the traceability of each of the IoT devices is another significant advantage of the integration of IoT with blockchain. This is possible since the participants in a blockchain network can easily identify every single device.

1.4.5 Blockchain platforms for IoT

The blockchain platforms, as well as applications, emerge from diverse areas due to the benefits of blockchain technology. This section analyzes blockchain applications and platforms. The blockchain technology is recognized as a disruptive technology that affects the financial services industry. The total number of platforms is so high, and with regular changes, it is not possible to analyze every platform sufficiently [1]. Bitcoin is a cryptocurrency and blockchain platform that provides a method to conduct monetary transactions in a reliable way that is included into applications as a protected payment system.

Based on IoT domain, the automated devices use Bitcoin to perform micropayments. Smart contracts are such a solution that is required at the time of integration of blockchain with IoT. The financial service sector is offering use cases for the blockchain technology, although the application is proliferating in other industries. Dorri et al. [11] stated that there are a number of areas where the company uses blockchain applications for financial services. The applications are used in domestic as well as international fund transfers. In finance, there is an emergence of alternative cryptocurrency, which builds a new market and furthermore facilitates new forms of payments. The new market leads to the creation of new applications for payment, swapover as well as trading infrastructures for new currencies. Malviya [19] argued that blockchain could increase the autonomy of the devices as it is easier to interact and coordinate by offering distributed open ledger where IoT devices have trusted information. Aigang is used for insurance network for IoT assets. This application has created a custom virtual currency. It offers investment chances in various goods with various risk points. The smart contracts are connected intelligent devices with assurance policies. With the addition of Oracles to the account events, the claim handling is performed mechanically.

MyBit is planned to construct an ecosystem for the services where IoT assets are owned by people and revenues are to be shared. Within the IoT devices, it generates income and the investors will receive the profit split equivalent to possession stake. Hassan, Aslam and Jang [14] discussed that smart contract is accountable for controlling and updating the IoT platform. This platform defines various asset types in addition to IoT devices connected to the assets; once installed, it is sent along with request information through the use of API. Oracles are used for the connection of devices to the network. The blockchain of things is provided with a secured open communication platform for industrial IoT integrations. Swan [28] reported that it was proposed by Catenis, a web service layer for the paid integration of blockchain technology with end-to-end encryption. In Catenis, IoT devices are represented as a virtual device into gateways. Each of the virtual devices is managed by a host of Catenis services for IoT devices. Those blockchain-IoT applications are examined to complete this research study, and a complete overview of interaction between blockchain technology and IoT paradigm is offered. The blockchain ledger is provided security to the Internet of things. With billions of devices linked together, the cybersecurity experts are worried about how the distributed information system can stay secure. Huh [15] discussed that the blockchain ledger system ensures that the information is established as well as unconfined to the trusted parties. This system is a management platform for examining a variety of amounts of data.

This section summarizes that blockchain is a decentralized way to record a list of digital transactions. It is best known as digital currencies such as Bitcoin. This currency is valued even higher than ever before. Due to the use of advanced technology, there are many challenges in the industry, but the integration of blockchain can overcome these security challenges. Because of the increase in the number of attacks in the IoT network, the data security in blockchain has to be increased by performing data quality check. The integration of IoT with blockchain is expected to improve the reliability of the data. It is possible to deploy the IoT network securely. It addresses the challenges which are associated with the protection of privacy. Decentralization is a benefit of integrating IoT and the blockchain technology. The integration of this particular technology ensures faster processing and saves time.

1.5 BLOCKCHAIN AS A SOLUTION

Cocco, Pinna and Marchesi [8] stated that blockchain technology is foreseen by the industry as a disruptive technology which plays a crucial role in managing, controlling and securing IoT devices. The security factors for the use of Bitcoin are introduced in this section. This chapter analyzes the use of blockchain technology as a solution to various problems in various industries so that the researchers can analyze its usage. Dudek [12] determined and reported its benefits in various marketplaces in real time. Kane [17] argued that blockchain can be a solution to challenges including intellectual property, art as well as contracts while reducing the paperwork, speeding up the transactions and lowering the cost.

1.5.1 Analyzing the use of blockchain in different industries

The blockchain is one of the advanced solutions to the challenges in various industries. With the use of blockchain, digital currency is able to change the way of handling money and performing transactions at the business level. Following are the industries where blockchain technology is used as a solution.

1.5.1.1 Insurance industry

Australia and New Zealand Banking Group Limited (ANZ) has announced blockchain solutions to improve the efficiency in the insurance industry. Working with the tech giant IBM as well as financial services of New Zealand, ANZ built a blockchain-based platform that aims to ease the data transfer as well as premium payments among the brokers [20]. The planned solutions stem from the proof of concept that can demonstrate the potential of the blockchain to solve the inefficiencies in the reconciliation of statements [2]. The proof of concept is built with Fabric, the blockchain-based platform developed by the Linux Foundation-backed Hyperledger consortium. The ANZ is involved in a number of blockchain projects and have successfully made some trial efforts in the year 2017, intending to digitize bank guarantee processes for the property leasing.

1.5.1.2 Information services industry

Due to the increase of Internet use, fingerprints are used to access services via mobile phones, and the users can seek access to websites in this way. Techgiant Google has decided to incorporate the speed of website into algorithm ranking factors. The search engine of this company considers a page to be slow if it is taking longer than 1.5 s to load. Blemus [7] stated that due to the use of blockchain technology, it is believed to transform the global Internet infrastructure [12]. The problems related to low Internet availability as well as pace in digital content progress because of higher content delivery costs are minimized with the use of blockchain as a solution. A single transaction is being automated only due to smart contracts enabled by the blockchain technology. Andreev [3] believed that blockchain is a power in Web 3.0 and offers faster speed as well as decentralization to develop in the Internet age.

1.5.1.3 Real estate industry

Due to the participation of buyers, brokers, sellers and real estate agents, the processes of the industry become too slow. There is also a transfer of information from one point to other, which causes data privacy issues. The blockchain reduces the risks and also increases trust [6]. With home purchases, people rely on the companies for the verification of real estate transactions as well as ownership. This technology is used to perform transactions with the use of cryptocurrency in an international real estate market. It demonstrated an option to buy homes with the digital assets [12]. This technology eliminates the need for a trusted party to conduct digital transactions, allowing the transactions to be done in a distributed and peer-to-peer network. It makes the transactions more secure.

1.5.1.4 Banking industry

The banking industry in New Zealand is shifted from closed unilateral systems to decentralized banks as platform approaches. Deposits, insurance accounts and exchanges besides crypto-holdings are done with the use of single interfaces. The industry uses blockchain to reduce the time needed to settle the transactions. Rather than the normal duration of 1–3 days to verify the fund transfers, the customers received verifications within an hour. As this technology is used in the banking applications, the transactions occur in real time. Ishmaev [16] believed that the strength of the blockchain technology is the elimination of the duplication of data. One of the companies that have capitalized on the blockchain technology to capture a share of the banking industry is Ripple that assists the bank with the processing of international payments. The real-time gross settlement (RTGS) system is constructed on a modified blockchain model. Shared ledgers help the banks in transaction information. The blockchain enables the transactions to be completed quicker than the centralized systems. The time required to capture information is very less [13]. Two security keys exist for the transactions: The public key is available for each user and private keys are owned only by parties for transactions.

1.5.1.5 Retail industry

The data provided by the blockchain help the clients to keep track of each end in the supply chain. For example, when a retail store is advertising of chocolate cake, then the blockchain data will let us to recognize when and wherever as well as by whom the cake is being consumed [30]. It tracks the individual ingredients used to formulate the cake. With the help of these data, the retailers can identify whether the company has used fresh ingredients and confirm no expired ingredients have been used. It helps to offer customers a fresh chocolate cake each time without being anxious about the selling of expired cake. The blockchain technology can offer complete confidence as well as clearness to the clients and also sellers as they are able to prove that the products are naturally sourced [23]. The technology also helps to deal with stealing of luxury items as well as resale of stolen items through tracking the owner. The retailers are able to track goods from the dispatch of the product to the delivery of shipments in addition to customer delivery. Finally, it benefits the retail industry as it is a trusted means of payments due to Bitcoin

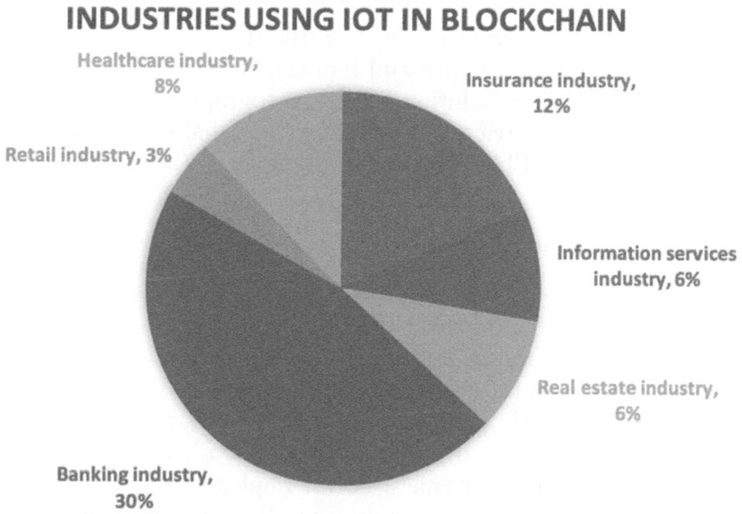

INDUSTRIES USING IOT IN BLOCKCHAIN

Healthcare industry, 8%

Insurance industry, 12%

Retail industry, 3%

Information services industry, 6%

Real estate industry, 6%

Banking industry, 30%

Figure 1.3 Statistical analysis of industries using IoT in blockchain technology.

[7]. It allows retailers to agree to cryptocurrencies with digital accounts that assist in reorganizing the refunds as well as return procedures. The companies such as Expedia and Newegg accept Bitcoin as payment methods.

1.5.1.6 Healthcare industry

The digitalization of the healthcare records provides a significant change in the healthcare sector, but it is criticized for centralization as well as associated with ethical issues. The blockchain technology helps to take care of the public health by creating a secured as well as flexible ecosystem for the exchange of electronic health records [9]. The technology makes space by creating provenances for critical drugs, organs and others. In addition to the medical licenses on the blockchain technology, fraudulent doctors can be prevented from working (Figure 1.3).

1.5.2 Blockchain cryptography solution

Hassan, Aslam and Jang [14] discussed that need for blockchain-based identity management for use in the Internet age, in the form of the identity of the project documents and passports, and there is no such alternative system to secure online authentication and identity of the digital entities. Blockchain technology provides a secure solution to the problem. It is used to create an identity on the blockchain, makes it easier to manage and has control over the personal information. By a combination of decentralized blockchain and identity verification, a digital ID card is created, which acts as a digital watermark that is assigned to online transactions. The challenges related to security deployment are solved by the use of blockchain cryptographic solutions. The integration of IoT and blockchain is a challenge; therefore, among all the blockchain solutions, the cryptographic method is the best solution for all the industries. Following are the challenges and respective solutions with the use of blockchain technology.

1.5.2.1 Storage capacity and scalability

Referring to one of the issues with blockchain, the number of transactions in a Bitcoin blockchain can process is limited. The transaction processing capacity is 7 tx/s maximum, and the Ethereum network has 15 tx/s. The confirmation time in the Bitcoin network is fixed at 10 min. The heavily loaded networks have a problem related to full blocks, which can trigger the problem of higher fees. For the Bitcoin blockchain, the proposed solution to the problem is SegWit, a name used for implementing soft fork change in the transaction format of cryptocurrency Bitcoin [24]. This function is added to support fast off-chain transactions and to increase the block size to 4 MB.

1.5.2.2 Security

Based on the security issues, the cryptographic method is used, and it is also known as encryption and decryption of information through complex mathematics. Miau and Yang [21] discussed that an example of cryptography is Caesar cipher. Each of the letters in a message is substituted with a letter that is 3 places to the left of the alphabet; then, the message is encrypted. Sun, Yan and Zhang [27] criticized that the blockchain technology uses cryptography to protect the identities of the users, encrypts the digital transactions and secures the information in addition to storing the values. Therefore, the blockchain technology has the confidence that something is recorded in the blockchain, and in the same manner, it is preserved with security. The cryptography method used in the blockchain is named as public key cryptography, which is best suited to associate with technology as compared to systematic key cryptography.

1.5.2.3 Anonymity and data privacy

The Bitcoin blockchain protocols use cryptographic methods for digital signatures as well as cryptographic hash functions [25]. The cryptographic algorithm used in Bitcoin is termed as elliptic curve cryptography. It provides the same level of the as RSA; it requires less computation, smaller key size and reduced storage and transmission requirements. Kim and Hong [18] explained that the digital signatures prove the ownership of assets and also allow controlling the funds. The digital signature is based on two functions:

Sign (Message, Private Key) → Signature

This message was sent to sign as well as the private key; this particular function produces an innovative digital signature for the messages.

Verify (Message, Private Key, Signature) → True/False

This message is used to verify the signature as well as the public key; this particular function provides a binary output based on whether the signature is authentic or not.

1.5.2.4 Legal

The blockchain with its digital ledger function is promised to be effective, secure as well as immutable for storing the data required for property rights such as land ownership. The technology is applied not to track the custody of the documents, but to store documents. With the use of digital ledger, there is a permanent record of the chain of custody while the evidence is digitally preserved, such that no evidence is thrown out [29]. The legal industry applies the blockchain technology to protect their legal documents, which offers timestamps as well as fingerprints into the media files.

1.5.3 Disadvantages of blockchain technology

Following are the disadvantages of blockchain technology:

Extreme volatility: The virtual currency based on blockchain technology, such as Bitcoin, is subject to extreme volatility as there is a fluctuation in the price of the currency. As the blockchain technology is new to the market, extreme volatility is caused. The price of Bitcoin dropped to around $200 when China decided to ban the companies from raising ICO in the year 2017.

Crime: Due to anonymity, illegal transactions are caused. People have used this platform to perform illegal transactions based on virtual currency.

It is summarized that cryptographic methods contribute toward the security of the network by creating it hard for data manipulation along with providing personal security for the end users. It enables translucent transactions while retaining the privacy of the individuals. The Bitcoin uses public key cryptography to reach the project goal. Most of the industries use blockchain ideas in the value-producing network with higher security using the open-source power of the blockchain platforms. It will reduce the development time and will back the operations to support the critical workloads.

Therefore, in order to overcome security issues, the blockchain technology is used in most of the industries.

1.6 CONCLUSIONS

It is concluded that Internet of things (IoT) is an exciting paradigm in the emerging technology. It has significant problems in its current stage; IoT is infeasible and also hazardous. IoT devices are connected with a web of devices that can operate with minimal computational power along with embedded chips for connectivity purposes. It has significant security flaws, and the researchers can demonstrate the capability as well as creativity in the breaching of IoT devices. The hackers can manage to control implanted devices, disable the cars remotely and prevent the launch of the DDoS attacks. It is analyzed that IoT security flaws revolve around three areas such as authentication, transaction and connection. The distributed ledgers can seem such as there are some minor changes into IoT networks to consider how physically distributed the systems are being, and the blockchain is used as killer applications. IoT devices interact with recognized as well as unrecognized devices. The application is tracking actions of network components that can verify that the record is another big goal for the IoT. The auditable feature of IoT and blockchain technology improves data analytics, network performance and the safety of the data. The blockchain is ideal to create consistent networks. With the use of blockchain applications, transactions are useful for IoT. They are performed by machine-to-machine interactions; micro-interactions ensure economic probability as well as optimality. The blockchain is considered an alternative to track registrations as well as system updation.

BIBLIOGRAPHY

1. Tareq Ahram, Arman Sargolzaei, Saman Sargolzaei, Jeff Daniels, and Ben Amaba. Blockchain technology innovations. In *2017 IEEE Technology Engineering Management Conference (TEMSCON)*, 137–141, 2017.
2. Waseem Akram. Necessity and implementation of blockchain technology. *International Journal of Scientific Research and Management*, 5:6279–6280, 2017.
3. R Andreev, P Andreeva, L Krotov, and E Krotova. Review of blockchain technology: Types of blockchain and their application. *Intellekt. Sist. Proizv*, 16:11, 2018.
4. Arshdeep Bahga and Vijay Madisetti. Blockchain platform for industrial internet of things. *Journal of Software Engineering and Applications*, 09:533–546, 2016.
5. Ahmed Banafa. 2 *The Industrial Internet of Things (IIoT): Challenges, Requirements and Benefits*, pages 7–12. 2018.

6. Kamanashis Biswas and Vallipuram Muthukkumarasamy. Securing smart cities using blockchain technology. In *2016 IEEE 18th International Conference on High Performance Computing and Communications; IEEE 14th International Conference on Smart City; IEEE 2nd International Conference on Data Science and Systems (HPCC/SmartCity/DSS)*, pages 1392–1393, 2016.

7. Sttphane Blemus. Law and blockchain: A legal perspective on current regulatory trends worldwide. *Revue Trimestrielle de Droit Financier (Corporate Finance and Capital Markets Law Review) RTDF*, 4:1–15, 2017.

8. Luisanna Cocco, Andrea Pinna, and Michele Marchesi. Banking on blockchain: Costs savings thanks to the blockchain technology. *Future Internet*, 9:25, 2017.

9. Ali Dorri, Salil Kanhere, and Raja Jurdak. Blockchain in internet of things: Challenges and solutions. *arxiv*, 2016.

10. Ali Dorri, Salil S. Kanhere, and Raja Jurdak. Towards an optimized blockchain for IoT. In *2017 IEEE/ACM Second International Conference on Internet-of-Things Design and Implementation (IoTDI)*, pages 173–178, 2017.

11. Ali Dorri, Salil S. Kanhere, Raja Jurdak, and Praveen Gauravaram. Blockchain for iot security and privacy: The case study of a smart home. In *2017 IEEE International Conference on Pervasive Computing and Communications Workshops (PerCom Workshops)*, pages 618–623, 2017.

12. Dariusz Dudek. Possibilities of using blockchain technology in the area of education. *Informatyka Ekonomiczna*, 3:55–65, 2017.

13. Mohamed Tahar Hammi, Badis Hammi, Patrick Bellot, and Ahmed Serrhouchni. Bubbles of trust: A decentralized blockchain-based authentication system for IoT. *Computers & Security*, 78:126–142, 2018.

14. Taimur Hassan, Saleem Aslam, and Ju Wook Jang. Fully automated multiresolution channels and multithreaded spectrum allocation protocol for iot based sensor nets. *IEEE Access*, 6:22545–22556, 2018.

15. Seyoung Huh, Sangrae Cho, and Soohyung Kim. Managing iot devices using blockchain platform. In *2017 19th International Conference on Advanced Communication Technology (ICACT)*, pages 464–467, 2017.

16. Georgy Ishmaev. Blockchain technology as an institution of property. *Metaphilosophy*, 48:666–686, 2017.

17. Ethan Kane. Is blockchain a general purpose technology? *SSRN Electronic Journal*, 1–27, 2017.

18. Kyong Kim and Seng Hong. Study on rule-based data protection system using blockchain in p2p distributed networks. *International Journal of Security and Its Applications*, 10:201–210, 2016.

19. Hitesh Malviya. How blockchain will defend IoT. Available at SSRN 2883711, 2016.

20. Nallapaneni Manoj Kumar and Pradeep Kumar Mallick. Blockchain technology for security issues and challenges in iot. *Procedia Computer Science*, 132:1815–1823, 2018.

21. Scott Miau and Jiann-Min Yang. Bibliometrics-based evaluation of the blockchain research trend: 2008 – march 2017. *Technology Analysis & Strategic Management*, 30:1–17, 2018.

22. Oscar Novo. Blockchain meets iot: An architecture for scalable access management in iot. *IEEE Internet of Things Journal*, 5(2): 1184–1195, 2018.

23. Alfonso Panarello, Nachiket Tapas, Giovanni Merlino, Francesco Longo, and Antonio Puliafito. Blockchain and iot integration: A systematic survey. *Sensors*, 18(8), 2018.

24. Byeong-ju Park, Tae-jin Lee, and Jin Kwak. Blockchain-based iot device authentication scheme. *Journal of the Korea Institute of Information Security & Cryptology*, 27(2):343–351, 2017.

25. Josep Rosa, Víctor Torres-Padrosa, Andres El-Fakdi, Denisa Gibovic, Oliver Hornyak, Lutz Maicher, and Francesc Miralles. A survey of blockchain technologies for open innovation. In *4rd Annual World Open Innovation Conference, WOIC*, 2017.

26. Khaled Salah and Minhaj Khan. Iot security: Review, blockchain solutions, and open challenges. *Future Generation Computer Systems*, 82:395–411, 2017.

27. Jianjun Sun, Jiaqi Yan, and Kem Zhang. Blockchain-based sharing services: What blockchain technology can contribute to smart cities. *Financial Innovation*, 2(1):1–9, 2016.

28. Melanie Swan. Blockchain thinking: The brain as a dac (decentralized autonomous organization). *Texas Bitcoin Conference*, pages 27–29, 2015.

29. Mark Wolfskehl. Why and how blockchain? *The Journal of the British Blockchain Association*, 1:1–5, 2018.

30. Quanqing Xu, Khin Aung, Yongqing Zhu, and Khai Yong. *A Blockchain-Based Storage System for Data Analytics in the Internet of Things*, pages 119–138. 2018.

31. Xiwei Xu, Ingo Weber, Mark Staples, Liming Zhu, Jan Bosch, Len Bass, Cesare Pautasso, and Paul Rimba. A taxonomy of blockchain-based systems for architecture design. In *2017 IEEE International Conference on Software Architecture (ICSA)*, pages 243–252, 2017.

32. Yu Zhang and Jiangtao Wen. The iot electric business model: Using blockchain technology for the internet of things. *Peer-to-Peer Networking and Applications*, 10(4):983–994, 2017.

33. Zibin Zheng, Shaoan Xie, Hongning Dai, Xiangping Chen, and Huaimin Wang. An overview of blockchain technology: Architecture, consensus, and future trends. In *2017 IEEE International Congress on Big Data (BigData Congress)*, pages 557–564, 2017.

34. Kazm zyılmaz and Arda Yurdakul. Integrating low-power iot devices to a blockchain-based infrastructure. In *2017 International Conference on Embedded Software (EMSOFT)*, pages 1–2, 2017.

Chapter 2

Energy data lakes
An edge Internet of Energy approach

Abdullah Alsalemi
De Montfort University

Abbes Amira
University of Sharjah
De Montfort University

Hossein Malekmohamadi and Kegong Diao
De Montfort University

Faycal Bensaali
Qatar University

CONTENTS

ABSTRACT

The Internet of Energy (IoE) paradigm is an advancing area of research in the field of energy efficiency encompassing data collection, processing, visualization, and decision making. Smart energy monitoring has witnessed technological advancements such as smart metering and IoE networking, allowing the expansion of smart energy networks in smart households. In this book chapter, we aim to understand energy behavior through big data collection and classification and improve energy efficiency using data

DOI: 10.1201/9781003304203-2

21

lakes. A specialized case study is reported on the ODROID-XU4 multicore platform to realize a setup developed at De Montfort University (DMU), UK, at the Energy Lab and Artificial Intelligence (AI) Lab. It is aimed to build a novel appliance-level energy data lake with contextual ambient environmental data. Also, a novel labeling system is introduced for classifying domestic energy consumption coupled with data visualization examples. In conclusion, the proposed work aids in exploiting energy efficiency technologies for improving energy efficiency via an innovative, automated energy efficiency framework.

2.1 INTRODUCTION

Energy efficiency, in the realm of domestic building, is in ever-increasing importance [1]. Individuals, societies, cities, and governments are taking bold steps toward reducing adverse effects of global warming on planet earth. Before the point of no return [2], the world must unite to curb pollution and take superb advantage of renewable energy resources, and most importantly, transform the behavior of individuals from energy consumerism to conscious energy saving [3, 4].

One of the approaches to battle end-user energy consumerism is through the utilization of smart technology, namely the use of big data and Internet of Things (IoT) [5,6]. To effectively manage and improve energy consumption, an understanding of the consumption and its surrounding context is required, whereby sensory devices are employed to collect power consumption data as well as ambient environmental conditions, together to gather a broad yet precise understanding of each specific environment's consumption patterns. Therefore, when enough data are collected, useful insights can be extracted, and more constructive energy decisions can be made with respect to the underlying context. Collectively, this engenders the term Internet of Energy (IoE), where IoT is used for energy efficiency purposes [7–9].

In essence, the application of IoE without the use of data analytics would not yield effective outcomes. Since the nature of the collected datasets is large, artificial intelligence (AI) algorithms are applied to yield meaningful conclusions that help shape energy consumption toward higher efficiency. Hand in hand with AI, visualizing the data can be a powerful tool for extricating relevant knowledge from data.

As a subset of AI concerned with learning from data without explicit instruction [10], machine learning (ML) algorithms may require powerful computing platforms. Sometimes, ML tasks can be outsourced to cloud servers, a cost-effective, scalable, and high computational power option [11]. Despite the benefits, data privacy and application-sensitive latency can be potential pitfalls of relying on cloud computing for AI [12–14]. Henceforth, the "edge" comes into play, where local computational resources are securely exploited to train ML algorithms at high performance. After overcoming the initial setup cost of edge computing platforms, computational costs can potentially drop to a viable minimum, coining the term edge AI.

Edge AI for IoE is a vast unplotted map of research opportunities, comprising three main sub-areas: (1) IoE data collection that involves sensors, embedded systems, wireless communication, and backend server configuration; (2) IoE data analytics with edge AI comprising pre-processing, classification, and data visualization; and (3) IoE decision making and integration where there are personalized recommendations based on the extracted meaning, coalescing to form a suitable energy-saving solution.

In terms of related work, a number of recent contributions can be found. First, Kafle et al. [7] addressed recent IoE solutions applied in several fields as well as technical challenges including security and commercialization. The key technologies are introduced with respect to the energy router as a significant element of the IoE network as well as storage devices, distributed renewable energy sources, plug-and-play interface, and electric vehicle integration. The article also presents similarities and differences between IoE and current distributed Internet infrastructures.

Moreover, targeting building energy management systems (BEMS), Hannan et al. [8] investigated the challenges and recommendations for such systems employed with IoE. The article addresses the drawbacks of other existing systems, such as the net Zero Energy Buildings (nZEBs) to comply with issues including the complexity of large-scale BEMS data and network obstacles. The article also introduces a critical review over the IoE-based BEMS for the energy efficiency improvement.

On the other hand, Shahinzadeh et al. [15] specifically addressed IoE for the applications of smart power systems, as they are considered the main element of the energy ecosystem. The article addresses several aspects including renewable energy generation, large-scale energy storage, thermal power plants, system operations and protection, and end-user consumption management in smart buildings.

The authors of [16] highlighted that the availability of renewable energy sources, along with advances in sensing and communication technology, has resulted in the long-term functioning of contemporary energy systems. Also, main difficulties and unresolved concerns with the IoT when integrated with energy systems in a review are examined. They evaluated the feasibility of several IoT/IoE data transmission and communication protocols for implementation in a contemporary grid system. Furthermore, various wireless IoT communication technologies are evaluated for their applicability in multilayer network architecture and energy system applications. Because an IoE system may produce a significant quantity of data, the appropriateness of certain current IoT-supported device message protocols and wireless connection or communication protocols is evaluated. Figure 2.1 illustrates how IoT and IoE can shape smart cities.

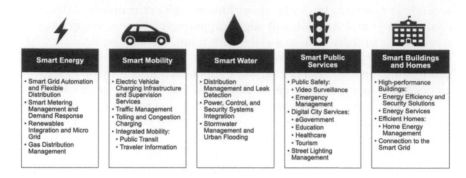

Smart Energy	Smart Mobility	Smart Water	Smart Public Services	Smart Buildings and Homes

• Smart Grid Automation and Flexible Distribution
• Smart Metering Management and Demand Response
• Renewables Integration and Micro Grid
• Gas Distribution Management
	• Electric Vehicle Charging Infrastructure and Supervision Services
	• Traffic Management
	• Tolling and Congestion Charging
	• Integrated Mobility:
	  • Public Transit
	  • Traveler Information
		• Distribution Management and Leak Detection
		• Power, Control, and Security Systems Integration
		• Stormwater Management and Urban Flooding
			• Public Safety:
			  • Video Surveillance
			  • Emergency Management
			• Digital City Services:
			  • eGovernment
			  • Education
			  • Healthcare
			  • Tourism
			• Street Lighting Management
				• High-performance Buildings:
				  • Energy Efficiency and Security Solutions
				  • Energy Services
				• Efficient Homes:
				  • Home Energy Management
				  • Connection to the Smart Grid

Figure 2.1 IoT and IoE architecture for smart cities. (Adapted from [16].)

Similarly, utilizing the capabilities of sensor-based IoE technology, user behavior is anticipated, and their energy usage habits are detected and controlled. In [17], an IoE-based architecture is proposed to resolve the existing challenges in energy management in order to use and generate energy in the most efficient way possible, as well as provide guidelines for the development of a sustainable energy structure that will present both opportunities and solutions for current types of challenges with the help of IoE.

A BEMS design proposed in [18], is an efficient technique for monitoring and managing a building's energy requirements. To address the present building energy management system's existing difficulties, such as huge quantities of BEMS energy data, energy data loss, and energy overload, a BEMS based on the IoE has been suggested. In this article, the potential of IoE-based BEMS for improving building energy usage performance in the future has been discussed.

Furthermore, smart sensor networks provide a plethora of possibilities for smart grid applications such as power monitoring, demand-side energy management, distributed storage coordination, and the integration of renewable energy producers. The gathering of ever-increasing quantities of data presents new difficulties for big data storage and processing. As a result, suggestions and techniques for usage in the future of smart grid and IoE are discussed in [19]. The uses of smart sensor networks in the smart power grid sector are investigated as well as the methods for managing large data produced by sensors and meters for application processing.

From another control theory point of view, it is important to be able to predict the correct state of an IoE system with adequate accuracy; henceforth, in [20], an IoE-focused H-infinity centralized state estimation model is proposed for microgrids. It shows that the authors' method can achieve superior evaluation metrics than existing approaches. Thusly, the proposed model can assist IoE smart grid communication systems by providing dynamic state estimations effectively.

Moreover, Shahzad et al.'s study focused on the deployment of IoE in industrial IoT applications [9]. The article highlights the significance of factory and industry applications, challenges, and architectures for the implementation of novel technologies. Challenges include the types of communication, cyberattacks, middleware, mobility, data integrity, and scalability and also:

1. Lightweight security features that work around the computational constraints of edge devices and fine-grained security features;
2. Extended investigation of potential cyberattacks and more effective physical intrusion detection mechanisms;
3. Revamped utilization of distributed computing as in secure mesh networks and blockchain systems;
4. Optimized communication latency as well as bandwidth usage for edge devices;
5. More thorough consideration of data management and aspects such as collection, accumulation, aggregation, processing, and storage strategies, whether offline or online (e.g., cloud backups);
6. Developing context-aware edge devices that act based on ambient conditions, geolocation, preferences, etc.;
7. Enhancements to the software tools used to develop edge computing applications and algorithms; and
8. Standardized schemes for large-scale deployments of edge networks.

Moreover, big data problems provide a significant challenge to conventional data management and analysis methods. To solve these issues, the idea of a data lake was developed. A data lake is a vast unstructured data repository that stores and manages all data in any format [21]. It is a research area of interest, especially to IoE, where data storage is a crucial prerequisite to producing effective classification and recommendations. As illustrated in Figure 2.2, data lakes can be an effective means to feed classification algorithms and data visualization programs. It also illustrates, in a Lego blocks metaphor, the different forms of data lakes in terms of raw unprocessed data, processed data, and visualized data through a story.

Henceforth, this work deals with using edge AI for IoE data collection as well as data analytics with particular interest in data lakes for preparing for ML classification. A case study on an IoE testbed at a UK institution is reported in terms of design, dataset, implementation, and discussion. By the end of this book chapter, the reader will identify the following contributions:

1. The use of IoE sensing for collecting power consumption as well as temperature, humidity, presence, light level, and barometric pressure in a novel appliance-level dataset;
2. The employment of edge computing platforms for managing collected data in a data lake form; and
3. Managing and visualizing energy date lakes locally on an edge computing platform.

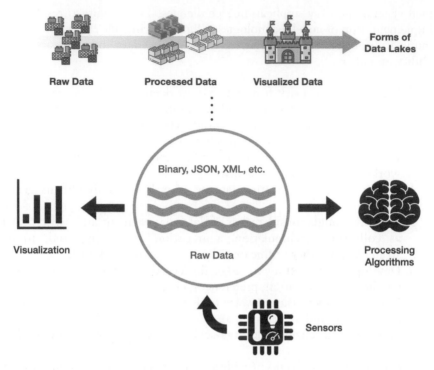

Figure 2.2 Overview of a data lake and its forms.

The remainder of this book chapter is organized as follows: Section 2.2 gives an overview of the larger energy efficiency framework. Section 2.3 discusses the testbed used to create an energy data lake and the means of labeling it. The current results are reported and discussed in Section 2.4, and the work is concluded in Section 2.5.

2.2 THE BIG PICTURE: FRAMEWORK OVERVIEW

As part of an umbrella project encompassing different aspects of energy behavioral economics, the grand aim is to unleash building energy efficiency opportunities with the use of IoE technology packaged in a cohesive, integrated framework. In a nutshell, the overall energy efficiency framework's aims can be summarized as follows:

1. Effective, privacy-preserving, yet cost-effective contextual energy data collection system;
2. Robust classification and recommendation system accessible by energy end-users; and
3. A rich, open-access dataset of context-aware appliance-level data.

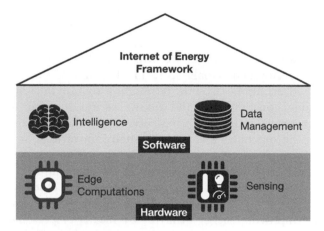

Figure 2.3 Overview of the IoE framework.

More specifically, as shown in Figure 2.3, the proposed system is composed of two cores: a hardware core that corresponds to sensors and IoT devices, and a software counterpart that relates to logic (e.g., data acquisition and management) and intelligence (e.g., AI-based algorithms).

The hardware part comprises a testbed of an edge computing device connected to a sensing board for ambient condition sensing. Being connected to a wireless network, the edge device collects temperature, humidity, light level, barometric pressure, and occupancy. Also, a number of smart electric plugs gather voltage, current, and power data, wirelessly transferred to the edge computing device. In this work, an ODROID-XU4 is chosen as the edge computing platform, where it stores, processes, and makes the data available in an accessible data visualization interface on the web and mobile devices.

On the flipside, the software counterpart involves programming the sensing board to correctly sense ambient conditions, store them in a secure manner on the ODROID-XU4, make a copy at a cloud server, and process the data using a number of algorithms. The software part also deals with receiving power consumption data from smart plugs as well as configuring the data visualization interface.

Retrospectively, the most important developmental aspect is the integration between hardware and software to harmoniously achieve the intended aims of the project. Moreover, in the seminal article by Kafle et al. on the future of IoE [7], parallels between the Internet and IoE infrastructures are indicated as well as contrasts. Extending the analogy further, we are adding a "data lake analytics" module to the existing infrastructure to close one of the biggest gaps in IoE research, namely the use of data lakes for transforming energy behavior. In the upcoming sections, the creation of a novel contextual energy dataset is discussed, followed by a succinct description of the processing and visualization aspects.

In this work, we aim to understand energy behavior through big data collection and classification to improve energy efficiency using behavioral economics, deep learning (DL)-based recommender systems, and intuitive data visualizations. Hence, we will contribute to United Nation's Sustainable Development Goals 7, 8, 11, 12, and 13 on clean energy, contributing to economic growth, developing sustainable cities, endorsing responsible consumption, and taking serious climate action [22]. Therefore, in terms of impact, urban living standards can significantly benefit from the outcomes and tools of such innovations, in addition to the immense social value gained from utilizing recommender systems in reducing energy consumption to the convenient minimum.

Motivated by the ever-evolving need for smart energy efficiency solutions, a study at De Montfort University (DMU) is taking place to investigate the use of AI in improving energy behavior by means of personalized, data-driven recommendations. The study is located in both the Energy Lab in the Institute of Energy & Sustainable Development (IESD) and the AI Lab at the Institute of AI (IAI) as data collection and analysis hot spots.

2.3 ENERGY DATA LAKES

2.3.1 Introduction

Conventionally, data come in three main representations: structured, semi-structured, and unstructured. Also, big data is used to identify datasets that are so large in entries that exceed traditional computational capabilities of managing them [23]. Correspondingly, data lakes are repositories of raw-formatted data, stored as their natural file types, whether binary, blob, JavaScript Object Notation (JSON), comma-separated values (CSV), Structured Query Language (SQL), etc. As less organized data representations, data lakes allow facilitated processing using ML and visualization purposes. As the names hint, data lakes are designed to hold big data repositories that are usually unstructured [23].

In a data lake, a flat structure dominates the repository, where raw values are semantically identified using a unique identifier (e.g., a timestamp) coupled with metadata tags. In spirit, data lakes support real-time or near-real-time data acquisition speed and are quite cost-effective in preliminary analysis of raw data using ML algorithms.

In this context, we follow a similar approach to collecting contextual appliance-level energy data. Using *energy data lakes*, power consumption information coupled with ambient conditions of the environment can be conveniently accumulated into an ever-expanding raw-formatted dataset. Specifically, Table 2.1 describes the energy data lake.

Accordingly, such an energy data lake is created to facilitate knowledge extraction via ML algorithms as well as effective data visualization.

Table 2.1 Energy data lake overview

Data format	JSON
Datastore location	Stored in both edge computing device and cloud datastore
Frequency	5 sec–2 min
Data duration	Minimum 3–6 months
Data size	100–500 MB
Acquisition site	DMU AI and Energy Labs
Data contents	• Power consumption data (V, A, W) • Temperature (°C) • Humidity (%) • Barometric pressure (Pa) • Light level (lux) • Carbon dioxide (CO_2) level (PPM) • Room occupancy (binary) • Outdoor conditions (e.g., temperature, humidity, ultraviolet (UV) index, from an online weather service)[a]

[a] https://www.accuweather.com/en/gb/leicester.

Therefore, the hardware aspects of the data generation and storage are described next.

2.3.2 Edge computing platform and sensing testbed

Before delving into the sensory testbed used to fill up the energy data lake, we provide a brief introduction to the single-board, multicore edge platform employed as the datastore and manager, the ODROID-XU4 [24]. It is a single-board computing platform that has low power usage and has a rather compact form factor relative to most other built-in ARM units. It houses the combination of an ARM Cortex-A15 and Cortex-A7 big.LITTLE CPU, and an ARM Mali-T628 GPU, which is advantageous when running deep ML algorithms locally in terms of processing time.

The ODROID-XU4 board does not only store data, but is directly connected to ambient environmental sensors and to the smart plugs to collect environmental and power consumption data, respectively. It also creates a cloud backup of the data, following hybrid edge-cloud approach. Also, the ODROID-XU4 handles all the means to process and visualize the energy data lake. This is considered an advancement in the field where all the acquisition and processing stages are efficiently consolidated in one edge device. Figure 2.4 illustrates the edge computing platform role and the hybrid edge-cloud approach employed for creating the energy data lake.

As a complementary board used alongside the ODROID-XU4, the Google Coral Dev Board is a single board computer equipped with a quad Cortex-A53, Cortex-M4F, integrated GC7000 Lite Graphics, and a tensor processing unit (TPU) capable of conducting ML edge operations with a relatively higher speed [25]. The board is equipped with built-in wireless

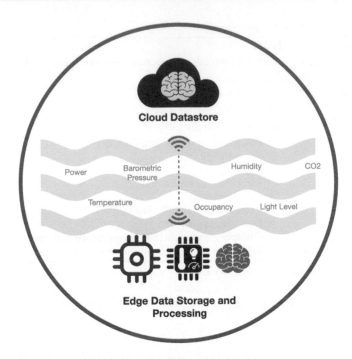

Figure 2.4 Hybrid edge-cloud for creating an energy data lake.

capability and can be connected to an external Environmental Board developed by the same manufacturer.

In a testbed developed at DMU at the Energy Lab and AI Lab, it is aimed to build a novel appliance-level dataset with contextual ambient environmental data. Power consumption data are collected via smart plugs that transfer the data locally to the ODROID-XU4 board. The ODROID-XU4, on the other hand, accumulates temperature, humidity, luminosity, and barometric pressure via an externally connected WEATHERBOARD. After the ODROID-XU4 performs edge AI computations on the collected data, to clean it, summarize it, anonymize it, and classify it, it transmits them to a cloud server for further deep processing and storage. Henceforth, the innovation lies in the use of the mentioned platforms to collect, process, and visualize energy and environmental data via edge AI. Figure 2.5 illustrates the heterogeneous sensing setup.

Collected energy and ambient environmental data are stored both in the ODROID-XU4 and in a backup cloud server (i.e., Google Firebase Database). This allows for both local processing and cloud offloading of selected classification tasks. Moreover, as signified in Table 2.1, the energy date lake is stored in a raw JSON format, the default structure of Firebase Database.

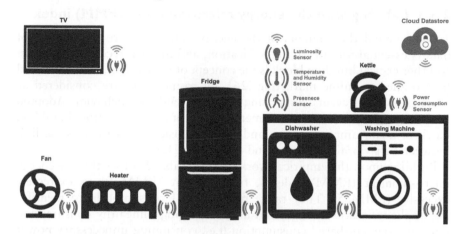

Figure 2.5 Proposed heterogeneous sensing setup.

Table 2.2 Sensing reference apparatuses

Sensing apparatus	Component name	Sensor used	Datasheet accuracy
Temperature	BME280	WEATHERBOARD	±1 C
	ThermoPro TP52	Reference meter	±1 C
Humidity	BME280	WEATHERBOARD	±4%
	ThermoPro TP52	Reference meter	±2%–3%
Light level	Si1133	WEATHERBOARD	±100 mlx (milli-lux)
	V·RESOURCING W-U113	Reference meter	±3%
Power	Energenie MiHome Energy Monitor Plug - MIHO004	Smart plug	N/A
	Energy Saving Appliance Power Monitor for Household Use - ENER00	Reference meter	±2%

It is worthy to mention that when running deep ML algorithms the data may be converted to CSV format via a script.

In order to ensure data correctness, a number of reference meters are used for temperature, humidity, light level, and power consumption to obtain accuracy metrics of the sensors used to build the data lake. As enumerated in Table 2.2, sensing reference apparatuses are compared with the employed sensors in terms of accuracy.

2.3.3 Labeling with the energy micro-moment (EMM) index

To understand the contents of the energy data lake, proper labeling of data is essential for effective classification, and in turn, recommendations. Another critical building block is the concept of micro-moments. Pioneered by Google for online marketing [26], micro-moments are considered as short contextual events comprising a specific end-user behavior. Adopted to the energy context, micro-moments represent an informational building block of a consumption action and can be considered as the missing link between behavioral economics and AI systems [1,27].

Building upon the empirical work of [28], Table 2.3 lists the five energy micro-moment (EMM) indexes, from healthy (EMM 0) to extremely excessive (EMM 5). They range from normal consumption to identifying appliance status change, and also classifying unhealthy consumption into environment-based consumption (i.e., consuming unnecessary power because of ambient environment), no-presence-based consumption (e.g., leaving heating on while outside room or house), and extreme consumption levels in terms of power magnitude.

To illustrate the EMM index further, let us take a case study of Adam living in an urban apartment. During the morning, Adam turned on the kettle (EMM 1) to make tea and retrieved milk from the fridge (EMM 0). Then Adam went for errands and forgot the heater is on (EMM 2). Later in the afternoon, Adam returned, turned off the heater (EMM 2), and switched on the lights (EMM 3) despite the fact that there was bright daytime light. In the evening, Adam fetched a meal from the fridge and cooked it in the microwave (switch on: EMM 1), but he forgot to close the fridge door, which increased its power consumption beyond normal levels (EMM 4). This example, despite its simplicity, reflect common healthy and unhealthy end-user energy habits. Thus, the EMM index can be used as a powerful tool to classify energy data lakes into meaningful cluster for further analysis. It is noteworthy to mention that this example involves a specific case study of a domestic end-user using a specific set of appliances in a given indoor and outdoor environment. In order to scale the example to span more case studies for a variety of appliances, behaviors, and environments, a large, rich dataset is required to train ML classifiers to be able to adapt accordingly.

Table 2.3 The EMM index

Index	Description
0	Normal consumption
1	Switch appliance on/off
2	No-presence normal consumption
3	Context-based excessive consumption
4	Extremely excessive consumption

2.4 RESULTS AND DISCUSSION

2.4.1 Testbeds overview

This book chapter is an introduction to the use of data lakes for IoE applications, with particular interest in computing edge platforms. In this section, we overview some preliminary results concerning the sensing testbed and expound upon data visualization of a sample of energy data lake.

It is worthy to mention that the data are stored using a hybrid cloud-edge methodology where sensing data are uploaded to the cloud Firebase Realtime Database (as a NoSQL JSON database) as well as a local SQLite database on the ODROID-XU4 edge unit at the AI Lab using Home Assistant (HA). It is notable to highlight that two broadband 4G routers are used for connecting the ODROID-XU4 boards and the other sensing units to the Internet, placed at the AI Lab and the Energy Lab.

AI Lab: As shown in Figure 2.6, the testbed demonstrated in the AI Lab is designed to collect and analyze indoor ambient conditions such as temperature, humidity, light level, and barometric pressure. It also acts as an edge AI computing platform, where the collected information from WEATHERBOARD chip is classified using a DL algorithm on the ODROID-XU4. The ODROID-XU4 in the AI Lab acts as the master datastore of the energy data lake. It also creates continuous backups of the lake on Firebase Database.

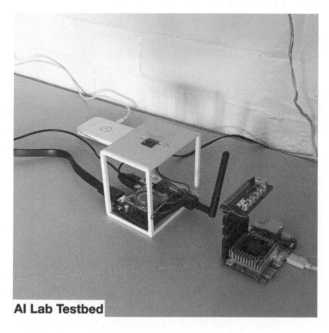

Figure 2.6 AI Lab testbed.

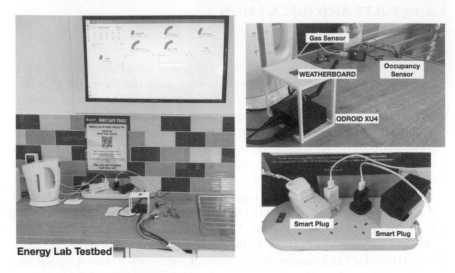

Figure 2.7 Energy Lab testbed.

Energy Lab: Similar to the setup of AI Lab, the testbed includes an ODROID-XU4 that collects ambient conditions as well as voltage, power, and current from smart plugs connected to domestic appliances. It also gathers CO_2 concentration levels as well as occupancy data. Also, a TV screen is connected to the ODROID-XU4 board for real-time data visualization purposes. When the ODROID-XU4 is turned on, it runs an automated script that operates a HA-based real-time data visualization dashboard on the TV screen. Figure 2.7 shows the Energy Lab setup.

2.4.2 Sensing accuracy

Tables 2.4 and 2.5 summarize the sensing accuracy for the employed smart plugs and ambient environmental sensors, respectively. With respect to ODROID-XU4, the values have been compared with a similar setup of the Coral Dev Board and its Environmental Board.

As per the reported results, both power and ambient reading yielded relatively accurate data for the purpose of creating an energy data lake for data analysis purposes. Indeed, further measurements with a variety of appliances would improve data validation, which is the blueprint of future work.

Further, it has been noticed that a pronounced accuracy discrepancy between the Coral Dev Board and Environmental Board is witnessed for temperature, humidity, and ambient light level. Initially, the errors have been induced by the emitted heat of the Coral Dev Board, due to its physical proximity with the Environmental Board. After distancing the Environmental Board by installing additional header connectors, the discrepancy decreased, yet it remains considerable and not reliable enough for longitudinal studies.

Table 2.4 Smart plug metering accuracy

Appliance	Average power (W)	Accuracy (%)
Vodafone R219 Mobile Wi-Fi hotspot (fully charged)	1.4	±5.26
Coral Dev Board	3.8	±2.56

Table 2.5 Sensor accuracy

Parameter	ODROID-XU4 WEATHERBOARD accuracy (%)	Coral Dev Board Environmental Board accuracy (%)
Temperature	±13.50	±26.57
Humidity	±0.90	±11.85
Ambient light level	±1.54	±57.3

With regard to the ODROID-XU4 WEATHERBOARD, it provides higher accuracy for the measured parameters; however, it is important to tighten its wiring to the ODROID-XU4 as loose wiring drastically affects reading fidelity.

2.4.3 Data visualization

Following data collection and analysis, interactive visualizations can aid in obtaining insights that highlight patterns and anomalies. For this purpose, we have utilized HA[1], an open-source home automation system. HA enables connecting multiple data sources (sensors, cloud, public data, etc.) all in a singular data repository. On HA, data are compiled into one SQLite database [29], another form of data lakes. Running on AI Lab's ODROID-XU4, HA includes a dashboard named LoveLace [30], which enables a number of useful visualizations of the energy data lake collected from the testbed sensors. LoveLace enables organizing data visualization as pages (i.e., AI Lab page and Energy Lab page) and offers different visualization options (known as cards) based on the nature of data (e.g., time series, binary, scale, and occupancy). Also, custom cards can be developed to allow for innovative visualizations.

Figures 2.8 and 2.9 show an example of a JSON representation of an energy data lake entry and sample visualizations created using the HA LoveLace, respectively. The history of a given parameter can be retrieved by taping on its corresponding card, as illustrated in Figure 2.10.

To illustrate some of the data recordings in the AI and Energy Lab data lakes, Figures 2.11–2.13 show ambient environmental conditions collected at the AI Lab for 8 hours on a given day, CO_2 and occupancy data at the

---

[1] https://www.home-assistant.io/.

```
..., "1619545158" : { // 1619545158 is the Unix timestamp for April 27, 2021
    "bar"     : 99.986,
    "hum"     : 27.641,
    "lux"     : 367.36,
    "temp"    : 35.765,
    "occ"     : 1,
    "co2"     : 406.31,
    "power"   : 1.400,
    "outdoor": {…},
},  ...
```

Figure 2.8 JSON representation of an energy data lake entry.

Figure 2.9 Smart data visualizations enabled by the collected data.

Energy Lab for 8 hours, and power consumption data for a full cycle of a washing machine at the Energy Lab, respectively.

2.5 CONCLUSIONS

In the pursuit of understanding energy behavior through big data collection and classification and improving energy efficiency using behavioral economics, an edge IoE system for creating a novel energy data lake has been proposed. Specifically, a specialized case study is reported on the ODROID-XU4 platform at DMU at the AI Lab and Energy Lab.

Future work involves deeper data validation and developing ML algorithms for data classification into EMM indices and producing personalized energy-saving recommendations on a mobile application.

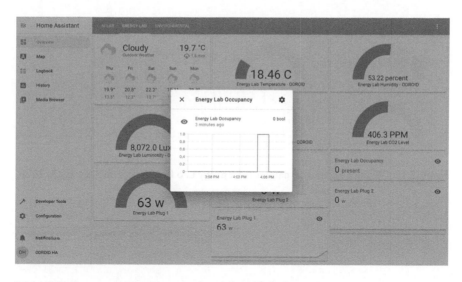

Figure 2.10 Parameter history example on the HA dashboard.

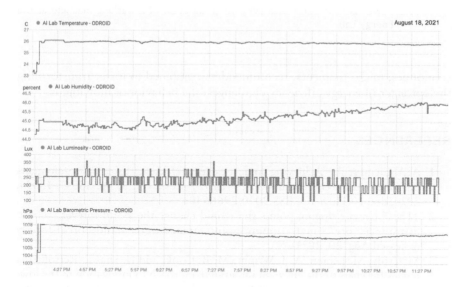

Figure 2.11 Ambient condition data at the AI Lab for 8 hours on August 18, 2021.

In terms of impact, urban living standards can significantly benefit from the outcomes and tools of such innovations, in addition to the immense social value gained from utilizing recommender systems in reducing energy consumption to the convenient minimum. To conclude, vast positive impact can be created when innovation meets technology, in other words, when behavioral

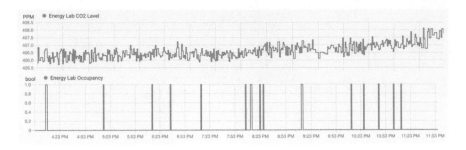

Figure 2.12 CO$_2$ and occupancy data at the Energy Lab for 8 hours on August 18, 2021.

Figure 2.13 Power consumption data (W) for a full cycle of a washing machine at the Energy Lab.

economics, micro-moments, recommenders combined to foster transforming the epicenter of energy efficiency challenges: the behavior of individuals.

REFERENCES

1. A. Alsalemi et al., "Achieving domestic energy efficiency using micro-moments and intelligent recommendations," *IEEE Access*, vol. 8, pp. 15047–15055, 2020, doi: 10.1109/ACCESS.2020.2966640.
2. "The 7 climate tipping points that could change the world forever," *Grist*. https://grist.org/climate-tipping-points-amazon-greenland-boreal-forest/ (accessed Aug. 20, 2021).
3. M. Crilly, M. Lemon, A. J. Wright, M. B. Cook, and D. Shaw, "Retrofitting homes for energy efficiency: an integrated approach to innovation in the low-carbon overhaul of UK social housing," *Energy & Environment*, vol. 23, no. 6–7, pp. 1027–1055, Oct. 2012, doi: 10.1260/0958-305X.23.6-7.1027.
4. R. Bull, G. Stuart, D. Everitt, N. Jennings, J. Romanowicz, and M. Laskari, "Competing priorities: lessons in engaging students to achieve energy savings in universities," Oct. 2018, doi: 10.1108/IJSHE-09-2017-0157.
5. S. B. Atitallah, M. Driss, W. Boulila, and H. B. Ghézala, "Leveraging deep learning and IoT big data analytics to support the smart cities development: review and future directions," *Computer Science Review*, vol. 38, p. 100303, Nov. 2020, doi: 10.1016/j.cosrev.2020.100303.

6. L. Shao, R. Foster, M. Coleman, K. Irvine, M. Lemon, and Y. Hao, "Wireless energy behaviour monitoring (Wi-be) for office buildings," *International Journal of Low-Carbon Technologies*, vol. 12, no. 2, pp. 181–188, Jun. 2017, doi: 10.1093/ijlct/ctv031.

7. Y. R. Kafle, K. Mahmud, S. Morsalin, and G. E. Town, "Towards an internet of energy," in *2016 IEEE International Conference on Power System Technology (POWERCON)*, Sep. 2016, pp. 1–6. doi: 10.1109/POWERCON.2016.7754036.

8. M. A. Hannan et al., "A review of internet of energy based building energy management systems: issues and recommendations," *IEEE Access*, vol. 6, pp. 38997–39014, 2018, doi: 10.1109/ACCESS.2018.2852811.

9. Y. Shahzad, H. Javed, H. Farman, J. Ahmad, B. Jan, and M. Zubair, "Internet of energy: opportunities, applications, architectures and challenges in smart industries," *Computers & Electrical Engineering*, vol. 86, p. 106739, Sep. 2020, doi: 10.1016/j.compeleceng.2020.106739.

10. M. S. Badar, S. Shamsi, M. M. U. Haque, and A. S. Aldalbahi, "Applications of AI and ML in IoT," in S. K. Sharma, B. Bhushan, R. Kumar, A. Khamparia, N. C. Debnath (Eds). *Integration of WSNs into Internet of Things*, CRC Press, Boca Raton, 2021. https://www.taylorfrancis.com/books/edit/10.1201/9781003107521/integration-wsns-internet-things-sudhir-kumar-sharma-bharat-bhushan-raghvendra-kumar-aditya-khamparia-narayan-debnath?refId=0df43981-cc07-46d2-a236-959ca1164de2&context=ubx

11. M. Antonini, T. H. Vu, C. Min, A. Montanari, A. Mathur, and F. Kawsar, "Resource Characterisation of Personal-Scale Sensing Models on Edge Accelerators," in *Proceedings of the First International Workshop on Challenges in Artificial Intelligence and Machine Learning for Internet of Things*, New York, NY, USA, Nov. 2019, pp. 49–55. doi: 10.1145/3363347.3363363.

12. V. Mothukuri, R. M. Parizi, S. Pouriyeh, Y. Huang, A. Dehghantanha, and G. Srivastava, "A survey on security and privacy of federated learning," *Future Generation Computer Systems*, vol. 115, pp. 619–640, Feb. 2021, doi: 10.1016/j.future.2020.10.007.

13. H. Li, J. Yu, H. Zhang, M. Yang, and H. Wang, "Privacy-preserving and distributed algorithms for modular exponentiation in IoT with edge computing assistance," *IEEE Internet of Things Journal*, vol. 7, no. 9, pp. 8769–8779, Sep. 2020, doi: 10.1109/JIOT.2020.2995677.

14. J. Chi et al., "Privacy partition: a privacy-preserving framework for deep neural networks in edge networks," in *2018 IEEE/ACM Symposium on Edge Computing (SEC)*, Oct. 2018, pp. 378–380. doi: 10.1109/SEC.2018.00049.

15. H. Shahinzadeh, J. Moradi, G. B. Gharehpetian, H. Nafisi, and M. Abedi, "Internet of energy (IoE) in smart power systems," in *2019 5th Conference on Knowledge Based Engineering and Innovation (KBEI)*, Feb. 2019, pp. 627–636. doi: 10.1109/KBEI.2019.8735086.

16. P. K. Khatua, V. K. Ramachandaramurthy, P. Kasinathan, J. Y. Yong, J. Pasupuleti, and A. Rajagopalan, "Application and assessment of internet of things toward the sustainability of energy systems: challenges and issues," *Sustainable Cities and Society*, vol. 53, p. 101957, Feb. 2020, doi: 10.1016/j.scs.2019.101957.

17. H. D. Mohammadian, "IoE – a solution for energy management challenges," in *2019 IEEE Global Engineering Education Conference (EDUCON)*, Apr. 2019, pp. 1455–1461. doi: 10.1109/EDUCON.2019.8725281.

18. V. T. Nguyen, T. Luan Vu, N. T. Le, and Y. Min Jang, "An overview of internet of energy (IoE) based building energy management system," in *2018 International Conference on Information and Communication Technology Convergence (ICTC)*, Oct. 2018, pp. 852–855. doi: 10.1109/ICTC.2018.8539513.

19. M. Jaradat, M. Jarrah, A. Bousselham, Y. Jararweh, and M. Al-Ayyoub, "The internet of energy: smart sensor networks and big data management for smart grid," *Procedia Computer Science*, vol. 56, pp. 592–597, Jan. 2015, doi: 10.1016/j.procs.2015.07.250.

20. M. Rana, "Architecture of the internet of energy network: an application to smart grid communications," *IEEE Access*, vol. 5, pp. 4704–4710, 2017, doi: 10.1109/ACCESS.2017.2683503.

21. P. Sawadogo and J. Darmont, "On data lake architectures and metadata management," *Journal of Intelligent Information Systems*, vol. 56, no. 1, pp. 97–120, Feb. 2021, doi: 10.1007/s10844-020-00608-7.

22. "THE 17 GOALS | Sustainable Development." https://sdgs.un.org/goals (accessed Feb. 18, 2021).

23. N. Miloslavskaya and A. Tolstoy, "Big data, fast data and data lake concepts," *Procedia Computer Science*, vol. 88, pp. 300–305, Jan. 2016, doi: 10.1016/j.procs.2016.07.439.

24. S. L. Fernandes and G. J. Bala, "ODROID-XU4 based implementation of decision level fusion approach for matching computer generated sketches," *Journal of Computational Science*, vol. 16, pp. 217–224, Sep. 2016, doi: 10.1016/j.jocs.2016.07.013.

25. "Dev Board," Coral. https://coral.ai/products/dev-board (accessed Sep. 12, 2021).

26. S. Ramaswamy, "How micro-moments are changing the rules," *Think with Google*, Apr. 2015. https://www.thinkwithgoogle.com/marketing-resources/micro-moments/how-micromoments-are-changing-rules/.

27. A. Alsalemi, C. Sardianos, F. Bensaali, I. Varlamis, A. Amira, and G. Dimitrakopoulos, "The role of micro-moments: a survey of habitual behavior change and recommender systems for energy saving," *IEEE Systems Journal*, vol. 13, pp. 3376–3387, 2019.

28. A. Alsalemi et al., "Endorsing domestic energy saving behavior using micro-moment classification," *Applied Energy*, vol. 250, pp. 1302–1311, Sep. 2019, doi: 10.1016/j.apenergy.2019.05.089.

29. H. Assistant, "Database," *Home Assistant*. https://www.home-assistant.io/docs/backend/database/ (accessed Aug. 20, 2021).

30. H. Assistant, "Lovelace," *Home Assistant*. https://www.home-assistant.io/lovelace/ (accessed Aug. 20, 2021).

Chapter 3

Cyberattack detection and prevention on resource-constrained IoT devices based on intelligent agents

Huy-Trung Nguyen

People's Security Academy

Vietnam Ministry of Public Security

Quoc-Dung Ngo

Posts and Telecommunications Institute of Technology

CONTENTS

ABSTRACT

Internet of things (IoT) has become a trend that attracts many scientists, businesses, and application research and development organizations in recent years. However, security for IoT devices in general and resource-constrained IoT devices, in particular, has become an important issue. This chapter will present an overview of resource-constrained IoT devices and explain the characteristics of resource-constrained IoT devices that make integrated information security and safety solutions currently

DOI: 10.1201/9781003304203-3

unavailable, such as traditional electronic devices (i.e., PCs, laptops, and servers). This chapter will also go through the issues related to the traditional electronic device agents and the resource-constrained IoT device agents. Unlike traditional electronic devices with mostly i386-based processors and Windows operating systems, resource-constrained IoT devices use a variety of different processors such as MIPS32, MIPS64, ARM, ARM64, PowerPC, and SPARC and need limited resources (i.e., storage and processing). The data collected by the agent on the resource-constrained IoT devices are of different varieties (i.e., from network traffic data (PCAP) to system data of the device (syscalls, PID, etc.)); therefore, detecting and preventing cyberattacks against resource-constrained IoT devices is effective and practical when preventing cyberattacks is handled directly on resource-constrained IoT devices.

3.1 INTRODUCTION

The Internet is one of the most typical achievements of the Third Industrial Revolution (the 1990s). Humanity has been strongly using the Internet for different purposes in their daily life until the Fourth Industrial Revolution or Industrial Internet rapidly transformed the industry in every country, taking place globally. This revolution is characterized by a fusion, without boundaries between technology, physics, digital, and biology domains. The core technologies in the Industry 4.0 are artificial intelligence (AI), Internet of things (IoT), and big data. In this chapter, the authors will focus on IoT.

Throughout the Fourth Industrial Revolution, several fields and applications utilize the IoT for providing better services, such as education, medical healthcare, politics, society, and economy, with remarkable achievements in a short time [1]. IoT plays an important role in these applications and fields by providing multiple solutions to improve people's lives. For example, in the medical healthcare sector, IoT improves medical quality by enabling remote medical consultation, continuous monitoring of a patient's condition, or automatic transmission and analysis of collected data by devices. In addition to the conveniences brought by the Industrial Revolution 4.0, information security in cyberspace is becoming increasingly complex, potentially posing many risks that directly affect national security, the legitimate interest of the citizens. These threats are increasingly present as supply chains, factories, consumers, and related activities are interconnected.

Different from traditional computers, IoT devices are very diverse in hardware types and architectures, so it is the diversity of IoT devices that makes the number of IoT devices explode. It is expected that by 2025, there will be about 75 billion devices used in many fields and industries, which will bring many experiences to users such as smart homes, transportation, and healthcare. According to Gartner's research [2], by 2020, there will be an estimated 25% of attacks on centralized information systems and IoT devices, and more and more industries and fields will apply IoT technology, which will cause the number and scale of cyberattacks to continue to increase. In addition, a research by OWASP (Open Web Application Security Project) also shows that 75% of IoT devices are at risk of intrusion attacks. From an attacker's perspective, IoT devices are an attractive environment because, unlike traditional computers, IoT devices operate 24/7/365, are hard to be installed with anti-malware solutions, and use weak authentication, which makes it easy for attackers to get deep-level access to IoT devices (e.g., BusyBox). With that fact, many domestic and foreign individuals and organizations have paid attention to and invested in researches on ensuring information security for IoT devices.

Addressing the problems above, the chapter aims to: (1) present an overview of resource-constrained IoT devices and explain the characteristics of resource-constrained IoT devices that make integrated information security and safety solutions currently unavailable, such as traditional electronic devices, and (2) present the traditional electronic device agent and the resource-constrained IoT device agent.

In order to achieve the stated research objectives, this chapter will focus on answering three research questions posed, which are as follows:

- Research Question 1 (RQ1): What is the difference between resource-constrained IoT devices and traditional electronic computing devices?
- Research Question 2 (RQ2): What are the current methods to effectively detect IoT devices cyberattack? Are these methods suitable for resource-constrained IoT devices?
- Research Question 3 (RQ3): Based on the information presented in RQ2, which method can be built for resource-constrained IoT devices for detecting and preventing cyberattacks and solving the resource-constrained IoT device differentiation problems outlined in RQ1?

This chapter describes the basic security principles that must be understood and addressed in intelligent agent deployment on resource-constrained IoT devices. It begins by exploring IoT device type classification and explains at an accessible level for resource-constrained IoT devices. Constrained IoT devices will have properties and architecture that affect the development of intelligent agent integrated on IoT devices in cyberattack detection and prevention. The chapter concludes by looking into future developments in security for constrained IoT devices using the intelligent agent.

3.2 BACKGROUND

To answer RQ1, in this section, we will focus on presenting three main contents: Internet of things devices, constrained IoT device operating systems, and constrained IoT device cyberattacks. In this section, we will provide the readers with the awareness about IoT devices, in general, and resource-constrained IoT devices, in particular, thereby seeing the difference between resource-constrained IoT devices and traditional electronic computing ones.

3.2.1 Internet of things devices

The term "Internet of things" (IoT) in recent years has become popular and attracted a lot of attention from the technology world. In 1999, the idea of the term Internet of things (IoT) was first defined by Kevin Ashton, co-owner and CEO of Auto-ID Center [3]. However, as early as the 1980s, the first Internet-connected device was the Coke vending machine at Carnegie Mellon University. The term IoT was really popular after the 4th world conference on information technology (Internet Protocol version 6 or Internet Protocol 6th generation) took place in France in 2014, on the basis of the concept of IoT that has been defined by many professional standardization bodies, organizations, and associations in the field of IK technology, as well as many previous researchers. They include, for instance, International Telecommunication Union, IoT European Research Cluster, Cisco, and Oxford Dictionary. In this chapter, the authors use the term IoT to refer to *a platform that includes "things" (physical and virtual) integrated on objects, people, environments, and the ability to connect, collect, share, and process data for services of different purposes.*

According to the forecast results of market research company Statista (Germany) [4], the number of IoT devices will explode. In 2025, it is estimated to reach nearly 75 billion devices, 2.4 times higher than in 2020, as illustrated in Figure 3.1.

As can be seen, IoT is the fastest growing field in the recent history of computing. At the same time, through the concept of IoT, it is found that in the IoT environment, there are many different types of devices such as smartphones, personal computers, laptops, smartwatches, smart TVs,

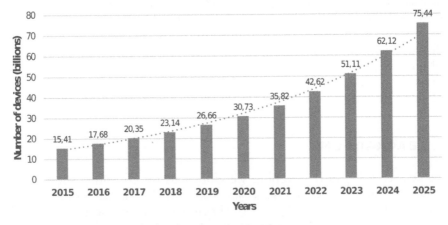

Figure 3.1 Number of IoT devices from 2015 to 2025 [4].

Figure 3.2 Illustration of the application of the Internet of things in real life.

printers, scanners, IP cameras, and routers. The explosion of IoT devices has a strong impact on human life, work, and society. IoT devices are present everywhere, in most industries and fields such as healthcare, production line management, energy management, intelligent transportation system, and power transmission system, as illustrated in Figure 3.2.

Applications of IoT devices are diverse, and there are many criteria to classify IoT devices [5], such as vendors, protocols, and connected objects. However, the above classifications are not comprehensive because the IoT is a relatively new and evolving field, and this classification is extensible to take new types into account. Therefore, to categorize IoT devices in a general way, suitable for the evolution and development of IoT devices in the future, IoT devices are broadly classified into two categories [6], constrained and high-capacity IoT devices, as shown in Figure 3.3.

- Constrained IoT devices: These are IoT devices with limitations such as low code storage (ROM/flash), low cache and state storage (RAM), low processor capacity, limited power availability, small device sizes, and low production cost, for example IP camera, routers, and SmartBox.
- High-capacity IoT devices: These are IoT devices that use the grid power and are capable of implementing power security features because the device configuration allows enough deployment resources (CPU, memory, and storage disk), for example server computer and personal computer.

Constrained IoT devices are divided into two subgroups [7], low-end IoT devices (Class 0) and middle-end IoT devices (Class 1). Class 0 or low-end

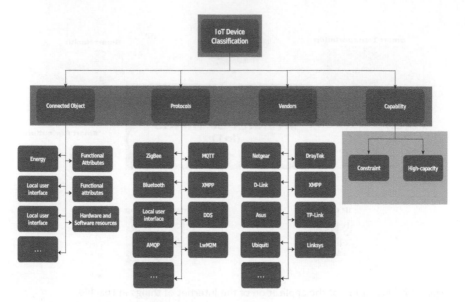

Figure 3.3 Categorization of IoT devices.

IoT devices are devices with confined resources such as power, memory, architecture, and computational competence. These IoT devices have sensing and actuating functions through lightweight communication protocols. They use a minimalist operating system with random access memory changing from 1 to 10 KiB (KiB=1024 bytes) and flash memory changing from 10 to 60 KiB. With such resources, these IoT devices rarely deploy security solutions and hence become easy targets for cyberattacks. Class 1 or middle-end IoT devices are devices that have more resources as correlated to low-end devices. The RAM changes from 100 KiB to 100 MiB, and the flash memory ranges from 10 KiB to 100 MiB. Having more resources, these devices have abilities such as data filtering (i.e., router devices) and image processing (i.e., IP camera) and can be partially secured utilizing encryption of data. In this chapter, the authors focus on security research for constrained IoT devices with intelligent agents.

Constrained IoT devices have characteristics that differentiate them from current traditional computing technologies, such as [8]:

- Uncontrolled Environment: Constrained IoT devices are highly portable and self-propelled (IP cameras, routers, etc.). These devices can physically access multiple locations, depending on environmental conditions, and perform pre-programmed tasks without the need for user involvement.
- Heterogeneity: Unlike traditional data processing devices such as personal computers with x86 processors, constrained IoT devices use a

variety of processor architectures such as MIPS (Microprocessor without Interlocked Pipeline Stages), ARM (Advanced RISC Machines), and PowerPC (Performance Optimization With Enhanced RISC – Performance Computing). In addition, the heterogeneity is also reflected in the fact that IoT devices are based on different networks such as the Internet, telecommunications networks, and satellite networks. Therefore, universal research for IoT devices is not easy.

- Constrained Resources: The constrained IoT devices are rarely deployed with security mechanisms to reduce production costs and reduce the size of devices, which makes constrained IoT devices resource constrained, such as low memory, small computing power, and low battery power capacity.
- Dynamic State: The state of constrained IoT devices changes dynamically, such as the time when they become active and asleep and the time when connected and disconnected, depending on the circumstances of the devices, such as location, function, and moving speed. Furthermore, the number of IoT devices may also vary.
- Connectivity: Through IoT, things can be connected and interact with the global communication and information infrastructure regularly. Resource-constrained IoT devices are often active and connected 24/7 over a variety of protocols and large-scale interactions.

Typically, constrained IoT devices have a structure that includes the main components shown in Figure 3.4.

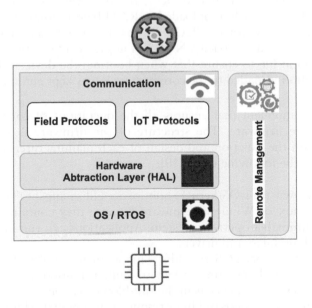

Figure 3.4 Structural overview of constrained IoT devices [9].

Things are often very constrained in terms of size or power supply. Therefore, they are often programmed using microcontrollers that have very constrained capabilities. The software running on microcontroller-based devices aims at supporting specific tasks. Major component key blocks on resource-constrained IoT devices include operating system (OS/RTOS); hardware abstraction – a software layer that enables access to the hardware features of the microcontrollers, such as flash memory and serial interfaces; communication – driver and protocol allowing to connect the device to a wired or wireless protocol (i.e., Bluetooth, CoAP, Z-Wave, and XMPP) and enabling device communication; and remote management – the ability to remotely control the device to upgrade its firmware or to monitor its battery level. In addition, there are some other components in the HAL block, which are as follows:

- CPU: It controls all device operations based on operating system executables.
- ROM: It contains programs that check automatically and may have the most basic components such that the device can perform a minimum number of operations even without an operating system or when the operating system is damaged.
- RAM: It allocates memory for processes such as buffers, configuration files when running, and parameters to ensure the operation of the device.
- Flash: It is a memory capable of writing and erasing, with no data loss when power is lost. Usually, the device's firmware is stored here. Depending on different devices, the operating system will be run directly from flash or uploaded to RAM before running.
- NVRAM (non-volatile RAM): It has the same function as flash, but with less storage capacity. NVRAM usually contains the device's configuration file to ensure that when booting, the device's default configuration is loaded to the correct state it was kept automatically.

The main component that ensures all the operations of constrained IoT devices is the firmware. The structure of the firmware is very diverse, depending on the function and design of each manufacturer. Firmware is divided into the following types [10]:

- Full-blown (full-OS/kernel+bootloader+libs+apps): These are usually Linux or Windows firmware because they contain a complete, but minimalist operating system. Applications can run in user mode, kernel modules, and drivers.
- Integrated (apps+OS-as-a-lib): This is an incomplete firmware; the functions and operating system are built as a library, not with all the necessary components as in the full-blown version.
- Partial updates (apps or libs or resources or support): This type of firmware contains only files used in updating the firmware to be upgraded.

3.2.2 Constrained IoT device operating system

To build programs, in general, and agents, in particular, to execute on IoT devices, the files need to satisfy the execution conditions for operating systems on IoT devices.

The operating system is a collection of programs that act as a link between an application or user and devices. Programs are constructed and run on the operating system platform. In other words, the operating system acts as a resource manager for complex systems. In a typical information system, these resources include processors, memory, timers, disk drives, network interfaces, security, and support for multimedia and power consumption. The operating system is installed on IoT devices to allow executable files to run on IoT devices and help operate and manage the devices. Therefore, it can be said that the operating system is responsible for managing and monitoring power consumption, allowing to run commands, programming the IoT device for its properties, and allowing devices to communicate back and forth. Due to the heterogeneous nature and strict constraints on the characteristics of IoT devices such as energy capacity, capacity, memory capacity, and computation, the operating system needs to be customized to meet the requirements of constrained IoT devices. Therefore, operating systems such as Windows, Linux, Android, and iOS are dominant on the laptops, servers, PCs, and mobile devices that are not directly suitable for devices in the constrained IoT space. Instead, the operating system should be lightweight to meet the requirements of constrained IoT devices with minimal hardware, yet following the security requirements. However, the operating system must ensure the three properties of IoT devices, including controlling, connecting, and communicating [11]. Thus, with the characteristics of constrained IoT devices, the commonly used operating system, based on the Linux platform, has been appropriately customized [12]. For example, through the Shodan.io search engine, the authors found that most network devices use the Kernel Linux 2.6.x kernel-based operating system. According to a review by Eclipse Foundation, Linux variants are the most utilized operating systems for constrained IoT devices, as shown in Figure 3.5.

In addition, points to pay attention to when designing an operating system for constrained IoT devices are the following:

- Architecture: There are many architectures to choose from for operating system design, such as monolithic (utilized for multilayer application system), microkernel (only the major functionalities run on kernel-land; other functionalities run in thread), modular (allows automatic addition and replacement of components to the kernel at runtime), and virtual machine (virtual system over the actual running system).
- Programming model: The programming model of the operating system affects the development of applications and the selection of

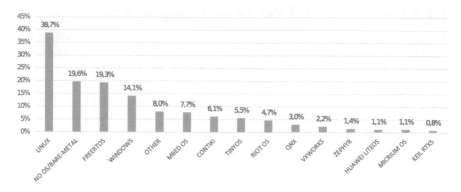

Figure 3.5 Ranking of operating systems for constrained IoT devices [13].

application programming languages. There are two main types of programming models, event-driven and multi-threaded.

- Scheduling: Scheduling strategy directly affects operating system capabilities.
- Memory management: It is the allocation and deallocation of memory resources. Memory can be divided into two types, static and dynamic memory. Static memory is allocated fixedly, while dynamic memory is flexibly allocated when it is required.

3.2.3 Constrained IoT device cyberattack

In this section, the risks associated with cyberattacks for resource-constrained IoT devices are presented. Many studies have presented information security threats to IoT devices [14]. However, such an approach to cyberattack risks will not be general, so this chapter presents an overview approach according to security requirements. For any information system or computing device, the three major security requirements that need to be satisfied are confidentiality, integrity, and availability, or the CIA triad [15]. Confidentiality ensures that messages are only accessed (read) by authorized objects (people, computer programs, etc.), and others are impossible. Integrity ensures that deleting or editing messages is impossible for any object except the targeted recipients and ensures that messages remain accurate when stored or transmitted. In addition, integrity maintains the authenticity of the data in the IoT system. Availability ensures that the system can be accessed anytime and can work in hostile situations. The CIA triad is not sufficient to take into account new attacks that arise on IoT devices. Therefore, in addition to the CIA triad, there are plenty of other security requirements that are specifically important for IoT devices, such as non-repudiation, privacy, accountability, audit, and credibility, as shown in Table 3.1.

Table 3.1 Major security requirements for IoT systems [16]

Requirements	Description
Confidentiality	It is strictly forbidden to disclose information to unauthenticated objects or to enter other systems, including the viewing of data in the real device or the cloning of device firmware itself.
Integrity	Needed to ensure the data cannot be modified without detection.
Availability	All devices must be accessible while being used. The system is always ready when needed, even during the attack. High availability and clustering solutions can support devices and services availability.
Non-repudiation	It prevents data owners (or data generators) from the denial of previously created data.
Privacy	IoT devices have widespread connectivity. Recently, it has become easier to track and identify objects, thus raising privacy concerns. For example, with BYOD devices, our bodies will be connected to the Internet, and with IP cameras, indoor space will be transmitted over the Internet. Therefore, the user's private information must be kept confidential and prevent unauthorized disclosure.
Audit	The ability of devices to implement defined privacy rules that allow control of sensitive data.
Accountability	The ability of devices to assign the responsibility of actions and decisions to an entity.
Credibility	The ability of devices to establish identification and ensure trust between third parties (users/processes).

There are different types of attacks to damage and breach security elements. Conceptually, cyberattacks on constrained IoT devices may be grouped into two complementary categories – active and passive attacks [17].

Active attacks are those where an attacker tries to modify the information or create a false message. Preventing these attacks is not easy because there are many potential physical, network, and software vulnerabilities. Rather than prevention, it emphasizes detecting the active attack and recovering from any disruption or delay caused by it. In contrast, passive attacks are attacks where the attacker performs unauthorized eavesdropping, simply monitoring the transmission or gathering information. The eavesdropper does not make any changes to the data or the system. In passive attacks, prevention is more concerned with detection. The significance of these attacks in constrained IoT device security is the basis for providing specific security solutions applied on constrained IoT devices for active and passive attacks.

Active attacks require state-of-the-art security mechanisms to prevent risks and mitigate damage, impact on the device, and network performance deterioration. Unlike active attacks, the defense mechanism deployed for passive attacks is limited to monitoring and mainly uses data encryption methods, so it has little impact on device and network performance. Some common attack forms under active attack and passive attacks against constrained IoT devices are as follows:

- Denial-of-service attack [18]: A denial-of-service attack is one of the techniques to prevent legitimate users from accessing and using any information technology service, leading to loss of system availability. In order to perform an effective denial-of-service attack that can bypass the defense of the attacked object, the attacker organizes an attack with simultaneous participation from many different devices (usually from various IP ranges). This form of attack is often referred to as a distributed denial-of-service (DDoS) attack. DDoS attacks are the most common and easiest to perform attacks on constrained IoT devices due to the enormous amount of devices scattered all over the globe. It is greatly dangerous in military communication, energy transmission sectors (e.g., electricity, oil, and gas), and emergency operations (e.g., fire and medical facility).
- Traffic sniffing attacks [19]: Traffic sniffing attacking in general terms refers to secretly gathering working data in order to find confidential information. From an information security perspective, sniffing refers to capturing the traffic or routing the traffic to a target and later utilizing it for attacks such as DDoS attacks. This information can be usernames, passwords, unencrypted data info, authentication types, hardware details, or any information that is of value to the attacker. There are two kinds of sniffing – active and passive. Sniffing in the switch is active sniffing, and the process of sniff through the hub that has no memory to store data and can only run in half-duplex mode is passive. Most of the constrained IoT devices currently on the market do not have enough security mechanisms to mitigate such attacks and easily fall victim to such attacks.
- Masquerade attack [20]: A masquerade attack is any attack that uses a fake identity, such as a network identity, to gain unauthorized access to the target device or system through legitimate access identification. If an authorization process is not wholly protected, it can become immensely vulnerable to a masquerade attack, as it helps the attacker gain access much more easily. Once the attackers gain access, they can get into all the device or system data to delete or modify them, steal sensitive data, or alter routing information and network configuration. Most constrained IoT devices are used by users using the manufacturer's default authentication info, which are values that hackers easily bypass. Therefore, constrained IoT devices with weak authorization processes are highly vulnerable and at high risk. Masquerade attacks perpetrate utilizing either stolen passwords or user credentials to gain unauthorized access to information systems through existing legitimate authentication processes. Access levels over masquerade attacks depend on the level of permission the penetrator achieves. Therefore, such attacks are usually triggered by someone inside or outside the organization. Therefore, such attacks are usually triggered by someone inside or outside the organization. For example, most of

the constrained IoT devices are from outside the organization since they are always connected to the Internet.

- Message replay attack [21]: A replay attack is a category of network attack that can be organized in three steps, including eavesdropping on the secure network communication or data transmission between IoT devices or gateway, interception, and then fraudulently delaying or retransmitting it to misdirect the receiver into doing what the attacker wants (i.e., duplicate transactions). The danger of replay attacks is that an attacker doesn't even need high-level skills to decrypt the data transmitted after capturing because the entire message can be resent to gain access to the server.

- Port scanning [22]: A port is a point on a computing device where information exchange between programs and the Internet to other devices takes place. A port scanning is a typical method that attackers use for determining open ports or weak points on a device or network. This method also helps discover whether an organization is using active security devices such as firewalls. With constrained IoT devices, the port scanning has the following elements – SYN requests, source, target port, packets, firewall, open nodes, and listening nodes. There are several techniques of port scanning, but with constrained IoT devices, the half-open scan or SYN (short for synchronize) scan method is the most used. In this tactic, the attackers only send an SYN message and wait for an SYN-ACK response message, but don't complete the connection. Since the TCP connection was not completed, the system doesn't log the communication and leaves the target hanging. It's a quick and sneaky technique aimed at learning if the port is open or not on target devices.

To combat the attacks on constrained IoT devices, employing a firewall is considered as the first layer of defense, but it is not an effective solution as the alteration and complication of IoT architectures [23] (e.g., diverse communication protocols). Therefore, an intelligent agent solution that is integrated right on constrained IoT devices to detect and prevent network attacks is necessary.

3.3 INTRUSION DETECTION AND PREVENTION

Despite having a large and direct impact, security studies for IoT devices, in general, and resource-constrained IoT devices, in particular, have not been given due attention from security individuals and organizations. One of the effective approaches to secure IoT devices is to use intrusion detection systems. In the early 1980s, Anderson performed intrusion detection studies [24]. An intrusion detection system (IDS) is one of the main techniques utilized for the protection of traditional computer networks and adaptation to diverse technologies in the IoT environment [25]. The operations of an

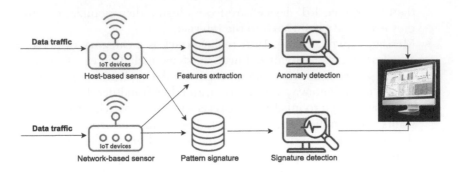

Figure 3.6 Overview of IDS operations [27].

IDS are illustrated in Figure 3.6. The activities of an IDS are divided into three phases. The first phase is the collecting and monitoring stage, which relies on host-based or network-based sensors. The second phase, the analysis phase, relies on feature extraction techniques or pattern identification techniques. The last phase, the detection phase, relies on anomaly or signature intrusion detection. The IDS observes the stream of network traffic to determine potentially harmful activities, and possible attempts may be logged or trigger an alert for system administrators [26].

Based on the first phase, the IDS is classified as host-based IDS (HIDS) and network-based IDS (NIDS). NIDS links to one or more network segments to observe network traffic for malicious activities. HIDS is combined with a computer device and monitors abnormal activities happening within the device. Unlike NIDS, the HIDS analyzes both network-level information and system-level information, such as system calls, file system changes, and running processes.

Typically, agents are deployed on devices with high computing capacity. IoT device networks are composed of devices with constrained resource. Therefore, finding devices with the capacity to support IDS agents are more complex in IoT devices networks. The second distinct characteristic is relevant to the network architecture. In a traditional computer network, servers connect directly to particular nodes (e.g., routers and access points) that are responsible for delivering the message packets to the destination. Meanwhile, the network of IoT devices is multi-hop. Based on the second phase, detection methods are classified into three main classes: signature-based, anomaly-based, and specification-based methods [28].

- Signature-based or misuse-based methods: This IDS detects a cyberattack when a system or network activity matches a cyberattack signature (a set of predefined rules) stored in the IDS database [29]. If any system or network behavior matches the stored signatures database, alerts are triggered, and the behavior will be treated as an intrusion. The advantage is that it is highly accurate and effective in detecting known threats (high detection rate with low false alarm rate), and its mechanism of action is easy to understand. However, unfortunately, it cannot detect zero-day/unknown/unseen attacks due to a lack of signatures. Therefore, the signature database in the signature-based IDS needs to be continuously updated, which results in low performance because of its need to store an enormous amount of cyberattack signatures [30].

- Anomaly-based methods: The anomaly-based IDS has knowledge of normal behavior, and it compares the activities of a system at an instant against normal activities to look for anomalies and generates an alert whenever the difference from normal behavior surpasses a threshold. The advantage of using this approach is that it enables the detection of new and unknown attacks, particularly those attacks related to misuse of resources. However, the primary limitation is that it might result in high false-positive alarms because knowing the entire range of normal behaviors is not a simple task [31] and normal profile activities are customized for each device and each network. So, in order to construct a set of normal behaviors, researchers often use statistical techniques, or mining or machine learning algorithms to improve the robustness of this kind of method, but these techniques are often resource-intensive for constrained IoT devices.

- Specification-based methods: The concept of a specification-based IDS was first proffered in 1997 [32]. Specification-based methods have the same logic as anomaly-based detection. It looks for usage anomalies by sampling normal activities and an alert of abnormal behaviors [33]. Specification is a set of predefined rules and thresholds by the system administrators (human experts). These security specifications are generated based on the functions and security policies for the computer system. If the rules are violated or the threshold is exceeded, the IDS will detect the anomaly and take appropriate action. This approach reduces high false alert rates as compared to anomaly detectors because each specification is defined manually by a human expert. However, this may not adapt to diverse environments and is time-consuming and error-prone.

- Hybrid: The hybrid method refers to utilizing a combination of signature-based, specification-based, and anomaly-based detection methods in the same IDS to overcome the shortcomings of a single method and maximize their advantages. However, the obvious weakness is that the entire IDS will become very large and complicated. This makes the whole system more difficult to operate and also more resource-intensive.

Besides IDS, intrusions can be prevented with IPS (intrusion prevention system). IPS is an IDS that responds to a potential threat or cyberattack to prevent it successfully or minimize damage. Some of the blocking responses are device reset, killing malicious processes on the device, dropping sessions, and blocking packets. However, an IDS only responds after detecting passing cyberattacks. Thus, it can be seen that in IDS systems, it is necessary to fully collect data from IoT devices and then process the data to detect and prevent cyberattacks against IoT devices [34]. Current studies have also been interested in the heterogeneity between IoT devices in terms of interoperability between different standards, data formats, heterogeneous hardware, etc. Currently, most IoT devices use Simple Network Management Protocol (SNMP) in collecting data on devices to detect abnormalities. However, for resource-constrained IoT devices, most do not support SNMP. Data collected from SNMP are application-level data only, not system-level data such as system calls. In addition, current solutions only partially meet the requirements of resource-constrained IoT devices. There is no overall system that addresses all three phases, including data collection, data preprocessing, and detection and prevention of cyberattacks against resource-constrained IoT devices. Therefore, building intelligent agents that can be directly installed on IoT devices and fully meet the above three phases is necessary. The proposed approach details are presented in the next section.

3.4 INTELLIGENT AGENTS FOR CYBERATTACK DETECTION AND PREVENTION

At this point, RQ1 and RQ2 have been answered in the content presented above. And to answer RQ3, this section will present a cyberattack detection approach aimed at resource-constrained IoT devices based on developing an agent that can be installed directly on the constrained IoT devices. There are many studies on agent software, such as [35] and [36], but this chapter finds that according to Wooldridge's research, a software agent is a computer system that can interact with its environment and is capable of making autonomous decisions on behalf of its owner to meet its certain objectives that are relevant and general. Agent software has many characteristics such as mobility, interaction, cooperation, adaptability, coordination, and negotiation [37]. Software agents enjoy a wide range of other characteristics, making it impossible for any researchers to include all of these in a single type. However, three distinguished characteristics of software agents include reactivity, proactiveness, and social ability.

- Reactivity: Software agents have the ability to sense their surroundings and interact with them in a customized way to achieve a goal.
- Proactiveness: Software agents have the ability to change their behavior toward a goal by initiating a request in order to achieve their objectives and goals.
- Social ability: Software agents have the ability to socialize and interact with other agents to achieve their goals.

To detect cyberattacks against resource-constrained IoT devices effectively, the first thing to do is to collect data for cyberattack detection, which is also an important function of the intelligent agent in this context. A cyberattack can be defined as a set of actions that compromise the integrity, security, and availability of a resource. Therefore, it is necessary to apply measures to detect network attacks to protect the participants in a network system. Data collection for detecting cyberattacks is divided into two main categories: system-level and network-level. System-level data such as system calls, CPU usage metrics, RAM, power consumption, and running processes are logged so that a predictive model can be generated for constrained IoT device attacks. However, on-device monitoring consumes many resources and can affect device operation, which may not be suitable for constrained IoT devices, so network-level data collection is required. Network-level data collection can be performed individually on each device as system-level data collection or the entire system (reducing resource consumption in the operating system). In network-level data collection, information of the network flow is to be collected, including services, source/destination addresses, source/destination ports and status flags, which will make it easier to detect cyberattacks in constrained IoT devices. The disadvantage of this method is that the manifestation of a network attack will be shown on network traffic only if the device has been compromised. Therefore, it is not as effective as monitoring the device at the system level and detecting immediately when the IoT device is attacked. Each data collection method has its advantages and disadvantages and helps in detecting cyberattacks. Therefore, developing an intelligent agent that can be installed directly on a limited IoT device to collect system call data, system information, and network flow data from IoT devices will help take advantage of the above two methods.

An overview of the model of the network attack detection and prevention system targeting constrained IoT devices using intelligent agents is shown in Figure 3.7. The system consists of three main subsystems as follows: data collection; data processing and analysis; and centralized monitoring, warning, and preventing cyberattacks.

3.4.1 Data collection segment

This segment includes the chain of agents installed on constrained IoT devices. An IoT agent is software that can control groups of constrained IoT devices and aggregate the data they collect into a combined stream and send it back to the central IoT analyzer. The intelligent agent is a decisive component to the management quality of the whole constrained IoT devices network monitoring system. The intelligent agent has a prerequisite role in determining the outcome of the entire information management process. The task of the intelligent agent is to actively monitor the information of the installed device, such as system information, system calls, and network flow information. To install agents into constrained IoT devices, there are two common methods:

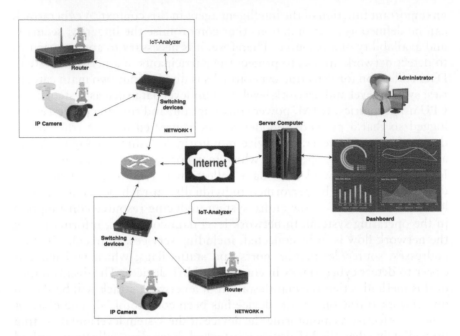

Figure 3.7 Overview model for detecting and preventing network attacks on constrained IoT devices using IoT agent.

- The first is through the agent's executable file: With the method of installing the agent through an executable file (such as ELF format on Linux operating systems or EXE on Windows operating systems), the executable file needs to be downloaded to the internal memory of the IoT device through a physical or an Internet connection. In other words, the agent is installed indirectly through network service ports such as SSH and Telnet. The method of passing the agent's executable file has the advantage that it does not require intervention, modification of the firmware, and kernel of the constrained IoT device. This method ensures that the agent is installed in RAM and will be lost when the IoT device crashes, loses power, or restarts.
- The second is through agent-built firmware: This method requires the intelligent agent to be built into the IoT device's firmware before it is released to the market and shipped to the end-users. The built-in agent will run with the IoT device system. However, when you want to update to a new version of the agent, you need to repeat the agent integration process and load the new firmware directly into the device. Simple firmware is stored in read-only memory, or OTP/PROM, while more complex firmware is stored in flash memory. The usual reasons for updating the firmware include fixing bugs or adding functionality to the device [38]. This method helps the agent work stably on the constrained IoT

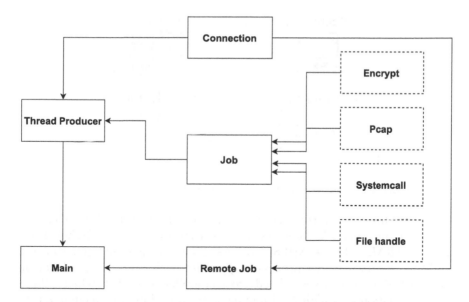

Figure 3.8 Components in the architecture of agent operations on constrained IoT devices.

device and not lose when the device reboots. However, integrating the agent into the firmware is not straightforward because it affects the integrity of the firmware and the operating system kernel.

From the perspective of monitoring and ensuring network security for constrained IoT devices, the agent first needs to collect system-level and network-level information of IoT devices placed in the network. The module is designed according to the model shown in Figure 3.8, and the components have specific functions as follows:

- Thread producer: This component is responsible for creating threads that collect data and process synchronously between threads.
- Connection: This component is responsible for handling features that build and maintain Internet connections.
- Job: This component is responsible for building information collection features on the device. This component is subdivided into the main workgroups that include the following:
  - Encryption: The work is related to encryption and decryption of data.
  - PCAP (packet capture): The work is related to network-level data collection.
  - System call: Jobs related to the collection of system calls are being called on the device (under construction).
  - File handling: Jobs related to the collection of system-level device parameters, which are stored in system files.

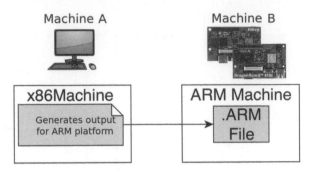

Figure 3.9 Cross-compiler translates from x86 to ARM.

Unlike traditional electronic computers, most of which use Intel x86 processor architectures, IoT devices use a variety of processor architectures such as ARM, ARM64, MIPS, MIPS64, PowerPC, and SPARC. To avoid building agents for each processor type and each firmware platform on limited IoT devices, a specialized cross-compiler is needed, which allows the compilation of a high-level language program into an executable program to run on numerous processor architectures. For example, as shown in Figure 3.9, a cross-compiler compiles a program developed on the X86 architecture into an executable program on the ARM architecture.

Given resource constraints, an agent developed on constrained IoT devices must also meet size constraints after compilation and resource consumption on the device during execution. For example, the agent after compiling on the IP camera (ARM architecture) is 322KB and, on the router (MIPS architecture), it is 418KB; the resource consumed when executed on the device here is the RAM information that the agent occupies, which is about 300KB. The file is executed on an IoT device capable of collecting system- and network-level data, and the data collected are illustrated in Figure 3.10.

After the collection process, raw data will be sent and processed at the data processing and analysis segment.

3.4.2 Data processing and analysis segment

This segment is developed in a distributed direction with each independent management pointing a set of IoT devices. From the obtained data, the segment analyzes and warns against network attacks before sending them to the centralized monitoring segment. Each of these analysis points consists of two main modules:

- Module for preprocessing and normalizing data collected from devices under the management of each point in the system;
- Module for applying machine learning model in analyzing and detecting cyberattacks.

Figure 3.10 Information collected by the agent at the system level (a) and network level (b) on the IoT device.

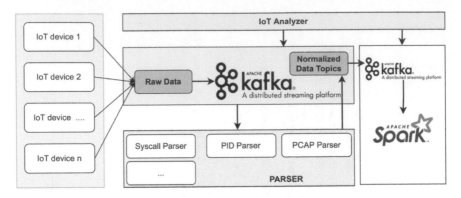

Figure 3.11 Proposed data acquisition and preprocessing model.

To avoid data loss during preprocessing and analysis, data processing models based on Apache Kafka, Spark, and MongoDB can be used. Using Kafka as a buffer helps to avoid bottleneck situations when the amount of data to be processed is too large and affects device resources (Figure 3.11).

3.4.3 Centralized monitoring, warning, and preventing cyberattacks segment

In order to improve the system's ability to analyze and warn about the risks of network attacks, the centralized monitoring server is responsible for updating abnormal network/system behaviors, new malware samples, and IP addresses, etc. from trusted open-source sources. These data sources are used to train the model before updating the scatter points. In addition, the monitoring server is also a bridge to update new agent patterns and help administrators manage their devices through the threat broadcast module.

- Integrate cyberattacks prevention measures into the agent installed on constrained IoT devices with termination of abnormal processes on the device: Distinguishing between anomalous processes and legitimate processes on the system involves looking at how the processes are running. In some cases, anomalous processes will immediately show suspicious characteristics, such as an established network connection with an Internet Relay Chat (IRC) server or an executable file stored in a hidden folder. More subtle signs of a malicious process include files it has opened, a process running as root without permission, and the amount of system resources system in use [39]. Identifying a malicious process leads to many other properties. Killproc is a command-line utility to terminate or kill Unix processes by PID. During a memory dump, a process's name and its process identifier (PID) are associated with other things such as [40]:

- Loaded DLLs: This may include attacker-provided libraries that you have not previously identified and where they are stored.
- File handling: This can include other files provided by the attacker.
- Handling the registry: This will tell you what registry keys are being accessed by the process, possibly including registry keys used to start the executable files at startup automatically.
- Sockets and network connections: The PIDs are all associated with active sockets or network connections. This helps to identify which servers are connected to limited IoT devices.

- Set up constrained IoT device restart: One of the most effective ways to prevent the spread and impact of devices when attacked is to disconnect that device from the network.
- Automatically update security patches, specifically firmware updates from manufacturers' websites.
- Automatically change/update strong passwords for Telnet/SSH protocols after a certain period. With the characteristics of compact devices and especially lack of awareness from users, limited IoT devices often keep their default passwords, which are simple and easy to guess such as admin, 123456, and root. Therefore, changing strong passwords will make attacks through remote administration protocols such as Telnet or SSH more difficult for hackers.

3.5 FUTURE RESEARCH DIRECTIONS

This chapter has provided an overview of IoT devices, highlighting the unique characteristics and security challenges of constrained IoT devices. For resource-constrained IoT devices, the level of system information collection currently stops at user-land, while collecting system calls from IoT devices is limited to kernel-land by implementing hooking function to system call table. In addition, this chapter also paves the way for the exploration of various intrusion detection and prevention solutions and constrained IoT devices protection mechanisms using agents installed directly on the devices.

3.6 CONCLUSIONS

The Industry 4.0 era, also known as the 4th Technological Revolution, can be understood as the breakthrough development of a series of new technologies that blur the lines between people and technology. At the same time, it also greatly affects the development of the economy, society, education, and politics. The main areas of interest in the 4.0 Revolution can be mentioned as artificial intelligence (AI), nanotechnology, biotechnology, big data, and especially IoT that makes everything possible, including more convenient connection and data exchange, helping users have more experiences in life. Besides these advantages, ensuring safety and information security for constrained IoT devices is very urgent in today's time. Moreover, to prolong battery life, constrained IoT devices typically possess low processing capabilities and limited memory and storage on flash or RAM. These characteristics lead to a lack of security designs inside these devices, thus leading to security issues of leaking private data as operating system disruption, attack of IoT botnet, and so on. This work assumes that the agent is essentially a viable solution for cyberattack detection and prevention in constrained IoT devices. In general, the segments in the general model are described in detail, in which the agent development segment plays an important role in determining the accuracy in detecting and preventing cyberattacks integrated directly on the device. In this chapter, we cover constrained IoT device characteristics, structure, and cyberattacks against constrained IoT devices to have necessary features in building and developing agents on the appropriate IoT device. Focusing more on data collection on constrained IoT devices, we identify system-level and network-level information that has different meanings and roles in detecting network attacks, such as DDoS attacks and port scanning attacks. This chapter also outlines the components required for agent development on constrained IoT devices and how to represent and transmit data for cyberattack detection and prevention.

ACKNOWLEDGMENTS

The authors would like to acknowledge the financial support of Vingroup Joint Stock Company and the support of Domestic Scholarship Program of Vingroup Innovation Fund (VINIF) and Vingroup Big Data Institute (VINBIGDATA).

REFERENCES

1. Hajjaji, Y., Boulila, W., et al., "Big data and IoT-based applications in smart environments: A systematic review," *Comput. Sci. Rev.*, vol. 39, p. 100318, 2021, doi: 10.1016/j.cosrev.2020.100318.
2. Hung, M., *"Gartner insights on how to lead in a connected world."* Gartner, Inc., Stamford, CT, Tech. Rep., 2017.
3. Kevin Ashton, "That 'Internet of Things' thing," *RFID J.*, vol. 22, no. 7, pp. 97–114, 2009.
4. Statista, R. D., "Internet of Things - number of connected devices worldwide 2015–2025." Statista Research Department. statista.com/statistics/471264/iot-numberof-connected-devices-worldwide., 2021.

5. Dorsemaine, B., Gaulier, J. P., et al., "Internet of things: a definition & taxonomy," *In 2015 9th International Conference on Next Generation Mobile Applications, Services and Technologies*, Sep. 2015, pp. 72–77. doi: 10.1109/NGMAST.2015.71.

6. Lévy-Bencheton, C., Darra, E., et al., *"Security and Resilience of Smart Home Environments."* European Union Agency for Cybersecurity, Publications Office of the European Union, 2015.

7. Bormann, C., Ersue, M., et al., "Terminology for constrained-node networks," *Internet Eng. Task Force IETF Fremont*, pp. 2070–1721, 2014.

8. Zhou, W., Jia, Y., et al., "The effect of iot new features on security and privacy: New threats, existing solutions, and challenges yet to be solved," *IEEE Internet Things J.*, vol. 6, no. 2, pp. 1606–1616, 2018, doi: 10.1109/JIOT.2018.2847733.

9. Nagasai, "Classification of IoT Devices." https://www.cisoplatform.com/profiles/blogs/classification-of-iot-devices, 2017.

10. Andrei Costin, *"Large Scale Security Analysis of Embedded Devices' Firmware'."* 23rd USENIX Security Symposium (USENIX Security 14), TELECOM ParisTech, 2014.

11. Musaddiq, A., Zikria, Y. B., et al., "A survey on resource management in IoT operating systems," *IEEE Access*, vol. 6, pp. 8459–8482, Feb. 2018, doi: 10.1109/ACCESS.2018.2808324.

12. Bansal, S., & Kumar, D., "IoT ecosystem: A survey on devices, gateways, operating systems, middleware and communication," *Int. J. Wirel. Inf. Netw.*, vol. 27, pp. 340–364, 2020, doi: 10.1007/s10776-020-00483-7.

13. E. Foundation, "IoT developer survey 2018." https://iot.eclipse.org/community/resources/iotsurveys/assets/iot-developer-survey-2018.pdf, 2018.

14. Xiao, L., Wan, X., Lu, X., Zhang, Y., & Wu, D., "IoT security techniques based on machine learning: How do IoT devices use AI to enhance security?" *IEEE Signal Processing Magazine*, vol. 35, no. 5, pp. 41–49, 2018.

15. Jang-Jaccard, J., & Nepal, S., "A survey of emerging threats in cybersecurity," *J. Comput. Syst. Sci.*, vol. 80, no. 5, pp. 973–993, Aug. 2014, doi: 10.1016/j.jcss.2014.02.005.

16. Cherdantseva, Y., & Hilton, J., "A reference model of information assurance & security," *In 2013 International Conference on Availability, Reliability and Security*, Sep. 2013, pp. 546–555. doi: 10.1109/ARES.2013.72.

17. Abdul-Ghani, H. A., Konstantas, D., & Mahyoub, M., "A comprehensive IoT attacks survey based on a building-blocked reference model," *Int. J. Adv. Comput. Sci. Appl.*, vol. 9, no. 3, pp. 355–373, 2018, doi: 10.14569/IJACSA.2018.090349.

18. Salim, M. M., Rathore, S., & Park, J. H., "Distributed denial of service attacks and its defenses in IoT: a survey," *J. Supercomput.*, vol. 76, no. 7, pp. 5320–5363, Jul. 2020, doi: 10.1007/s11227-019-02945-z.

19. Stiawan, D., Idris, M., Malik, R. F., et al., "Investigating brute force attack patterns in IoT network," *J. Electr. Comput. Eng.*, 2019, doi: 10.1155/2019/4568368.

20. Shen, H., Shen, J., Khan, M.K. et al., "Efficient RFID authentication using elliptic curve cryptography for the internet of things," *Wirel. Pers. Commun.*, vol. 96, no. 4, pp. 5253–5266, 2017, doi: 10.1007/s11277-016-3739-1.

21. Na, S., Hwang, D., et al., "Scenario and countermeasure for replay attack using join request messages in lorawan," *In International Conference on Information Networking (ICOIN)*, 2017, pp. 718–720. doi: 10.1109/ICOIN.2017.7899580.

22. Kumar, C. O., & Bhama, P. R. S., "Detecting and confronting flash attacks from IoT botnets," *J. Supercomput.*, vol. 75, no. 12, pp. 8312–8338, Dec. 2019, doi: 10.1007/s11227-019-03005-2.

23. Liang, C., Shanmugam, B., et al., "Intrusion detection system for the internet of things based on blockchain and multi-agent systems," *Electronics*, vol. 9, no. 7, p. 1120, Jul. 2020, doi: 10.3390/electronics9071120.

24. Anderson, J. P., "Computer security threat monitoring and surveillance." Technical Report, James P. Anderson Company, 1980.

25. Zarpelão, B. B., Miani, R. S., et al., "Survey of intrusion detection systems towards an end to end secure internet of things," *In 2016 IEEE 4th International Conference on Future Internet of Things and Cloud (FiCloud)*, Aug. 2016, pp. 84–90. doi: 10.1109/FiCloud.2016.20.

26. Anwar, S., Mohamad Zain, J., et al., "From intrusion detection to an intrusion response system: Fundamentals, requirements, and future directions," *Algorithms*, vol. 10, no. 2, p. 39, Jun. 2017, doi: 10.3390/a10020039.

27. Elrawy, M. F., Awad, A. I., et al., "Intrusion detection systems for IoT-based smart environments: A survey," *J. Cloud Comput.*, vol. 7, no. 1, pp. 1–20, 2018, doi: 10.1186/s13677-018-0123-6.

28. Sobh, T. S., "Wired and wireless intrusion detection system: Classifications, good characteristics and state-of-the-art," *Comput. Stand. Interfaces*, vol. 28, no. 6, pp. 670–694, 2006, doi: 10.1016/j.csi.2005.07.002.

29. Bul'ajoul, W., James, A., & Pannu, M., "Improving network intrusion detection system performance through quality of service configuration and parallel technology," *J. Comput. Syst. Sci.*, vol. 81, no. 6, pp. 981–999, 2015, doi: 10.1016/j.jcss.2014.12.012.

30. Abduvaliyev, A., Pathan, A. S. K., et al., "On the vital areas of intrusion detection systems in wireless sensor networks," *IEEE Commun. Surv. Tutor.*, vol. 15, no. 3, pp. 1223–1237, 2013, doi: 10.1109/SURV.2012.121912.00006.

31. Mitchell, R., & Chen, I. R., "A survey of intrusion detection techniques for CyberPhysical Systems," *ACM Comput. Surv. CSUR*, vol. 46, no. 4, pp. 1–29, 2014, doi: 10.1145/2542049.

32. Ko, C., Ruschitzka, M., & Levitt, K., "Execution monitoring of security-critical programs in distributed systems: A specification-based approach," *In Proceedings. 1997 IEEE Symposium on Security and Privacy (Cat. No. 97CB36097)*, May 1997, pp. 175–187. doi: 10.1109/SECPRI.1997.601332.

33. Santos, L., Rabadao, C., & Gonçalves, R., "Intrusion detection systems in Internet of Things: A literature review," *In 2018 13th Iberian Conference on Information Systems and Technologies (CISTI)*, 2018, pp. 1–7. doi: 10.23919/CISTI.2018.8399291.

34. Zarpelão, B. B., Miani, R. S., Kawakani, C. T., & de Alvarenga, S. C., "A survey of intrusion detection in Internet of Things," *J. Netw. Comput. Appl.*, vol. 84, pp. 25–37, 2017, doi: 10.1016/j.jnca.2017.02.009.

35. Wooldridge, M, *An Introduction to Multiagent Systems*. John Wiley & Sons, New York 2009.

36. Laarabi, M. H., Roncoli, C., et al., "An overview of a multiagent-based simulation system for dynamic management of risk related to dangerous goods transport," Apr. 2013, pp. 830–835. doi: 10.1109/SysCon.2013.6549980.
37. Hyacinth S. Nwana, "Software agents: An overview," *Knowl. Eng. Rev. Camb. Univ. Press*, vol. 11, no. 3, pp. 205–244, Sep. 1996, doi: 10.1017/S026988890000789X.
38. I. C. Martínez, "The key to everything: Firmware on IoT devices." https://www.puffinsecurity.com/the-key-to-everything-firmware-on-iot-devices, 2020.
39. C. H. Malin, E. Casey, and J. M. Aquilina, "Malware forensics field guide for Linux systems: digital forensics field guides," *Newnes*, Elsevier, 2014.
40. E. Casey, *Handbook of Digital Forensics and Investigation*. Academic Press, 2009. doi: 10.1016/C2009-0-01683-3.

Chapter 4

Artificial intelligence system for intelligent monitoring and management of water treatment plants

Jamal Mabrouki, Ghizlane Fattah,
Siham Kherraf, and Younes Abrouki
Mohammed V University in Rabat

Mourade Azrour
Moulay Ismail University

Souad El Hajjaji
Mohammed V University in Rabat

CONTENTS

DOI: 10.1201/9781003304203-4

69

ABSTRACT

In the field of clean water treatment, the use of artificial intelligence is becoming imperative to achieve two main objectives at present, the control of water quality and the reduction of operating cost constraints. Treatment plant output quality variables play an important role in water control and monitoring. Although some parameters can be measured continuously using low-cost physical sensors, the software sensor-based system can provide an efficient and cost-effective means of addressing these issues. Our work can be considered as a contribution to the proposed solutions to problems of strategic interest of national and international concern, using modern tools based on advanced techniques and artificial intelligence. In this context, we present a contribution to the study of intelligent sensors used in the monitoring and control and management of processing stations. These algorithmic sensors based on artificial intelligence techniques and representing a very attractive way to cope with the lack of specific sensors have become highly coveted.

4.1 INTRODUCTION

Today, clean water, as a source of life, is one of the most closely watched food products in the world. Indeed, in recent years, the importance of modern technologies for its treatment has increasingly attracted the attention of developing countries [1,2]. Adding to this, lower-quality treatment activities further increase the risk of disease through the use of polluted surface water [3,4]. In order to improve the quality of this vital resource, the use, development and dissemination of increasingly modern treatment technologies are becoming a priority in countries' strategic choices.

Indeed, the field of water monitoring is often under increasing pressure to produce drinking water of higher quality at lower cost. This represents a saving not only in terms of cost, but also in terms of environmental friendliness. These are very specific characteristics that must be taken into account in the construction of an overall risk prevention approach. Controlling the sanitary quality of water undoubtedly alleviates the serious consequences that materialize in terms of the risks to public health. The requirement for very strict regulation by the public authorities in this area is therefore well and truly justified. It should be emphasized at this point that a modern drinking water plant has two main functions: to meet the demand for water and to ensure a uniformly high level of quality [5]. Permanent monitoring systems must therefore ensure the control of the various treatment processes and facilities, especially those parameters related to the quality of the water leaving a production plant [6].

When we talk about water monitoring, we are in fact talking about knowing its state on a continuous basis, based on various parameters, known as descriptors, relating to its quality. Traditionally, a number of useful measurements of the descriptor parameters are usually made of raw water for quality testing, such as bacteriological control, disinfection control and physical disinfection and physicochemical control, to finally decide on its clean condition after applying the appropriate techniques and methods to make it potable. The disadvantage of this procedure is that it requires non-stop interventions and travel on site by the operator. It does not in fact allow the evolution of the quality of the raw water to be followed in detail and has the disadvantage of having a relatively long response time. This is the advantage of having an automatic control system for better treatment efficiency and reduced operating costs. Water control at production plants must therefore be immediate, based on continuous monitoring of quality parameters throughout a treatment chain that ensures both monitoring and control. Automated monitoring can in fact eliminate certain human weaknesses, increase reliability and improve the operating conditions and performance of the installation by eliminating a maximum number of repetitive and tedious tasks for the operator. Automating treatment processes can therefore have various objectives, the most common of which are to increase the performance of the production system, to guarantee product quality, to monitor treatment plants and equipment, to reduce production costs and to improve the safety of the industrial plant and its environment. Furthermore, automation coupled with information storage allows statistical studies of the data collected, opening the way to modeling studies and therefore to the optimization of treatment processes. In this context, automation and computer supervision have led to an increase in comfort by allowing better control, even at a distance, of a large amount of information, which simplifies the tasks of operation, monitoring, maintenance and management. The use of techniques from the field of artificial intelligence appears to be the main alternative for tackling these problems when it is necessary to take into account the intervention of experts in the field or to process information of a qualitative nature.

In water quality monitoring, as in other similar fields, effective monitoring depends mainly on the accuracy and depends mainly on the accuracy and reliability of the measurement sensors used [7]. On the other hand, water is considered as a process input and has several descriptor parameters to be controlled and monitored. Moreover, the heterogeneity of these parameters measured by the sensors is considered a real challenge for water quality [8,9]. These quality parameters actually play a fundamental role in ensuring clean water quality. Although some of these parameters can be measured continuously with low-cost sensors, there are other parameters that require specific and costly laboratory analyses due to the lack of dedicated sensors [10,11]. In fact, and for several reasons, such as the high cost of some sensors, their number, the time spent on their control, cleaning, calibration and replacement routines, it often becomes difficult for them to function properly.

In view of the above-mentioned problems, soft sensors based on algorithms inspired by artificial intelligence techniques have become an effective and very attractive way to overcome the lack of physical and/or specific sensors [12]. Indeed, the deployment of microelectronic devices has led to a drastic reduction in costs, which has allowed the emergence and development of these software sensors and their software sensors and their widespread application, such as in biochemical systems [13], bioprocess monitoring [14], biological wastewater treatment [15] and treatment and process prediction [16].

This research work is an evaluation study of several regression techniques derived from artificial intelligence and a new method for the prediction of the water treatment process in the field of wastewater treatment, in order to improve the efficiency of the process. The objective is to implement a monitoring system architecture based on the use of software sensors based on these techniques that can be integrated into intelligent sensor platforms. These hybrid sensors can be used more economically to make appropriate decisions in the control and monitoring of processes for better water quality.

4.2 LITERATURE REVIEW

The transformation of surface wastewater into water fit for consumption involves a wide range of treatment processes that must be assembled in a specific sequence to provide a finished product that meets drinking water standards. The effectiveness of the treatment adopted will also depend on the way in which the plant is operated. In order to achieve the desired objective, the operator will need to respect certain basic principles to ensure the control of the treatment process and control of the treated water and, on the other hand, to have a certain number of technical and human resources. However, existing techniques are being developed and improved. This evolution is reflected in the search for new processes and in the implementation of numerous automatic systems. Below, we present the most complete and most common water treatment methods, particularly without going deep into the fine details of the processes. From these processes, it can be assumed that the complete typical chain consists of five main stages (Figure 4.1) [17].

Monitoring of certain parameters of drinking water quality means knowing the state of the water on a continuous basis (at any given moment), based on the various parameters related to its quality. A number of useful measurements of the various parameters that describe the quality of raw water are generally carried out, such as bacteriological, disinfection and physicochemical controls, in order to decide on its proper state after applying the techniques and methods to make it drinkable [18,19]. The disadvantage of this technique is that it requires non-stop interventions and travel on site by the operator. In fact, it does not allow the evolution of the quality of the raw water to be followed in detail and has the disadvantage of having a relatively long response time. Here is the advantage of having an automatic control of this process for better treatment efficiency and a

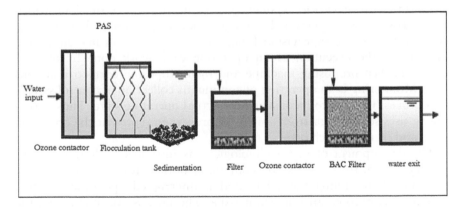

PAS

Water
input →

Ozone contactor   Flocculation tank

Sedimentation   Filter   Ozone contactor   BAC Filter   water exit

Figure 4.1 System of surface water treatment.

reduction of the operating costs. Water control at production plants must therefore be immediate, based on continuous monitoring of quality parameters through a treatment chain that provides both monitoring and control. The automation of these processes for monitoring will make it possible to overcome certain human weaknesses, increase reliability and improve the operating conditions and performance of the installation by eliminating a maximum number of repetitive and tedious tasks for the operator [20]. Automating treatment processes can therefore have various objectives, the most frequent being to increase the performance of the production system, to guarantee the quality of the product quality, monitoring of processing plants and equipment, reducing production costs and production costs and to improve the safety of the industrial plant and its environment. In addition, automation coupled with information storage allows statistical studies of the data collected, opening the way to modeling studies and therefore process modeling and therefore optimization of treatment processes [21,22].

In more recent times, automation and supervision by means of computers have led to an increase in comfort by enabling better control and management, even from a distance, of a large amount of information, which simplifies the operation, monitoring, maintenance and control tasks [23]. The use of techniques from the field of artificial intelligence appears to be the main alternative to tackle these problems when it is necessary to take into account the intervention of domain experts or to process information of qualitative nature.

4.3 PROPOSED SYSTEM

The whole process, actuators, sensors and control part, constitutes the automated system. This loop exchanges information with the operator from whom it receives instructions and to whom it provides information.

An installation supervision system consists in carrying out this loop which passes through the operator. Data acquisition is a function that links the control part to the supervision function. This consists in managing and monitoring the execution of an operation or a work done by man or machine, then proposing machine and then proposing corrective actions [24]. Monitoring is an operation of continuous collection of control signals of a process in order to reconstruct the actual operating state. Thus, monitoring uses sensor data from system or process to represent the operating state and then detect changes.

The development of new technologies has introduced additional complexity to real-time systems by combining both hardware and software elements. Maintaining the safety and uninterrupted operation of these systems has become an important issue. The purpose of monitoring the process diagnosis is to identify the causes of a set of observed symptoms that indicate degradation or failure of certain system components leading to abnormal behavior of the physical system. Monitoring methodologies are generally divided into two categories: model-based and model-free monitoring methodologies [25]. As a result, it is often difficult to determine the most appropriate method for solving the monitoring problem. Model-based monitoring methods are often preferable, especially in a dynamic context. These methods and the type of model associated with them differ not only in the nature of the knowledge available about the physical system and its failures, but also in the way this knowledge is exploited.

The two approaches automatic and artificial intelligence can be combined for more advantages. Automatic methods are by nature close to the system being monitored, as they work directly from sensor data and are therefore mainly used for alarm generation. AI methods, on the other hand, are more oriented toward communication with the operator and focus on the transformation of a set of raw and unrelated information into information that can be directly interpreted by the operator in charge of the driving task; they are therefore used for the interpretation of alarms and decision support. In the case of the use of AI tools, the monitoring function is often seen as a pattern recognition application where the patterns represent the input vector composed of the different process parameters. However, a diagnostic problem can be defined as a pattern recognition problem [26].

4.4 MATERIALS AND METHODS

In industrial instrumentation, particularly in measurement chains, any physical or chemical quantity to be measured is first converted into an electrical signal by a device called a sensor. The latter acts as a transducer, delivering at its output a signal as an information carrier that can then be used in various operations such as acquisition, analysis, recording and transmission. Sensors are designed to be used in generally hostile environments.

These sensors must therefore be very robust. A harsh environment often combines several stresses applied to the sensor at the same time: shock, vibration, acceleration and temperature. In the field of water monitoring, the constraints imposed on sensors are mainly humidity and the nature of the water. These sensors, which are often immersed, require periodic cleaning of the measuring probes, as deposits on them cause more drift; hence, regular calibration is necessary. Reliability is defined as the ability of the sensor to function properly, i.e., to provide data with adequate accuracy and with a robust hardware design.

4.4.1 Multi-parameter probes

There are devices on the market for monitoring water quality, called water quality probes. These probes allow measurements of some parameters/descriptors of water quality. This probe is equipped with a set of six specific sensors designed to make measurements of fluid properties in water wells. The use of the latest smart sensor technology may avoid the need for complex on-site calibrations [27]. Corrections to standard temperature and pressure measurements are made automatically on surface systems.

4.4.2 Intelligent sensors

The integration of signal processing functions within physical sensors is representative of the concept of the "intelligent sensor". The continuous progress in this area is an archetype of technological innovation. The incorporation of dedicated signal processing increases the design flexibility of measuring devices and thus enables new complex functions to be realized. The other consequence is a reduction in the load on the central processing units and on the devices for transmitting the information obtained, by distributing the data to the central processing units. From the information obtained, it distributes the operations in the measurement systems themselves [28,29].

4.4.2.1 Conjunction of needs and technology

The contributions of intelligent sensors are related, in the first place, to their primitive functions and therefore concern performance improvements (accuracy, response time, etc.). As sensors are used in many systems for the production of goods (continuous or manufacturing processes) or services (tertiary sector), they are also used in the production of goods (continuous or manufacturing processes) or services (tertiary and embedded systems), and the contribution of intelligence is linked to the general performance and to the particular increase in the measurement credibility [30].

However, users have other information needs which concern the following:

- Monitoring and control, in order to be informed in real time in a qualitative or quantitative way the state of the system and/or the characteristics of the product manufactured or the service provided;
- Safety, with certain measures causing reflex arcs that make it possible to protect operators, equipment or the environment;
- Maintenance, to know the state of degradation of the system and consequently its state of operation;
- Production management, to obtain balances and characteristics of the various products or energy flows;
- Technical management, to know the availability of the process.

    For manufacturers, the intelligence of a piece of equipment leads to a reduction in the costs and timescales of its development, as well as the costs of its production. Once the investment in equipment and personnel has been amortized, the interests lie essentially in improved performance (self-compensation, taking into account nonlinearities, self-calibration, etc.);

- Traceability of the life of the equipment;
- Configuration and tuning aids. In summary, the main gains brought by intelligent sensors, in terms of both metrology and functionality are as follows [31].

4.4.2.2 Construction of smart sensors

A smart sensor is achieved by combining sensor technology, electronics and computing. An intelligent instrument is a piece of equipment that incorporates additional or advanced functionality to improve what it was designed to do. It is through the new services included that an intelligent instrument is distinguished from a standard component. Generally speaking, the evolution of instruments shows a graduation from analog to digital to intelligent. An instrument is often considered to be intelligent as soon as it incorporates at least one digital process (complex or not), regardless of its contribution in terms of services. Apart from marketing reasons, this is due to the great similarity between the hardware architecture of the digital instrument and that of the smart instrument. The distinction between "smart sensor" and "intelligent sensor" is illustrated in Figure 4.2 [32].

The smart instrument has features that improve its metrological performance, through on-board data storage and processing functions.

The smart instrument enriches this with a capacity to make its function credible, associated with a greater involvement in the realization of the functions of the system to which it belongs. The intelligent sensor corresponds mainly to the integration in the body of the sensor of an internal calculation device (microprocessor and microcontroller), a

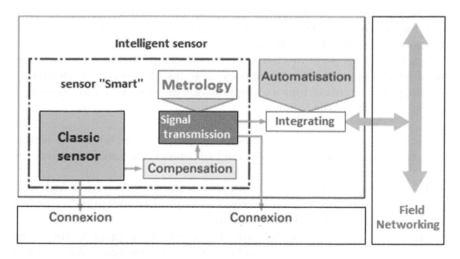

Figure 4.2 Smart sensor and intelligent sensor.

signal conditioning system (programmable or controlled) and a data processing system. From a hardware point of view, a smart sensor then consists of four units shown in Figure 4.2 [33].

A measure-specific main sensor has its signal acquisition and digitization devices such as a transducer, a conditioner that adapts the electrical signal for transmission, a multiplexer for transmission, amplifier, and sample and hold analog/digital converter. The transducer allows the detection of any variation of the physical quantity at the input of the sensor. Its design is closely linked to the field of application for which the sensor will be used.

A digital computing device (microcontroller, microprocessor or dsPIC) is used to calculate and manage the acquisition, correction of the effects of the influencing variables by means of parameters stored in PROM, linearization and diagnosis of the sensors.

A communication interface (radio or wired) links the sensor to a central computer and allows a bidirectional dialogue of digital data with the automation system. It also allows the intelligent sensor to receive the information from the system necessary for the elaboration of its measurement and its validation. It can also be used in the calibration and commissioning phases of a device in its working environment.

A power supply ensuring voltage stabilization is necessary for the instrument's electronics. A battery can be considered to maintain certain activities in the absence of an external power source (clock, memory, etc.). An intelligent sensor can therefore be considered as a real autonomous embedded system, which will have to have its own operating system allowing it to cooperate within an organization of other intelligent sensors.

The function-oriented design revolves around what the equipment does, without looking very closely at how it does it. Without paying much attention to how exactly it does it, the designer is interested in the output of a "black box". This point of view leaves the choice to the designer-producer to adopt the most suitable technology in terms of expected performance and cost [34]. There are four main application areas in which smart sensors are used, which are the following:

L'industrie manufacturière, caractérisée par des contraintes de temps-réel fortes et des contraintes environnementales variables suivant le type d'application;

The "continuous process" industry, characterized by rather low real-time constraints but must satisfy strong environmental constraints (chemical or thermal processes, etc.);

Embedded systems, which must also satisfy very variable time constraints depending on the application, but very strong environmental constraints;

Finally, the tertiary sector, which is most often the least constraining in terms of both real time and the environment.

4.4.2.3 Intelligent sensor networks for water quality monitoring

In a larger geographical area of deployment with a dimension beyond the range of the sensors radio frequency coverage, detection becomes a very difficult task. To overcome this difficulty, an ad hoc network of sensors called a wireless sensor network (WSN) is built up as and when the required resources are available and without infrastructure as shown in Figure 4.3.

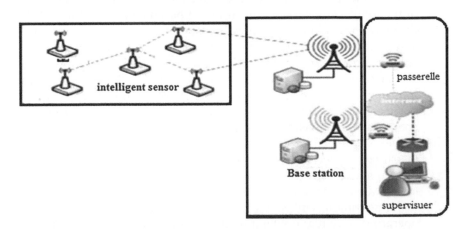

Figure 4.3 Multi-hop or cooperative communication in an FSCN.

In the literature, various studies have been carried out on the implementation of water quality monitoring systems using WSN technology [35]; for example, a distributed water quality measurement system is designed and implemented. Sensors for temperature, conductivity, pH and turbidity are connected to a field point, from which the data are sent via a GSM mobile telecommunications network to a ground station. This study focuses on processing the sensor data using Kohonen maps (auto-associative neural networks). In a water environment system based on WSN that detects and monitors video data of key areas and water parameters such as temperature, turbidity, pH, dissolved oxygen and conductivity, the data are sent from the data monitoring nodes and the video data base station to a remote monitoring center using Zigbee and CDMA (code division multiple access) technologies [36]. The parameters are measured with standard sensors, and the data are sent to a base station via GPRS (general packet radio service). A water quality monitoring and measurement system based on Zigbee WSN is presented. The system allows remote probing and real-time monitoring of descriptor parameters, as well as observation of current and historical water quality status [37]. A watershed-wide WSN for agriculture and water monitoring, called "Soil Weather", is implemented in [38]. The network uses GSM and GPRS technologies for the transmission of sensor data. The DEPLOY project is introduced to monitor the spatial and temporal distribution of water quality and environmental parameters of a river basin.

The aim is to demonstrate that an autonomous network of sensors can be deployed over a wide area and that the system measures parameters such as pH, temperature, depth, water quality, conductivity, turbidity and dissolved oxygen. The data collected from different sensor nodes are sent to a secondary base node and from there to a monitoring station using a GSM network. An inexpensive seawater probe, capable of measuring chlorophyll a, conductivity, turbidity and temperature, was used. The authors suggested that the implementation of the solution would result in an immediate improvement in the efficiency of surface water quality monitoring. However, the use of a single probe to detect all water parameters is not very reliable, as all data will be lost in case of malfunction. Data will be lost if the probe malfunctions.

The characteristics of the platform are as follows:

- Quick and easy sensor addition and/or change.
- Solar-powered external panel option.
- Available radios: 802.15.4, 868 MHz, 900 MHz, WiFi, 4G, Sigfox and LoRaWAN.
- Radio link programming (OTAP) of multiple nodes at once (via WiFi or 4G radios).
- Optional industrial protocols: RS-232, RS-485, Modbus and CAN bus.
- GPS receiver.
- External battery module.
- External SIM connector for 4G models.

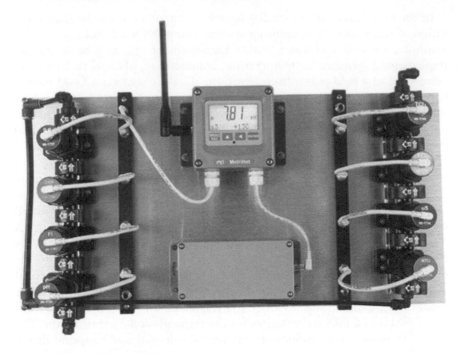

Figure 4.4 Smart sensor platform.

In view of the essential functions that can characterize an intelligent sensor, it would be quite possible, for the sake of flexibility and performance, to integrate sensors into the system. Possible to integrate possible software sensors into a smart sensor platform, or even into a sensor itself, for the sake of flexibility and performance. Software sensors within a smart sensor platform, or even at the level of a smart sensor.

4.4.3 Sensors software

Industrial processes are well equipped with a variety of sensors, designed for online supervision, monitoring and control, as well as for maintaining a constant product quality. Some variables, however, cannot be automatically measured online, due to the lack of sensors or the high cost of the sensor, resulting in a lack of sufficient information on the status of the system in real time. Usually, laboratory tests on product samples are carried out to measure the quality of the product offline on a real-time basis. In order to measure quality variables in real time, computer intelligence methodologies can be used to build intelligent/computational sensors to infer the target quality value or variables from other process variables measured online. The construction of such sensors is based on the fact that the values of the target variables have a functional relationship with other process variables that can be measured online. This type of sensor is generally referred to as a

Figure 4.5 Software sensor described as an input-output model.

"soft sensor". In general terms, soft sensors can be defined as inferential models that use measurements from sensors that are available online (easy-to-measure variables) for online estimation of quality variables (hard-to-measure variables) that cannot be measured automatically at all, or can only be measured at high cost, sporadically or with long delays (e.g., laboratory analysis).

It is worth noting that over the past two decades, researchers have begun to use the data measured and stored in industry to design and develop predictive models based on these data. These models have thus been called soft sensors. The term "soft sensor" is a combination of the word "software", because these models are based on computer programs, and the term "sensor", because these models provide information similar to that of hardware sensors. Software sensors are virtual instruments that can be used for similar purposes as their hardware counterparts. They are computer programs, and a model at the base will process information typically produced by hardware instruments [39].

A soft sensor is classically described as an input-output model. The inputs to the model are usually the secondary variables that can be easily and reliably measured, with reasonable costs (often presented as easy-to-measure variables). The outputs of the model consist of information associated with these primary variables that are difficult or very expensive to measure reliably (often reported as hard or difficult to measure). The information contained in the input and output variables are empirically modeled in the software sensor (Figure 4.5) [40].

The various physicochemical sensors used in the field of water were particularly presented. The intelligent sensor as a basic microelectronic element in a modern measurement chain was also introduced, a solution that could be beneficial for water quality control systems. According to the characteristics of this type of sensor, software sensors based on algorithmic approaches could possibly be integrated into these architectures to compensate for the lack of specific sensors and especially for more flexibility and performance.

4.5 RESULTS AND DISCUSSION

In a given field of application, the resolution of a regression and/or classification problem is carried out by comparing models in order to choose the most suitable one to solve the problem. The evaluation of models is therefore an unavoidable prerequisite for the selection. The state of the art proposed in the previous chapter shows the large number of approaches, both for classification and for regression.

This chapter is devoted to a simulation study and aims mainly at evaluating the performance of the proposed techniques as a solution in the design of software sensors used in the field of clean water quality monitoring. This work therefore presents a contribution to the study and development of soft sensors used in this field. A comparative study between MLP, RBF, SVM and ELM techniques in terms of learning time and other regression and classification parameters is then presented. The objective is to implement a multi-sensor system based on software sensors in order to make a decision suitable for the control and monitoring of water quality problems. An example of application is planned for this purpose; it is to develop a software sensor for chlorine seen as a regression problem, allowing the contribution to the control of the potability of water.

4.5.1 Architecture of the Monitoring System

Figure 4.6 shows the architecture of the multi-sensor system for monitoring and controlling the quality of clean water. It consists of an input of data obtained from physicochemical sensors and a data acquisition system and software for data processing and decision making on the quality of the monitored water. Software sensors are, in fact, used for various reasons (as already highlighted), namely the high price, the large number of sensors, the cleaning operation, the calibration routines, the replacement of sensors as well as the time spent on checking these sensors.

4.5.2 Description of input data

We seek to build the software sensor and decide on the quality of water through its descriptor parameters. We have no a priori knowledge of a type of model that perfectly represents this model and the process, but we can make our judgment on the quality of this water from some descriptive data. The objective behind collecting data on these parameters is to find a regression

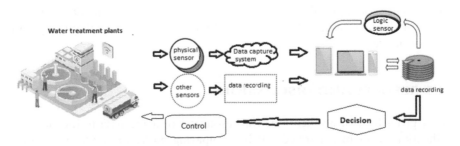

Figure 4.6 System architecture for clean water quality monitoring and control.

Table 4.1 Statistics of the parameters used

Parameter	Min.	Max.	Median	Standard deviation
pH	6.7	9.1	7.6	0.4
SS	0.50	625	21.2	47.1
BOD	0.3	7.8	3.3	1.5
Ca	2	71	16.2	9.2
Cl	0.01	38	10.2	6.1
Mg	0.5	9.5	4.5	2.1

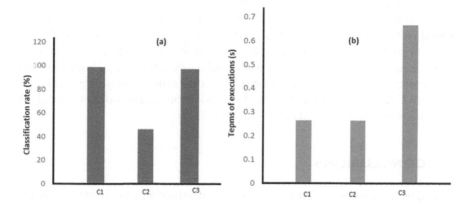

Figure 4.7. (a) Classification rates obtained; (b) execution times obtained for the three scenarios.

model to distinguish between the software sensor and a classification model after selecting the adopted technique. The quality of the water reflected by its potability is in fact based on a correlation that can only be identified statistically. Experimental descriptive data collected over a long period of time (several years) could achieve this goal. In this work, a total of 774 samples are obtained from 10 water quality data variables. Descriptive statistics of these physicochemical parameters are shown in Table 4.1. Figure 4.7 represents graphically the temporal evolution of these different parameters.

The input variables are pH, DO, SS, BOD, Ca, Cl and Mg, which represent the negative logarithm of the concentration of hydrogen ions in water, dissolved oxygen, suspended solids, biochemical oxygen demand, calcium, chlorine, magnesium, respectively. These inputs are selected for analysis because of their continuity of measurement over the timescale.

4.5.3 Sensor application for system

The results obtained, showing the classification rate for the potability decision for these three cases, are shown in Figure 4.7. It can be seen from this figure that there is a significant deterioration in the classification rate in the case of the second scenario (case of sensor failure), while in the third scenario, a high classification rate is obtained, i.e., 97.33% (case of replacement of the failed sensor by the software sensor for Cl). Comparing the execution times, it can be seen that in the case of the third scenario, the time is higher than that of scenarios 1 and 2, because it is the classification time that is added to the execution time of the soft sensor, whereas in scenarios 1 and 2, the execution time is only that of the classification time (Figure 4.7).

The results obtained showed that these four models were similar in terms of execution time, which gives them the advantage of being integrated into a dynamic monitoring system. However, the MLP, RBF and SVM models, in particular, showed a major drawback related to training time, which was fortunately overcome by the ELM model, chosen for this purpose for its speed in this training phase and its qualities presented in terms of RMSE and correlation coefficient. This model is well adapted to the learning of large databases and has, in fact, presented many advantages, both in terms of the use and application of this model to the training phase was very successful. The use and application of this model could have a direct impact on design, environmental and economic aspects.

4.6 CONCLUSIONS

The development of clean water quality monitoring and control systems based on software sensors was performed. Equipped with physicochemical sensors, such as temperature, pH, dissolved oxygen and conductivity, these systems ensure continuous online monitoring and control of water quality. The software sensor was deliberately introduced because some quality control variables cannot be measured automatically online, either because of sensor failures and the high cost of replacement, or the difficulty of the measurement itself, requiring travel to the site. The various physicochemical sensors used in the field were particularly described. The concepts of intelligent sensors and software were introduced. In the third chapter, software sensors, in particular, were discussed as an interesting means of bypassing the use of certain physicochemical sensors. The results obtained showed that the possibility of using both physical measurements and soft sensor estimates in a complementary way in the processing operation was demonstrated by means of the proposed switching system. Software sensor estimates are usually used as a backup option for existing instruments when they experience downtime or are used when physical sensors are not used at all to measure process variables. This proposal, in particular, opens up new opportunities for the scientific community, not only with regard to water treatment, but also for other industrial sectors. The application of the technique can have a direct impact on the economy, the environment, and the design and development of monitoring systems in general.

REFERENCES

1. Bell, M., & Albu, M. (1999). Knowledge systems and technological dynamism in industrial clusters in developing countries. *World Development*, 27(9), 1715–1734.
2. Morrar, R., Arman, H., & Mousa, S. (2017). The fourth industrial revolution (Industry 4.0): A social innovation perspective. *Technology Innovation Management Review*, 7(11), 12–20.
3. Naidoo, S., & Olaniran, A. O. (2014). Treated wastewater effluent as a source of microbial pollution of surface water resources. *International Journal of Environmental Research and Public Health*, 11(1), 249–270.
4. Schwarzenbach, R. P., Egli, T., Hofstetter, T. B., Von Gunten, U., & Wehrli, B. (2010). Global water pollution and human health. *Annual Review of Environment and Resources*, 35, 109–136.
5. Giudicianni, C., Herrera, M., Di Nardo, A., Greco, R., Creaco, E., & Scala, A. (2020). Topological placement of quality sensors in water-distribution networks without the recourse to hydraulic modeling. *Journal of Water Resources Planning and Management*, 146(6), 04020030.
6. Zeinalzadeh, K., & Rezaei, E. (2017). Determining spatial and temporal changes of surface water quality using principal component analysis. *Journal of Hydrology: Regional Studies*, 13, 1–10.
7. Ahmed, A. N., Othman, F. B., Afan, H. A., Ibrahim, R. K., Fai, C. M., Hossain, M. S., & Elshafie, A. (2019). Machine learning methods for better water quality prediction. *Journal of Hydrology*, 578, 124084.
8. Pule, M., Yahya, A., & Chuma, J. (2017). Wireless sensor networks: A survey on monitoring water quality. *Journal of Applied Research and Technology*, 15(6), 562–570.
9. Mabrouki, J., Azrour, M., Dhiba, D., Farhaoui, Y., & El Hajjaji, S. (2021). IoT-based data logger for weather monitoring using arduino-based wireless sensor networks with remote graphical application and alerts. *Big Data Mining and Analytics*, 4(1), 25–32.
10. Mabrouki, J., Azrour, M., Fattah, G., Dhiba, D., & El Hajjaji, S. (2021). Intelligent monitoring system for biogas detection based on the internet of things: Mohammedia, Morocco city landfill case. *Big Data Mining and Analytics*, 4(1), 10–17.
11. Mabrouki, J., Azrour, M., Farhaoui, Y., & El Hajjaji, S. (2019, April). Intelligent system for monitoring and detecting water quality. *In International Conference on Big Data and Networks Technologies* (pp. 172–182). Springer, Cham.
12. Azrour, M., Mabrouki, J., Guezzaz, A., & Farhaoui, Y. (2021). New enhanced authentication protocol for internet of things. *Big Data Mining and Analytics*, 4(1), 1–9.
13. Mabrouki, J., Benbouzid, M., Dhiba, D., & El Hajjaji, S. (2020). Simulation of wastewater treatment processes with Bioreactor Membrane Reactor (MBR) treatment versus conventional the adsorbent layer-based filtration system (LAFS). *International Journal of Environmental Analytical Chemistry*, 1–11.
14. Mabrouki, J., Bencheikh, I., Azoulay, K., Es-soufy, M., & El Hajjaji, S. (2019, April). Smart monitoring system for the long-term control of aerobic leachate treatment: dumping case Mohammedia (Morocco). *In International Conference on Big Data and Networks Technologies* (pp. 220–230). Springer, Cham.

15. Bencheikh, I., Mabrouki, J., Azoulay, K., Moufti, A., & El Hajjaji, S. (2019, April). Predictive analytics and optimization of wastewater treatment efficiency using statistic approach. *In International Conference on Big Data and Networks Technologies* (pp. 310–319). Springer, Cham.

16. Mabrouki, J., Moufti, A., Bencheikh, I., Azoulay, K., El Hamdouni, Y., & El Hajjaji, S. (2019, July). Optimization of the Coagulant Flocculation Process for Treatment of Leachate of the Controlled Discharge of the City Mohammedia (Morocco). *In International Conference on Advanced Intelligent Systems for Sustainable Development* (pp. 200–212). Springer, Cham.

17. Azrour, M., Mabrouki, J., Fattah, G., Guezzaz, A., & Aziz, F. (2021). Machine learning algorithms for efficient water quality prediction. *Modeling Earth Systems and Environment*, 8(2), 793–2801.

18. Rohani, S., Went, J., Duvenhage, D. F., Gerards, R., Wittwer, C., & Fluri, T. (2021). Optimization of water management plans for CSP plants through simulation of water consumption and cost of treatment based on operational data. *Solar Energy*, 223, 278–292.

19. Hassan El Ouazzani, B. P. (2020). Study of the efficacy of coagulation-flocculation process in domestic wastewater treatment plant (WWTP) from the city of Hattane (MOROCCO). *Journal of Advance Research in Dynamical & Control Systems*, 12(7), 147–157.

20. Fayaz, H., Rahim, N. A., Hasanuzzaman, M., Nasrin, R., & Rivai, A. (2019). Numerical and experimental investigation of the effect of operating conditions on performance of PVT and PVT-PCM. *Renewable Energy*, 143, 827–841.

21. Mabrouki, J., Fattah, G., Al-Jadabi, N., Abrouki, Y., Dhiba, D., Azrour, M., & El Hajjaji, S. (2021). Study, simulation and modulation of solar thermal domestic hot water production systems. *Modeling Earth Systems and Environment*, 8(2), 2853–2862.

22. Zhang, M. H., Dong, H., Zhao, L., Wang, D. X., & Meng, D. (2019). A review on Fenton process for organic wastewater treatment based on optimization perspective. *Science of the Total Environment*, 670, 110–121.

23. Griebler, D., Vogel, A., De Sensi, D., Danelutto, M., & Fernandes, L. G. (2020). Simplifying and implementing service level objectives for stream parallelism. *The Journal of Supercomputing*, 76(6), 4603–4628.

24. Donnot, B., Guyon, I., Schoenauer, M., Panciatici, P., & Marot, A. (2017). Introducing machine learning for power system operation support. arXiv preprint arXiv:1709.09527.

25. Ren, J. C., Liu, D., & Wan, Y. (2021). Modeling and application of Czochralski silicon single crystal growth process using hybrid model of data-driven and mechanism-based methodologies. *Journal of Process Control*, 104, 74–85.

26. Mabrouki, J., Azrour, M., Dhiba, D., & El Hajjaji, S. (2021). High-Fidelity Intelligence Ventilator to Help Infect with COVID-19 Based on Artificial Intelligence. In Intelligent Data Analysis for COVID-19 Pandemic (pp. 83–93). Springer, Singapore.

27. Dehua, W., Pan, L., Bo, L., & Zeng, G. (2012). Water quality automatic monitoring system based on GPRS data communications. *Procedia Engineering*, 28, 840–843.

28. Azrour, M., Mabrouki, J., Guezzaz, A., & Kanwal, A. (2021). Internet of things security: Challenges and key issues. *Security and Communication Networks*, 2021, 1–12.

29. Azrour, M., Mabrouki, J., Guezzaz, A., & Farhaoui, Y. (2021). Survey of high school students' usage of smartphone in Moroccan rural areas. *International Journal of Cloud Computing*, 10(3), 265–274.

30. O'Connor, P. J., Hill, A., Kaya, M., & Martin, B. (2019). The measurement of emotional intelligence: A critical review of the literature and recommendations for researchers and practitioners. *Frontiers in Psychology*, 10, 1116.

31. Mabrouki, J., Benbouzid, M., Dhiba, D., & El Hajjaji, S. (2021). Internet of Things for Monitoring and Detection of Agricultural Production. *In Intelligent Systems in Big Data, Semantic Web and Machine Learning* (pp. 271–282). Springer, Cham.

32. Azrour, M., Mabrouki, J., Farhaoui, Y., & Guezzaz, A. (2021). Experimental Evaluation of Proposed Algorithm for Identifying Abnormal Messages in SIP Network. *In Intelligent Systems in Big Data, Semantic Web and Machine Learning* (pp. 1–10). Springer, Cham.

33. Zamora-Izquierdo, M. A., Santa, J., Martínez, J. A., Martínez, V., & Skarmeta, A. F. (2019). Smart farming IoT platform based on edge and cloud computing. *Biosystems engineering*, 177, 4–17.

34. Schmidt, O., Gambhir, A., Staffell, I., Hawkes, A., Nelson, J., & Few, S. (2017). Future cost and performance of water electrolysis: An expert elicitation study. *International Journal of Hydrogen Energy*, 42(52), 30470–30492.

35. Rahim, H. A., Zulkifli, S. N., Subha, N. A. M., Rahim, R. A., & Abidin, H. Z. (2017). Water quality monitoring using wireless sensor network and smartphone-based applications: A review. *Sensors & Transducers*, 209(2), 1.

36. Riese, F. M., Keller, S., & Hinz, S. (2020). Supervised and semi-supervised self-organizing maps for regression and classification focusing on hyperspectral data. *Remote Sensing*, 12(1), 7.

37. Pandey, L. K., Lavoie, I., Morin, S., Park, J., Lyu, J., Choi, S., & Han, T. (2018). River water quality assessment based on a multi-descriptor approach including chemistry, diatom assemblage structure, and non-taxonomical diatom metrics. *Ecological Indicators*, 84, 140–151.

38. Abioye, E. A., Abidin, M. S. Z., Mahmud, M. S. A., Buyamin, S., Ishak, M. H. I., Abd Rahman, M. K. I., & Ramli, M. S. A. (2020). A review on monitoring and advanced control strategies for precision irrigation. *Computers and Electronics in Agriculture*, 173, 105441.

39. Yao, L., & Ge, Z. (2017). Deep learning of semisupervised process data with hierarchical extreme learning machine and soft sensor application. *IEEE Transactions on Industrial Electronics*, 65(2), 1490–1498.

40. Jin, X. B., Yang, N. X., Wang, X. Y., Bai, Y. T., Su, T. L., & Kong, J. L. (2020). Hybrid deep learning predictor for smart agriculture sensing based on empirical mode decomposition and gated recurrent unit group model. *Sensors*, 20(5), 1334.

Chapter 5

Very long range (VLoRa) communication for the Internet of things

An imaginative proposal for Raspberry Pi transmitters and the WSPR protocol

Joshua D. Reichard

Omega Graduate School

CONTENTS

ABSTRACT

While inexpensive long-range (LoRa) transceivers have captured the imaginations of Internet of things (IoT) enthusiasts, existing protocols in the amateur radio community provide opportunities for very long-range communication (what may be termed "VLoRa"). Digital amateur radio protocols such as WSPR utilize different error correction algorithms and typically operate in the high-frequency (HF) bands of the electromagnetic spectrum. When imagining the future of IoT, engineers and enthusiasts might consider how promising protocols such as Joe Taylor's Weak Signal Propagation Reporter (WSPR) can be used to transmit and receive sensor data over distances in range of thousands of kilometers. In this chapter, I propose the use of Raspberry Pi (or other inexpensive microcontrollers such as Arduino) to create low-cost transmitters to advance the promise of IoT devices over very long ranges (VLoRa).

DOI: 10.1201/9781003304203-5

5.1 INTRODUCTION (WSPR VERSUS LoRA CSS)

LoRa operates in the non-licensed band below 1 GHz and uses a derivative of "chirp spread spectrum modulation" to achieve relatively long-range communications between devices (Sinha, et al., 2017, p. 16). Chirp spread spectrum (CSS) modulation has been used in military applications since the 1940s, but in recent years, small microcontroller devices have made CSS applicable to the burgeoning Internet of things (IoT) movement by providing manageable data and symbol rates for transmission of small amounts of data over several kilometers of distance. LoRaWAN allows remote sensors, monitored by inexpensive microcontrollers, to transmit data on battery or solar power back to receiving stations connected to the Internet. "The LoRaWAN network applies an adaptive modulation technique with multichannel multi-modem transceiver in the base station to receive a multiple number of messages from the channels" (Sinha, et al., 2017, p. 16). The most appropriate applications of LoRa are "with smart sensing applications working on the IIoT non-authored spectrum" (Nurelmadina, 2021, p. 338).

WSPR, the Weak Signal Propagation Reporter, is an amateur radio protocol used largely for antenna testing and monitoring propagation conditions. WSPR was created by Princeton Astrophysicist and Nobel Prize Laureate Joe Taylor, K1JT, in 2008. WSPR is now part of a suite of software for weak signal digital communications called WSJT-X. The WSJT-X suite is designed for studying radio propagation with low power under less-than-ideal conditions. Power is communicated in terms of dBm, such that 30 dBm=1W and 37 dBm=5W.

WSPR transmissions consist of a call sign, the maidenhead grid locator of the station, and the signal strength in dBm (transmit power). For example, see Table 5.1.

An encoded 50-bit WSPR message would be:

```
1 0 1 0 0 0 0 0 0 0 0 0 0 0 0 0 1 1 1 0 0 0 1 0 0 0 1 0 0 0 1 1 0 0 1 0 1 0
0 0 1 1 1 1 1 0 0 1 0 1 0 0 0 0 1 0 0 0 1 0 1 0 1 1 1 0 1 0 0 1 0 0 1 0
1 0 0 1 0 0 1 0 0 1 0 0 1 0 0 0 0 1 0 1 0 1 1 0 0 0 0 1 0 1 0 0 1 1 0 1 0
0 0 1 1 1 1 0 1 0 0 0 1 0 0 1 1 1 1 0 0 1 0 0 0 1 1 1 1 0 1 1 0 1 1 1 1 0
1 0 0 1 1 0 0 1 0 0 0 1 1 1
```

Receiving stations report "spots" of transmissions back to a central database called WSPRnet, via an Internet-connected computer decoding signals from a radio transceiver. Simple resources such as WSPRnet are "powerful tools for remote sensing the ionosphere. These voluntarily constructed and

Table 5.1 WSPR message bit configuration

28 bits	15 bits	7 bits	50 bits
Call sign	**Grid locator**	**Power**	**Total**
K8KJR	EN91	37	

operated networks provide real-time and archival data that could be used for space weather operations, forecasting, and research" (Frissell et al., 2014).

WSPR transmissions occur over a time synchronized period of two minutes at a rate of 25 bits per minute. The seven bits allocated to the transmitter power output report are expressed in decibels per milliwatt. Decibels are effectively "dimensionless", but when expressed relative to milliwatts, dbM is a logarithmic measure of relative power. For the purposes of WSPR transmissions, dBM is an appropriate report of power since the protocol is intended for minimal power. A Raspberry Pi GPIO pin can output approximately 10 mW or 37 dBM.

All GPIO pins on the Raspberry Pi support software-based pulse-width modulation (PWM). When PWM is applied, the GPIO pin produces a square waveform with a wide range of possible frequencies and duty cycles. The minimum and maximum PWM output frequencies are 10 Hz and 8 KHz, respectively. Duty cycles of 0 or 1 mean the waveform is always, respectively, high or low (MathWorks, n.d.). However, by simply modulating the voltage on a single pin via software, the Raspberry Pi GPIO pins can break free from the audio range into generating square waves between 0 and 250 MHz, thus making the possibility of a single-in digital transceiver possible.

WSPR and other tracking networks have generated a "MF and HF propagation data set with greater spatial, temporal, and spectral coverage than any prior amateur radio citizen science experiment" (Frissell et al., 2018). The WSJT-X software enables radio amateurs to experiment with antenna designs and propagation conditions by season or solar cycle and gather massive amounts of data for future analyses. "Radio activities including low-power DXing, meteor scatter, moonbounce, and precise frequency measurement — all of them possible with relatively modest station equipment" (Taylor, 2010, p. 31). Taylor insisted the WSJT-X suite of software is not intended to be robotic or automatic and should require a control operator to manage two-way communications.

Although the WSJT-X software expects to decode 50-bit messages restricted to the specified pattern, its encoding-decoding algorithms are open source and could be adapted for other purposes currently used by LoRaWAN networks. Because the algorithm used by WSPR expects data to conform to particular constraints within bit ranges of each transmission, IoT-type data otherwise transmitted via LoRa networks would either need to be constrained to the WSPR algorithm, or the WSPR algorithm would need to be adapted to accommodate more flexibility in encoding and decoding messages. The tradeoff for longer-range high-frequency communication may be worth the effort.

LoRa transceivers are intended for long-range and low-power distributed applications (Khutsoane, Isong, and Abu-Mahfouz, 2017). Mesh networks comprised of LoRa gateways from local and remote devices provide more complex data transfer (Lee & Ke, 2018). However, amateur radio-derived protocols such as WSPR can provide unconventional opportunities for very long range (VLoRa) data transmission using the characteristics of HF ionospheric propagation. Such applications could complement existing LoRa networks rather than supplant them. Amateur radio protocols may contribute a holistic vision for the future of IoT, which utilizes traditional wired Internet infrastructure, mesh networks, VHF, UHF, microwave, and even HF frequencies.

In the VHF, UHF, and microwave ranges, radio amateurs have employed packet radio protocols for decades. Terminal node controllers were once popular devices which connected amateur radio transceivers to personal computers via serial cables for over-the-air data communications. Currently, the AX.25 (Amateur X.25) protocol, which was derived from the X.25 data link layer protocol employed in the 1980–1990s, is used for location reporting such as APRS (Automatic Packet Reporting System). APRS packets can be routed to the Internet via an "igate" station, not unlike LoRa gateways. APRS is often used for transmitting telemetry data via weather balloons or space stations. DireWolf is a software-based solution, which essentially replaces the traditional TNC devices (in effect a "virtual TNC") and can be easily deployed on a Raspberry Pi. Much like LoRa transceiver chips, APRS transceiver chips (as stand-alone beacons or integrated with microcontrollers) are commercially available.

Although packet radio has a long history in amateur radio and modern solutions such as DireWolf are aiding a resurgence of relevance of packet radio, the advanced forward error correction, low power design, and vast popularity of the WSJT-X suite make the "JT protocols" interesting opportunities for expanding IoT applications into the HF bands, especially for very long range. For the purposes of this chapter, the simplicity of modulating a GPIO pin on a Raspberry Pi as a transmitter provides a unique opportunity for expanding the IoT to the HF (and even LF) bands without an additional amateur radio transceiver.

While HF frequencies introduce confounding challenges to transmissions to long-range communication such as ionospheric fluctuation and space weather disruptions, VHF, UF, and microwave frequencies typically employed with LoRa are not without their challenges as well. Zourmand et al. (2019) noted that within and between buildings, the range and quality of LoRA networks depend on "the distance from the gateway" and also "the effect of path loss due to the structural element". However, Zourmand et al. also demonstrated that "using a single receiver in the LoRa network, it is able to handle many nodes at multiple locations within the area, unlike Wi-Fi-based system which needs to have many access points to increase the coverage area" (p. 324). The most promising applications of both LoRa, WSPR, and WiFi are potentially integrative and complimentary rather than competing alternative technologies. Different circumstances and applications may warrant the implementation of LoRa transmissions, VLoRa transmissions, packet radio, and WiFi or cellular transmissions for a rich integration of IoT devices and ad hoc networks.

5.2 THE WSPR PROTOCOL AND IoT APPLICATIONS

Not unlike the CSS modulation used by LoRa to overcome interference and poor conditions, the WSJT-X suite, including WSPR, depends on strong digital message error correction to propagate signals in poor conditions. Digital messages propagate because of "controlled redundancy", so "transmission errors can be recognized and corrected". Of course, "simple repetition of each symbol is a trivial form of redundancy" (Taylor, 2017).

Instead of simple repetition, forward error correction (FEC) is used by the WSJT-X software suite. The WSJT-X suite, including WSPR, depends on encoding and decoding digital messages with error correction. After encoding, WSJT-X generates a code word, whereby "powerful redundancy can be arranged by mapping each sequence of k message symbols in a controlled way into a unique and longer sequence of n symbols called a codeword" (Taylor, 2017).

The code rate for WSPR is expressed as k/n; in that, for every k bits of useful information, the coder generates a total of n bits of data, of which $n - k$ are redundant. "The mathematics underlying design of such k-to-n mapping schemes and their corresponding n-to-k reverse transformations forms a major branch of modern communication theory". Redundancy can be "characterized by the ratio n/k, and its reciprocal k/n is the code rate" (Taylor, 2017). WSPR uses a constraint length of $K=32$ and rate $r=1/2$. Relatively speaking, 32 is a high K for a convolutional code algorithm, which is used by WSPR.

The algorithm is a finite state machine in computer science. Convolutional code algorithms for error correction are used in digital video, cellular data, and satellite transmissions (Griffiths, 2020; Harold, 2021). Convolutional algorithms can be recursive or non-recursive. WSPR is non-recursive. In convolutional code algorithms, "each output not only depends on the current input but also on previous inputs" (Taylor, 2017).

For WSPR, the convolution procedure extends the 50 user bits into a total of $(50+K - 1)\times2=162$ one-bit symbols. The WSJT-X protocols use block codes in which the values of n and k are fixed and labeled as (n, k) codes. WSJT-X uses a fixed length of 28 bits for a call sign and 15 for a grid locator (plus 7 bits for the power). A standard amateur radio call sign is usually a 1–2-character prefix followed by a number (i.e., K8 or KE8), followed by a 1–3-character suffix, (i.e., KJR). "Within these rules, the number of possible call signs equals $37\times36\times10\times27\times27\times27$, or somewhat over 262 million" (Taylor, 2017). "Similarly, the number of four-digit Maidenhead grid locators on Earth is $180\times180=32,400$ ... so a grid locator can be encoded uniquely with 15 bits" (Taylor, 2017).

WSPR operates on price two-minute cycles. The computer's clock must be accurate to within one second of UTC time (WSPR Manual, version 4.0). "Reception of transmitted symbols requires accurate synchronization of time and frequency between transmitting and receiving stations" (Taylor, 2017). Any remote IoT device in the field using the WSPR protocol would need GPS or atomic clock synchronization, which will inevitably put more demands on battery power. While such transmissions are far from instantaneous, the benefit of error correction over very long ranges, especially for non-critical monitoring of sensor data, may outweigh the constraints of slow transmission and a synchronized clock.

A two-way WSPR transmission consists of the following steps, whereby "steps 1–5 take place at the transmitting station, and steps 6–9 at the receiving end" (Taylor, 2017).

Transmitting station
1. Generate a message.
2. Compress message to k symbols of q bits per symbol.
3. Add error-correcting redundancy to produce code word of n symbols.
4. Add synchronizing pattern and modulate onto a carrier.
5. Transmit modulated waveform over a radio channel.

Receiving Station
6. Receive, synchronize, and demodulate to yield n symbols, some of which might be in error.
7. Decode n received symbols to recover k error-free message symbols.
8. Decompress k symbols to recover original message in human-readable form.
9. Deliver message to receiving user.

According to Taylor, "the most crucial are steps 3 and 7. Step 7 likely requires the most computational resources" (2017). Proof-of-concept WSPR transmitters have been created using ATMega/Arduino 328 microcontrollers, but processing and decoding received WSPR signal audio accurately and quickly may require more computing power, especially because the subsequent transmission window begins almost immediately. IoT applications may comprise of low-cost WSPR transmitters operating on microcontrollers in the field and more powerful Internet-connected computers receiving and decoding the transmissions.

WSPR and other "citizen science" initiatives aided in collecting valuable data during the 2017 solar eclipse. By having a global network of transmitting and reporting stations, scientists are able to gather more data about important space weather events. WSPR and the WSJT-X suite of software have opened new doors for radio amateurs to operate with low power and in weak propagation conditions.

Low-cost software-defined radio (SDR) receivers, available *en masse* in USB-dongle form factors, connected to low-end personal computers are sufficient to decode WSPR signals and report to the WSPRnet database. The US-based HamSCI organization, founded by physics professor Nathaniel Frissell (W2NAF), promotes a "citizen science" concept to collect data for studying ionospheric propagation from simple amateur stations. "An ideal station would be able to receive signals omnidirectionally and simultaneously with equal response across all bands of interest (typically 1.8–54 MHz)" (Frissell et al., 2014). Anyone interested in radio science can set up a WSPR monitoring station and participate in sending decoded signals to the WSPRnet servers. In like manner, anyone with a personal computer, an SDR dongle, an antenna, and appropriate software could receive and decode signals from a field device transmitting using the WSPR protocol.

5.3 A RASPBERRY Pi WSPR TRANSMITTER FOR VERY LONG RANGE (VLoRA) COMMUNICATIONS

Lee and Ke (2018) argued that while other technologies exist to transfer data from widely distributed sensors that comprise the IoT, they are cost-prohibitive and impractical for most applications. Because WSPR signals can be modulated on low-cost devices such as the Raspberry Pi with no additional microcontrollers or hardware for transmitting, such hardware-software combination has the potential to dramatically expand the range of IoT communications devices.

While the prospect of LoRa transceivers communicating over a few kilometers and reporting data to the Internet is intriguing, the notion of very long range (VLoRa) communications using amateur radio protocols such as WSPR expands the possibilities for the future of IoT. Imagine a low-cost, low-power transmitter sending data from a remote sensor in Antarctica and receivers around the world regularly decoding the signal and reporting it to the Internet. Instead of *ad hoc* networks of devices every few kilometers, a VLoRa system would use the propagation characteristics of the ionosphere, even if in poor conditions, to send and receive data over very long ranges, potentially globally at the peak of solar cycles.

Open-source WSPR transmission software is available for the Raspberry Pi (https://github.com/JamesP6000/WsprryPi/), by modulating voltage on general-purpose input/output (GPIO) pin 4. Originally developed by Dan Ankers (https://github.com/DanAnkers/WsprryPi), the implementation has been forked on GitHub a number of times. Other than a Raspberry Pi and a low-pass filter, no other commercial radio equipment, transceiver or otherwise, is needed. In this configuration, pin 4 is modulated and pin 5 is used for ground. The open-source command-line WSPR program for Linux can modulate a signal on pin 4 at a specific frequency at about 10mW power, which, with an adequate low-pass filter and efficient and resonant antenna, is more than sufficient for global propagation under right conditions. The *wsprrypi* command-line syntax is: wspr K8KJR EN91 10 20m.

The *wsprrypi* software can repeat transmissions and terminate after *x* transmissions have completed successfully. A random frequency offset can be added to each transmission (±80 Hz) to move the transmission window within the bandwidth of the waterfall to ensure the signal is not drowned

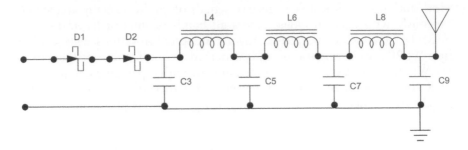

Figure 5.1 Raspberry Pi low-pass filter.

out by stronger adjacent signals or signals at the exact same frequency. The software can calibrate against an NTP server if the Raspberry Pi is Internet-connected.

Because the Raspberry Pi GPIO pin modulates a square wave, a low-pass filter is necessary to suppress harmonics. Practically, I have constructed a number of low-pass filters for various amateur bands (10, 12, 15, 17, 20, 40, and 80 m) for use with the Raspberry Pi WSPR transmitter. The filters consisted of two inductors in series and three capacitors in parallel pulled to ground. Two small-signal fast-switching Schottky diodes precede output to the center conductor of the antenna feedline to provide some measure of protection against stray voltage and electrostatic discharge from the antenna system returning to the GPIO pins of the Raspberry Pi. Any input voltage to GPIO4 exceeding the expected 3.3V logical-level range will damage the Raspberry Pi.

In my own experimentation, I have used an SMA connector from the filter board to my antenna. Figure 5.1 shows a schematic of the low-pass filter.

With a resonant antenna, I have received spotting reports by stations across the continental United States from my location in Northeast Ohio, the USA, at just 10 mW of power. I suggest using direct pin headers from the low-pass filter board to the Raspberry Pi to reduce spurious harmonic emissions even from the shortest of jumper wires. A small linear amplifier could improve the power, but with an efficient omnidirectional antenna system, 10 mW should suffice for most applications. For example, a 5 W wideband HF linear amplifier, on the front- or back-end of the filter board, can also aid in improving performance and preserving power consumption.

I have also transmitted WSPR signals on the LF bands, including 630 m (~475 kHz), which requires a more complex antenna system than the HF bands. The antenna system for the 630 m band consists of an impedance transformer, a tapped tuning coil, a loading coil (approximately 200–250 µH total), a ground rod and radial system, and a 100 foot tall vertical antenna wire. Using the Raspberry Pi, a low-pass filter built for 475 kHz, and a 5 W amplifier, I transmitted WSPR signals, which were heard hundreds of miles from my station, even with such a severely compromised antenna system. The potential applications of low-band WSPR transmissions include highly reliable ground wave and surface wave propagation, which are not subject to fluctuations in ionospheric propagation or the negative effects of space weather. Such highly reliable transmissions on the LF bands may be useful for emergency communications, where reliability is more important than speed. Even at such low frequencies, extraordinarily long ranges have been achieved; for example, currently, a distance of 16,832 km has been achieved via WSPR on the 630 m band (see 472khz.org).

It should be noted that a linear amplifier will likely be required to make the 630 or 2,200 m bands practical. Compromised antenna systems yield significant power losses because of shortened lengths, loading coils, transformers, and ground losses. Nonetheless, radio amateurs are restricted to 5 W EIRP (Effective Isotropic Radiated Power) on the 630 m band and 1 W EIRP on the 2,200 m band. Stations within 800 km (approximately 496 miles) of Russia (which only practically applies to locations in parts of the state of Alaska) are permitted 1 W EIRP maximum transmit power on the 630 m band. EIRP is calculated using the power supplied to the antenna multiplied by the gain of the antenna in a given direction, which is then considered relative to an isotropic antenna. EIRP can be calculated by multiplying the ERP of an antenna system by 1.64. Needless to say, at least 100 W of input power at 472 kHz would be needed to yield 5 W EIRP in most compromised 630 m antenna systems.

In the USA, amateur radio operators are required to notify the Utilities Technology Council (UTC) before operating on the LF bands (630 and 2,200 m). Because the 135.7–137.8 kHz (2,200 m) and 472–479 kHz (630 m) frequencies may overlap with Power Line Carrier (PLC) systems operating on the same or overlapping frequencies, the UTC must notify radio amateurs if the fixed latitudinal and longitudinal coordinates of their LF antenna systems are within 1 km of PLC transmissions. According to the American Radio Relay League (ARRL), "located beyond a minimum separation distance from PLC transmission lines, which will help ensure the compatibility and coexistence of amateur and PLC operations, and promote shared use of the bands" (2017). Operation on the LF bands are detailed in the Federal Communications Commission (FCC) rules Part 97 rule amendments, § 97.3, 97.15(c), 97.301(b) through (d), 97.303(g), 97.305(c), and 97.313(k) and (l) (Figure 5.2).

5.4 PRACTICAL EXAMPLES: MALAYSIAN AIRLINES FLIGHT MH370 AND SPACE WEATHER STATIONS

WSPR has been used for more than testing ionospheric propagation or amateur radio antenna systems. In an unpublished paper, Richard Godfrey (2021) suggested WSPR transmissions may hold the key to aid in the search for the missing Malaysian Airlines Flight MH370. Godfrey suggested WSPR transmissions logged in the WSPRnet database during the flight of MH370

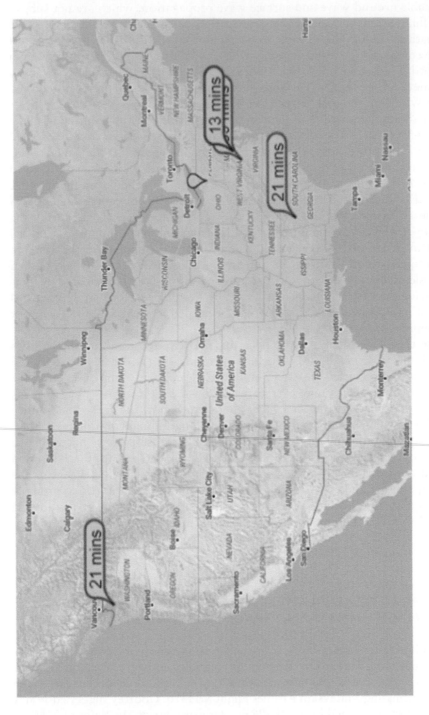

Figure 5.2 Example reporting from K8KJR at 10mW on the 20m (14MHz) band (https://about.google/brand-resource-center/products-and-services/geo-guidelines/).

may help locate the lost aircraft through the synchronization of multiple WSPR transmissions. Aircraft produce both forward and side scatter, and if the path of the aircraft is known, related phenomena in WSPR transmissions can be identified within the WSPRnet database during the flight of a particular aircraft. Godfrey and others demonstrated the use of anomalous data in both short-path and long-path WSPR transmissions to potentially locate aircraft.

In final analysis, Godfrey only found 12 possible WSPR DX detections of MH370, but did not attempt analyses of hypothetical flight paths of the aircraft (p. 22). Although Godfrey's work is *ex post facto*, the collection of massive amounts of propagation data from the WSPR transmissions and receptions of global radio amateurs provides unique opportunities for solving complex problems such as locating missing aircraft. While certainly not a unilateral solution, such data may prove useful for other similar problems in the future.

Another practical example of using WSPR for very long range communications is for collecting data related to space weather phenomenon. Fallen (2018) proposed experimentation with data from the High-frequency Active Auroral Research Program (HAARP) ionosphere heater and the Weak Signal Propagation Reporter (WSPR) network for the purposes of assessing the effects of space weather phenomena. Frissell et al. (2019) noted that because HF communications are often used in emergency situations, such as immediately following destructive hurricanes, studying the ionospheric propagation is critical not only to science, but to potentially saving human lives. Erratic space weather events "such as X-ray flares from the Sun and geomagnetic storms can alter the ionosphere to disrupt these communications" (p. 118).

Because thousands of radio amateurs around the world may be collecting and reporting data from WSPR transmissions at any given time, concerns about "consistency, verification, and validation of volunteer observer data" can mitigated through appropriate software and "the sheer number of available good observations, even with the presence of flawed observations, outweighs in scientific value a few perfect observations" (Fallen, 2018). In a study of the effects of solar flares, Frissell et al. (2019) found that "emergency communicators suffered both the short-term effects of solar flare-induced radio blackouts and the longer-term effects of geomagnetic activity-induced ionospheric storms" (p. 131).

Further, data primarily from the WSPRnet database revealed that single solar storms likely do not cause extended depressions in the propagation of HF signals, but a combination of multiple events is likely to be underlying causes The study also revealed that effective HF propagation recovered from solar flare radio blackouts in tens of minutes to hours, while recovery from geomagnetic storms did not happen for days. Although more research is necessary, understanding the behavior of ionospheric propagation by analyzing large quantities of data collected and reported by radio amateurs will have implications for emergency communications in the future.

5.5 OPPORTUNITIES AND CHALLENGES

Because no additional commercial hardware is necessary (not even the sx1276 LoRa chip), many new possibilities are opened for transmitting data using microcontrollers or single board computers such as the Raspberry Pi. The sophistication of Joe Taylor's convolutional code algorithm for error correction provides an alternative to spread spectrum transmissions with a proven track record of successful encoding and decoding of simple messages across a wide range of frequencies. Because the Raspberry Pi GPIO pin can be modulated at any frequency, non-licensed engineers and enthusiasts can experiment on non-licensed HF frequencies where available. The vision of the WSPR protocol extending the boundaries of LoRa networks should be received as an opportunity for advancing the IoT (Vangelista et al., 2015).

According to Frisell et al. (2019), "Radio communications using the high-frequency (HF) bands (3–30 MHz) is important for emergency communications because it is the only form of electronic communications that can travel over the horizon without relying on man-made infrastructure such as the Internet, satellite systems, or phone networks" (p. 118). However, while LF transmissions, such as on the 630 m band, are highly reliable due to ground and surface wave propagation, antenna systems are impractical and, for many radio amateurs, unreliable, even for adequately low power transmissions at such low frequencies.

Challenges of implementation will also include clock synchronization of the transmitting device, power management, and antenna implementation. Perhaps the greatest challenge will be the latter, since most HF antennas are either $1/2\lambda$ dipoles or verticals with extensive ground radial systems. To transmit efficiently at 10 mW in the HF spectrum, antennas will need to be constructed efficiently with few physical and electrical compromises. Although VHF LoRa applications accommodate smaller antennas because of operations at shorter wavelengths, they exchange skywave propagation for groundwave propagation and lose the benefits of global ionospheric refraction. A WSPR-based VLoRa IoT station would indeed require sufficient space for a resonant antenna, but specific transmitting stations for specific purposes may warrant such a footprint. The overall cost would remain low, as resonant wire antennas would suffice; extensive infrastructure would not be necessary. As in any technological application, a cost-benefit analysis relevant to the presenting need would be prudent.

Further, Zhou et al. (2019) conducted experiments to improve LoRa network architectures for scalability and flexibility. While WSPR-based VLoRa would not provide the same kind of gateway-bridge configuration most typically deployed in LoRa typologies, it could contribute to what Zhou et al. call "decoupled modules", whereby WSPR transmitters provide data to a LoRa network as independent decoupled modules independent from, but part of, the LoRa deployment itself. Such an integrative approach to available technologies may increase the reliability and robustness of IoT ad hoc networks.

Finally, that most of the world licenses the HF spectrum and prohibits automatic beacons on HF frequencies would create additional restrictions for implementation. The extent to which such WSPR transmissions for the purposes of reporting IoT sensor data would be considered a "beacon" is debatable, but any such station operating within licensed frequencies would require a licensed control operator for legal operation. Each country has its own licensing requirements in cooperation with the International Amateur Radio Union or commercial licensing within their own jurisdictions.

5.6 CONCLUSIONS

In this imaginative yet practical proposal, I suggest using the WSPR protocol for implementing very long range (VLoRa) low-power messaging systems to expand the IoT. Amateur radio has always been a force for innovation and experimentation. The WSPR protocol provides a software basis for transmitting short messages over very long ranges using a convolutional code algorithm for error correction and the natural benefits of HF ionospheric propagation. Combined with a low-cost Raspberry Pi transceiver, low-pass filter, and resonant antenna system, a WSPR transmitter could be part of an IoT application, whereby sensor data are transmitted over thousands of kilometers and uploaded to the Internet for processing. With open-source software, inexpensive hardware, and "low-tech" amateur radio engineering, VLoRa transmitters can become part of an ever-expanding future for IoT.

REFERENCES

Fallen, C. T. (2018). Citizen Space Science: A Preliminary Systematic Study of HF Radio Propagation from a Source in the Subarctic Using HAARP and the Ham WSPR Network, SA13C-2786. https://ui.adsabs.harvard.edu/abs/2018AGUFMSA13C2786F.

Frissell, N.A. E. S. Miller, S. R. Kaeppler, F. Ceglia, D. Pascoe, N. Sinanis, P. Smith, R. Williams, and A. Shovkoplyas (2014). Ionospheric Sounding Using Real-Time Amateur Radio Reporting Networks. *Space Weather*, 12, doi:10.1002/2014SW001132.

Frissell, N. A., Katz, J. D., Gunning, S. W., Vega, J. S., Gerrard, A. J., Earle, G. D., Moses, M. L., West, M. L., Huba, J. D., Erickson, P. J., Miller, E. S., Gerzoff, R. B., Liles, W., & Silver, H. W. (2018). Modeling amateur radio soundings of the ionospheric response to the 2017 great American eclipse. *Geophysical Research Letters*, 45(10), 4665–4674. https://doi.org/10.1029/2018GL077324.

Frissell, N. A., Vega, J. S., Markowitz, E., Gerrard, A. J., Engelke, W. D., Erickson, P. J., et al. (2019). High-frequency communications response to solar activity in September 2017 as observed by amateur radio networks. *Space Weather*, 17, 118–132. https://doi.org/10.1029/2018SW002008.

Godfrey, R. (2021). WSPRnet and Inmarsat Satellite data | The Search for MH370. https://www.mh370search.com/2021/04/03/wsprnet-and-inmarsat-satellite-data/

Griffiths, G. (2020, September 11). Griffiths and Robinett WSPR with TimescaleDB and Grafana ARRL-TAPR 2020.

Harold, G. (2021). *Using the WSPRnet and Inmarsat Satellite data in the search for MH370*. Unpublished Paper. Retrieved from https://www.dropbox.com/s/w43gu64vn7jvmxm/Using%20the%20WSPRnet%20and%20Inmarsat%20Satellite%20data%20in%20the%20search%20for%20MH370.pdf?dl=0.

Khutsoane, O., Abu-Mahfouz, A., & Isong, B. (2017). IoT devices and applications based on LoRa/LoRaWAN. https://doi.org/10.1109/IECON.2017.8217061.

Lee, H. and K. Ke, "Monitoring of large-area IoT sensors using a LoRa wireless mesh network system: Design and evaluation," in *IEEE Transactions on Instrumentation and Measurement*, vol. 67, no. 9, pp. 2177–2187, Sept. 2018, doi: 10.1109/TIM.2018.2814082.

Nurelmadina, N., Hasan, M. K., Memon, I., Saeed, R. A., Zainol Ariffin, K. A., Ali, E. S., Mokhtar, R. A., Islam, S., Hossain, E., & Hassan, Md. A. (2021). A systematic review on cognitive radio in low power wide area network for industrial IoT applications. *Sustainability*, 13(1). https://doi.org/10.3390/su13010338.

Sinha, R.S., Y. Wei, S.-H. Hwang (2017). A survey on LPWA technology: LoRa and NB-IoT, *ICT Express*, 3(1), 14–21, ISSN 2405-9595, https://doi.org/10.1016/j.icte.2017.03.004.

Taylor, J. (2010). WSPRing around the World: You'd be astonished at what you can do these days with just a few watts. *QST November 2010*: 30–33.

Taylor, J. (2017). Work the World with WSJT-X, Part 2: Codes, Modes, and Cooperative Software Development. *QST November 2017*:1–6.

The Raspberry Pi PWM - MATLAB & Simulink. (n.d.). Retrieved October 23, 2021, from https://www.mathworks.com/help/supportpkg/raspberrypiio/ug/the-raspberry-pi-pwm.html.

Vangelista L., Zanella A., Zorzi M. (2015). Long-Range IoT Technologies: The Dawn of LoRa™. In: Atanasovski V., Leon-Garcia A. (eds) *Future Access Enablers for Ubiquitous and Intelligent Infrastructures. FABULOUS 2015. Lecture Notes of the Institute for Computer Sciences, Social Informatics and Telecommunications Engineering*, vol 159. Springer, Cham. https://doi.org/10.1007/978-3-319-27072-2_7.

Zhou, Q., K. Zheng, L. Hou, J. Xing and R. Xu, (2019). "Design and implementation of open LoRa for IoT," *IEEE Access*, vol. 7, pp. 100649–100657, doi: 10.1109/ACCESS.2019.2930243.

Zourmand, A., A. L. Kun Hing, C. Wai Hung and M. AbdulRehman, "Internet of Things (IoT) using LoRa technology," *2019 IEEE International Conference on Automatic Control and Intelligent Systems (I2CACIS)*, 2019, pp. 324–330, doi: 10.1109/I2CACIS.2019.8825008.

Chapter 6

Analysis of applying blockchain technology to hospitality operation

Kei Au Yeung
University of Auckland

Mingwei Gong
Mount Royal University

Ranesh Naha
University of Adelaide

Aniket Mahanti
University of Auckland
University of New Brunswick

CONTENTS

DOI: 10.1201/9781003304203-6

ABSTRACT

Blockchain was first conceptualised in 2008 and drew attention from the general public since the introduction of one of its applications, cryptocurrency, in 2014. Blockchain consists of several revolutionary characteristics and has already been applied in different industries. Therefore, it is also deemed as a computer technology that has the potential to change the traditional business model. The hospitality industry is one of the significant economic supports to New Zealand; this industry could take advantage of the implementation of blockchain technology. Moreover, applying blockchain technology in various industries is a new arena in the existing research. The results of qualitative research indicate that blockchain technology could benefit the hospitality industry by building a more trustable reputation system, smoothening operation flow, reducing operation cost, enhancing customer experiences, enhancing food safety, and providing convenient payment methods without the necessity of intermediaries. This chapter is focused on investigating how the implementation of blockchain technology benefits the hospitality industry, together with its potential drawbacks.

6.1 INTRODUCTION

The blockchain is a new technology that consists of public ledgers storing transactions that are distributed in a network. Most of the transactions are validated by the nodes within the network according to a majority consensus method before being added to the ledger and stored in a list of blocks. The chain grows as newly verified transactions are appended continuously. Once the transaction is validated and added to the ledger, it cannot be modified and removed from the ledger at any time.

Initially, it was first mentioned in 1991 in a research paper written by Haber and Stornetta [28] who proposed the idea of sending a document through a timestamp server and having the server sign the document with the current timestamp. It also contains a pointer that links to the previous document. If the document is changed, the pointer will become invalid. By this mechanism, tamperproof is guaranteed, which is similar to the basic concept of the blockchain. However, it only started to attract the attention of the general public since one of its popular usages as a cryptocurrency (i.e. Bitcoin) in 2008.

Since 2014, researchers and investors switched their attention from Bitcoin to the blockchain technology itself. They started to realise that the blockchain technology itself can be separated from Bitcoin and used in various sectors and applications. According to Gatteschi et al. [27], the so-called Blockchain 1.0 is mostly related to Bitcoin or other cryptocurrencies. In Blockchain 2.0, smart contracts were started to be included in the blockchain. They are programmed to perform specific actions or transactions automatically without the interaction of a third party or intermediaries after certain conditions are met. In the state-of-the-art Blockchain 3.0, the application of blockchain is no longer limited to the finance sector. Researchers and investors are trying to address the advantages and possibility of implementing the blockchain technology in different sectors, such as government, supply chain management (SCM), health and IoT. The understanding of the potential about using blockchain in various fields is still at the beginning.

6.1.1 Advantage of the blockchain

The blockchain is deemed to be a revolutionary technology that will change most of the procedures in every sector of business nowadays. It provides several benefits. First, it can reduce the transaction cost and time needed by eliminating the intermediaries. In the blockchain, no central trusted authority is needed for the verification of transactions. The transactions are verified by the consensus mechanisms in the blockchain to maintain the data consistency. Second, all the transactions recorded in the blockchain can be validated quickly, and any invalid transaction will be rejected by the nodes participating in the consensus mechanisms. Moreover, it is almost impossible to alter or remove the transactions once they are validated and added to the blockchain. Thus, any attack or invalid transaction could be detected immediately before being added to the blocks for processing. Third, it provides anonymity. As all the users communicate with the blockchain by a generated address that does not include any real information about the identity of the users, the real identity information is being protected. Lastly, the blockchain provides better security; all the transactions are encrypted by cryptography. Moreover, a majority of nodes are required to add the data to the chain. Blockchain relies on a distributed network, and all the blocks are replicated between nodes to ensure consistency. When a single node is down, the other nodes will take responsibility and provide the ledger for verification.

6.1.2 How blockchain can solve the existing issues in the hospitality industry

As mentioned by Global Hospitality Portal [64], the whole hospitality and tourism industry accounted for around 8 trillion dollars in the global economy and will be expected to grow to more than 10 trillion by 2025. Nowadays, some issues still cannot be solved by the existing hospitality systems [22]. For example, the hospitality operator still relies on third-party trusted authorities for the payment process, which leads to a high transaction cost and time. The transactions may take days to verify and months for the amount to be debited into the operator's bank account. Moreover, the hospitality industry is still an employee-intensive industry as many of the operations are still done by humans. Also, it is hard to trace the food source and other handling parties in case of food safety incidents. For the hotel operators, guests are always complaining about the slow check-in and check-out process as well as the lack of attractive redeemable items in the loyalty programmes.

The hospitality operators want to deal with these issues to have smoothened business processes and maintain a good relationship with the guests. When using blockchain, there are no intermediaries to process the payments and transactions. The transactions are verified, approved and executed by a consensus mechanism, and usually, it takes a few minutes with a relatively low transaction fee. Moreover, using the trusted identity of the blockchain helps to make the check-in and check-out processes faster without the identity verification by hotel staffs and thus save the operation cost. Furthermore, the special request can also be shared with the partners in the blockchain to provide a personalised experience to the guests [67]. Also, the loyalty programme could be enhanced by providing more variety of redeemable products with the operation with other vendors within the same blockchain network. By using blockchain, the time needed to trace a node throughout the manufacturing process of a product in a supply chain could be reduced from days to seconds [36].

6.2 RELATED WORK

6.2.1 Information system used in hospitality and its advantages and challenges

In this section, the studies and researches are discussed. These articles pointed out the problem of the existing systems and the approaches for future developments. As far as 2005, Singh and Kasavana [62] conducted a survey using the data from a panel of 25 experts in the lodging industry and tried to find out how and what information technology could help the industry and forecast what and how information technology can be used from 2007 to 2027. The author has predicted that wireless technology will improve service delivery, lower the operating cost and enhance the overall guest satisfaction. Chathoth [18] studied the impact of information technology and developed a conceptual framework to describe how to use information systems to lower the operation cost and manage customer satisfaction, for a full-service hotel firm. The author also concluded that the legacy human-oriented system could be replaced by IT-based system to increase the efficiency, productivity and revenue. Muller [48] considered the use of technologies in hospitality, such as systems for information sharing, staff scheduling, credit card processing and inventory management. He mentioned that the use of Internet helps to speed up the operational processes as well as marketing to reach more customers. He also mentioned that the use of IoT could help to automatise a restaurant to build a smart kitchen, which in return lowers the operating cost by reducing the employees needed throughout the business processes. Law et al. [42] studied and outlined the benefits of implementing information technology in the hospitality industry, which focuses mainly on hotels and restaurants. They mentioned that IT systems could help to enrich customer experiences. They also highlighted the challenges of why the management of the operators resisted implementing IT to their businesses. Seric et al. [59] used the evidence from the hospitality industry to analyse the relationship between the advancement in technology and the enhancement of public relationship and the building of brand equity from the customer perspective. Schuckert et al. [58] reviewed and analysed the articles related to online reviews and reputation system in the tourism and hospitality industry. The study covered the studies about the online review platform in the lodging industries and restaurants. The handling methods of online complaints and conflicts were also studied. At last, the authors also highlighted that consumers intend to check online reviews before making any decision on buying products or booking hotels and restaurants and the importance of these systems is increasingly vital for the businesses. Hua et al. [31] indicated that nowadays hotels keep putting more capital to implement e-commerce systems after ample researches proved that it does help in reducing the operating cost, increasing the revenues, attracting new customers, and increasing customer loyalty, especially for chained hotel groups. However, it does not apply to some categories of hotels or resorts.

Dragonchain [56] was originally developed by Disney in 2015 and consisted of various functionalities aimed at the hospitality industry to make the business processes smoother and to lower the operating cost as well as improve the guest satisfaction. Then, it was released as an open source in the late 2016, which is a private blockchain platform developed for use in various use cases and applications in different industries. Zhou et al. [76] pointed out that guests in hospitality concerned about their privacy as traditional online marketplaces were collecting lots of valuable personal information such as passport number and credit card information. Thus, the authors proposed a technique that uses a Bitcoin blockchain network to secure personal information by interacting with those service providers anonymously. Dogru et al. [25] suggested that blockchain technology can make a change in the hospitality industry by providing a shared ledger and security and it can also be used to track customers and food and provide a better loyalty programme and a digital ID for identity verifications. Taylor [67] figured out some of the technologies that could enhance the guest experience which are mobile check-in, better Wi-Fi coverage, stronger cybersecurity, personalised customer experiences and robot. This also leads to the existing underlying issue that the customers want their experience to be improved by advanced technologies. Calvaresi et al. [15] suggested that trust is a critical element of the tourism industry. Trust can be built by transparency, loyalty and traceability, which are also the characteristics of blockchain technology. Thus, blockchain can be used for improving the loyalty programme, digital ID verification, guest and food tracking as well as online reviews and provide various benefits to both customers and suppliers.

6.2.2 Blockchain technology

In this section, the technical details of blockchain technology are discussed, such as the mode of operation and consensus algorithm. In recent years, blockchain has become a popular academic perspective; researchers believed that it has the potential to be a revolution in business processes in any industry.

In 2016, Cachin [14] studied the Hyperledger, which is used to develop a standard platform for blockchain technology including the ledger framework and code bases for different industries, and Hyperledger Fabric, a platform for the running of smart contracts and allowing pluggable functions to be implemented. The Hyperledger Fabric was developed as an open source blockchain platform targeting business uses. Lin and Liao [43] analysed the possible security issues and challenges that needed to be overcome. They first gave a brief description of blockchain technology and then pointed out six major challenges (majority attack, fork problem, scalability, time confirmation of blockchain data, current regulations of governments and relatively high integration cost) that might happen when implementing the blockchain technology. Xu et al. [73] discussed the details of the blockchain technology and proposed a design framework for a blockchain-based system. They also discussed the benefits and drawbacks of different consensus protocols as the protocol should be decided before building the system and will affect the performance and the stability of the whole blockchain system significantly. Keenan [37] highlighted the current and emerging security issues of blockchain along with a connection to a report from the European Union Agency for Network and Information Security in January

2017, which proposed recommendations for ideal blockchain practices. Zheng et al. [75] published a paper on the architecture, consensus and possible future trends in the blockchain technology in a conference. The paper described the details of different elements in the blockchain technology together with its challenges, possible solutions and the possible directions in which it can be developed. Kshetri [40] analysed the role of blockchain technology in enhancing cybersecurity as well as in protecting user privacy. The author explained how blockchain works towards security by various protective mechanisms and what blockchain is going to solve in different industries. Blemus [12] is a legal consultant and a PhD student in France; he discussed the legal status of blockchain in the USA and EU as well as the other countries. He focused on the regulations of virtual currencies. He found that none of the countries or major economic systems had clear guidelines or regulations related to blockchain, but the governments have already realised the importance of setting up rules for blockchain operators as this technology is growing rapidly.

Wolfskehl [71] analysed the reason why blockchain is not popularly implemented in business information systems and provided some examples of how blockchain can be used in some of the companies. Wüst and Gervais [72] analysed different blockchain systems used in different perspectives in different industries and developed a guideline to help the decision-makers to decide whether blockchain could help their business after outweighing the challenges. Puthal et al. [54] provided a general concept of blockchain including its characteristics, operation theories, consensus mechanisms, applications and challenges, which is suitable for anyone to gain some knowledge on blockchain technology. Košťál et al. [39] assessed different consensus mechanisms, such as PoW, PoS, chain-based PoS and BFT-based PoS, based on the energy efficiency of cryptocurrencies. After assessing different mechanisms, they concluded PoW is not suitable for cryptocurrencies because of its performance and efficiency. Thus, PoS could be used. Finally, Santos and Swan [57] pointed out that PoW is not hard to implement compared to other consensus mechanisms such as PoS. Thus, they proposed to determine whether it is possible to utilise the advantages of both PoW and PoS by combining them into a hybrid protocol, while another research by Ogawa et al. [50] introduced a new mechanism called "Proof-of-Luck-ID".

6.2.3 Different applications in different industries

In this section, how blockchain has been implemented and going to be implemented in different industries is studied. The applications of blockchain technology have become a hot topic in recent years. Researchers published lots of papers regarding how blockchain technology could be used to maximise the benefit in different aspects. These articles also provide some evidences and practical use cases to show how the blockchain system can be used to maximise the benefits, and some of them could also be implemented in the lodging industry. Sun et al. [66] proposed some suggestions that blockchain could be implemented to facilitate the operation of smart cities and sharing economies. It can be used as a medium for providing trust, enabling residents to maintain privacy during identity verifications and implementing smart contracts to finish transactions without human intervention. Lam [41] suggested a way to implement blockchain technology to an online review system to prevent the companies from removing any review that they think unfair and encouraging users to provide quality reviews by providing rewards for their participation through a reward system. Ahram et al. [6] suggested some ideas of what can be done with the help of some blockchain characteristics to enhance the existing practices in the healthcare industry using a blockchain system based on an IBM blockchain initiative. These concepts can also be transferred and inspire the other researchers to have an idea to implement blockchain in other industries. Shrestha et al. [61] proposed a solution that shares user profiles with privacy within different businesses in tourism, such as travel agencies, hotels, restaurants and shopping malls. In their idea, the user profile was collected in any of the business nodes with some validation on site, providing the users the ability to select which information they want to share in preserving their privacy. The concept can also be used in other industries in order to facilitate business processes and data sharing across different parties.

Loyalty programmes, which are used in airlines, hotels and shops, have been implemented for decades. However, the result was not satisfying. The limited number of items redeemable restricted the interest from the customers of loyalty programmes. Thus, Choi [20] wanted to propose a model on how to implement a loyalty programme for blockchain technology using credit card and making the tokens able to be spent in offline stores. The users use a credit card as a medium to store a personalised digital wallet that contains the loyalty tokens. When the user purchases at a shop, the credit card company will pay the amount to the retailers as a typical credit card transaction and will collect the user's tokens. The owner of the loyalty programme can pay the credit card company for the tokens, or the credit card company can sell the tokens to the market. Thus, the token can be used anywhere if the retailer accepts credit cards.

Marr [45] listed out many real blockchains practically used nowadays in different aspects and their applications, such as entertainment, social engagement, retail, cars, SCM, logistics, insurance, health care, real estate, charity and financial services.

Beck et al. [9] developed a proof-of-concept prototype for a coffee shop as an example and tried to find out the benefits and challenges of blockchain when switching from a trust-based punch card system to a trust-free blockchain-based system. The authors revealed that a trust-free blockchain-based system could minimise malicious or accidental exceptions, lowering the operation cost of printing and administering punch cards and providing transparency, trust as well as security. However, it does have its drawbacks, such as a longer block time compared to the existing punch card system. It was also quite complex to handle any change in smart contracts, and blockchain incurred a little transaction fee compared to the existing system. These findings also apply to another potential system that may be developed in the future in other industries.

Initially, a vast majority of researches were focused on the finance area, but another usage of blockchain technology rather than cryptocurrency has already started to draw more attention from the researchers. Cocco et al. [21] discussed how blockchain helped to save cost in the banking industry, promoting economic growth and developing green technology. They assessed the limitations of cryptocurrency in blockchain systems through Bitcoin and described how to overcome these obstacles to handle financial transactions in a more efficient way. Papadopoulos [52] studied the reason why he thinks cryptocurrencies can be used in the conventional payment system and the challenges. He mentioned that cryptocurrencies provided a high degree of identity protection and double-key cryptography to secure the transaction and hashing to protect from modification and provide privacy, which is essential for a payment system. However, cryptocurrencies are still illegal in some countries. Even cryptocurrencies can be used in the EU and USA; the governments concern about money laundering, financing crime and tax evasion due to their anonymity. Lastly, the author concluded that a reliable and professional solution is needed before cryptocurrencies can be used in the official payment system.

Yasin and Liu [74] proposed a framework that uses online digital identity and reputation information to generate a personal behaviour rating. The behaviour rating is linked to the digital identity only for using on online systems with the preservation of the real identity of the user. The user needs to sign on an account with real information to prevent fake account, and the account is stored on a blockchain network. Then the user grants permission to the reputation system to access the browser history, online social network account and email accounts; then, these historical data are used to generate an online behaviour rating for the specific user.

In recent researches, some researchers have focused on using blockchain for proving online identity. By using the pre-verified identity stored on the trustable platform in blockchain application, users can prove their identity easily without presenting any identification document to the checker to save time and cost when processing a transaction. Jacobovitz [34] discussed the applications and solutions focusing on digital identity management utilising the blockchain technology. When a user creates an identity through the blockchain system, their physical identity documents or biometric information was uploaded and the individual can control who can have their personal information accessed. It also helps the organisations to check the identity beforehand to authorise a transaction as well as signing and notarising documents. Nowadays, such blockchain-based digital identity systems are already in use for identifying individuals, devices, companies, software packages and websites. Rivera et al. [55] mentioned that blockchain-based digital identity helps to provide a secure platform with integrity and anonymous way to prove a citizen's identity, which is necessary to build a smart city. The identity can be used in storing health records, voting, making the government operations transparent, authorising payments and using financial services, and allowing the users to share their personal information with different organisations.

Many giants in SCM and logistics also implemented a blockchain system to speed up their processes and keep track of their transactions. Many researchers are also focusing on studying how blockchain can benefit SCM and logistics and future development together with its challenges and limitations. Abeyratne and Monfared [3] first explained what blockchain is and some current applications. They then explained how blockchain could be used in manufacturing SCM. They suggested different actors should register an identity on the blockchain, record the transaction of what they did and pass the ownership to others. By using the distributed nature and immutable record, it is efficient to provide a trustable record promptly. Korpela et al. [38] investigated and interviewed operators about the functions they wanted and the requirements of integrating blockchain into SCM systems. They considered four transformations are required in the organisation as well as the investment cost. They also described the four integration models and how blockchain can be used to lower the cost and speed up the transactions.

6.3 BLOCKCHAIN INHOSPITALITY

In this decade, the hospitality sector and hotel industry are two of the fastest growing industries all over the globe even though the global economy experiences some major crises. According to SOEGJOBS [63], hotel industries have enormous growth because many large enterprises have opened their headquarters in various locations in the world and the number of international visitors in recent years has increased. In 2018, the total revenue of the hotel industry reached USD 500 billion. Moreover, the hotel industry accounted for 5% of the global GDP and the hotel industry itself had a growth of 6%–7% in 2018. The hotel industry is more significant and is thus focused in this paper, especially how to use blockchain technology to facilitate the business processes of the lodging sector.

6.3.1 Existing system and limitations

Traditionally, hotel management system (HMS) or property management system (PMS) has played a vital role in making hotel operations smooth and efficient. Hotel operators tend to find a solution for smoothening all the operations, such as front office, booking, finance, human resource, inventory, security, housekeeping and customer relationship management. However, in recent decades, technology advancement has had a massive impact on hotel management. Various computer systems are used within the same hotel or hotel group to provide various functionalities for the guests and backend staffs due to the increasing number of technologies aimed at enhancing customer satisfaction and improving the efficiency of backend operations. However, using more than one system in the same organisation is inefficient as the systems cannot always be integrated and collaborated very well to each other in most of the cases. Many human resources are wasted for inputting and double-checking the data inputted and processed by different systems, which increases the rate of human errors.

6.3.2 How does it work?

Blockchain can work with several industries and helps to smoothen the business processes as well as to lower the cost of operations. Some features are also applicable to the hotel industry if some customisations were made.

6.3.2.1 Supply chain management system

Food safety is becoming a cause for concern for all the people in the developed countries. People are more concerned about whether the food they consume contains unnecessary harmful additives, such as chemical fertilisers and pesticides. Thus, there is an increasing demand for a traceable SCM of what raw materials are used in the cuisines provided in the restaurants. In addition, people are willing to pay more for a dish whose production was more environmentally friendly and socially responsible, especially in a fine dining restaurant in a hotel. The producers must provide evidence before their items could be sold as organic or fair-trade products fulfil all the requirements and attain the relevant certifications.

To go deeper, the blockchain will use a consortium model. It allows the owner to assign which parties are authorised to upload information and update the block data. In addition, the read permission is given to anyone in public to access the transaction history to trace the food. All the real identity of the producers, distributors and retailers are verified by the owner before granting the write permission to lower the risk of attacking by unknown adversaries. Thus, PBFT can be used for consensus in a consortium blockchain; as no mining is required, it can help to reduce the waste of energy and provide better efficiency. A block will be created for every batch of product or raw material. At first, the farmers are responsible for adding the first transaction with the batch information and timestamps of when they have harvested the crops or slaughtered the cattle together with any certificate information, nutritional information and allergens along with the farmer's blockchain address for identifying the producer, and thus, they create the block. They also add a transaction for recording when and where the produce will go with the information about transportation and their unique ID. When the food is received by the distributors, they update the status, check and verify the product as well as attach the time information and their ID to the block to indicate all the information is correct and thus append a transaction with a timestamp and the destinations of the batches to the existing block and transportation information. Similarly, when the items arrive at the retailers, they first update the status, check and verify the previous records and attach the time information, the retailer ID and destinations of where the food is to be sold, with the information of the transportation. All the transactions are digitally signed to ensure the integrity and make sure the transaction is submitted by the authorised parties in the blockchain. The records maintained should be immutable, transparent and tamperproof through every supply chain node. The restaurant operators and customers could check their ingredients in the cuisine are safe and certified as the producers claim. In case of a food safety incident, all the records can be traced easily by any parties, including the government authority effortlessly.

6.3.2.2 Digital ID system

Fraud identity is an important issue in modern security systems, especially due to the fact that previous terrorist attacks happened in world-famous hotels. Digital ID system is one way to verify and prove the true identity of a person without checking the physical identity documents. With a private blockchain solution, privacy could be protected as the data in the blockchain are only available for the participating parties and the guests themselves. Only a computer-generated address instead of the full name of the users will be linked to the specific identity to preserve their privacy. In Figure 6.1, the physical identity document must be verified by a government authority in order to ensure the genuineness of the identity. The identity verified will be uploaded as a new block in the private blockchain. Then the verified digital ID can be used in all the participating hotels and restaurants. The ID could be used to make a reservation of accommodation or restaurant. The customers can also view their personal profile and update any special request as needed through the application connected to the blockchain system with their login credentials for identity verification. When a customer wants to make a booking, they could check with the booking system in the blockchain platform and confirm the booking using their unique digital ID. The system could also assign the rooms, facilities or restaurant seats according to their preferences if they did not select a particular room or dining table. When the customer arrive at the hotel or restaurant and show their digital ID in the mobile application, the front desk staff could check the booking details and verify whether the digital ID belongs to the specific user without knowing additional unnecessary information from checking the physical identity documents, or the customers can do it by themselves through a self-check-in kiosk. During the check-in process, guests could also finish the check-in process through the kiosk by logging in with their credentials, biometrics or two-factor authentication without showing the travel documents. It could save the time needed for the verification of ID documents. After the identity is checked by the system, a payment history could also be loaded to determine whether the payment has already been settled. If the guest has any outstanding balance that needs to be paid, they can pay

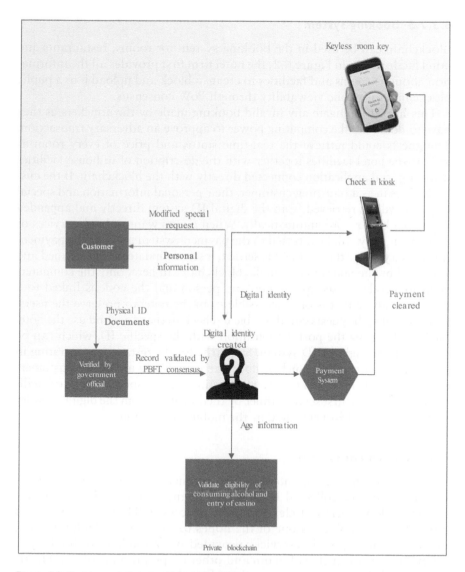

Figure 6.1 Framework for the digital ID system.

it with cryptocurrencies and the transaction could be finished in minutes. After all the payments are cleared, a system-generated door key is issued and it could be a contactless key stored in the mobile application to unlock the hotel room instead of the physical key cards, which is faster and more convenient for the guests and enhances the customer experience. When age validation is required to consume alcohol and to enter some facilities such as bars and casinos, the guest could prove the eligibility by showing a yes or no answer in the application instead of the actual age to preserve the privacy.

6.3.2.3 Booking system

Blockchain can be used in the booking system for rooms, restaurants and hotel facilities. As in Figure 6.2, the hotel firm first provides all the information about its rooms and facilities to create a block and upload it to a public blockchain for public viewability through PoW consensus.

This helps to mitigate any invalid booking made by the attackers as they have to dominate the computing power to approve an adversary transaction. The guests could retrieve the real-time status and price of every room as well as the hotel facilities together with the description of in-house facilities using a portal application connected directly with the blockchain. If the customer logs in as a returning customer, their personal information and special requests will be retrieved from the digital ID system directly and appended to the booking record automatically. When guests want to book services or equipment, they will be directed to the payment system to make the payment if necessary. After the payment is settled, a status update will be verified and validated by the nodes in the public blockchain. In here, only the computer-generated code is used as the booking person and the code is linked to a private database that is only accessible from the hotel to preserve the users' privacy. Thus, the guests could be able to check-in the room and use the hotel facilities by using the portal application with the specific ID, which can be verified in the digital DID system. Similarly, for the restaurants operating in hotels, more information such as floorplan can also be uploaded. Customers could choose their desired tables, which gain access to specific views or facilities in a first come first serve manner by their identity from the digital identity system stored and authenticated by the mobile application.

6.3.2.4 Payment system

The massive amount of international payment incurs a large amount of transaction fee collected by different financial intermediaries. It also requires a long period of clearing to be processed. There are voices that blockchain technology is one of the hopes to ease this difficulty. In fact, one of the most popular services provided by blockchain technology is cryptocurrencies, such as Bitcoin and other cryptographic tokens. Hotels could build their payment system based on the existing cryptocurrencies

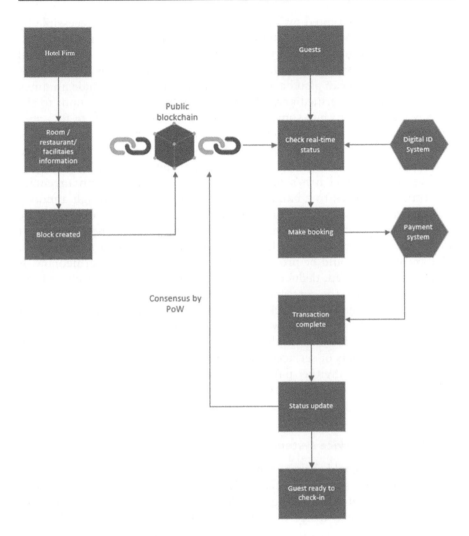

Figure 6.2 Framework for the booking system.

payment gateway to accept cryptocurrencies or tokens from other loyalty programmes. It could be used in transactions of purchasing and handling customers' reservations in restaurants and hotels as well as handling transactions in casinos. The system could be built in a public blockchain based on an existing cryptocurrency such as Bitcoin or Ethereum. A wallet application can be used to store and initialise transactions between cryptocurrencies. Users can protect their credentials by introducing two-factor authentication and authorising which devices could be used to access the account to prevent unauthorised access to the specific wallet and performing malicious transactions. Apart from this, all the sensitive information is encrypted by TLS and 192-bit AES and only accessible by the account holder. If there is any transaction, the digital signature will be checked before submitting the transaction for consensus. If both hotel firm and customers do not have their valid cryptocurrency wallet, a traditional credit card can also be accepted. However, it may include a money exchanger as an intermediary. The customers first pay the amount to the money exchanger to buy some cryptocurrencies and store them to a specific address on the public blockchain. Then, the cryptocurrencies will be verified and the transaction will reach consensus publicly by PoW. Then, the cryptocurrencies will be transferred from the sender's address to the address of the hotel firm's public blockchain and the cryptocurrencies are transferred back to a bank account by selling them through a money exchanger. After the payment is received, the hotel firm could provide products or services to their customers. Similarly, it is the best practice if both the customers and hotel firm do have a valid cryptocurrency wallet. The transaction could be processed directly without any intermediary. It can also be validated, deducted in a public blockchain and reach consensus by PoW. Then, the corresponding number of cryptocurrencies will be deducted from the users' blockchain address and sent to the hotel firm's blockchain address directly within seconds or minutes (depends on the block time of the blockchain they are using), and then, the customers can receive the products or services they wanted in an almost immediate manner. Nevertheless, if either party (customer/hotel firm) does not have any cryptocurrency wallet, they can still use the payment system with the help of money exchangers without any issue.

6.3.2.5 Room service system

Room service could bring considerable income for hotel operators. Figure 6.3 shows a system framework for the guests to log their room service orders, complaints and enquires directly to the blockchain system with the terminal located inside the room, which is already connected to the blockchain network as a trusted and approved node. A private blockchain can be used since all the transactions do not need to be verified by the public. Guests and front desk staff can check all the verified transactions through the terminals located in a room or the front desk. Moreover, it mitigates the risk of adversary transactions and leak of information to any outsiders. PFBT could also be used in a private blockchain to save the energy used for consensus. After the guest checks in and arrives at their room, the status of the in-room terminal is changed to "activated". Transactions can then be uploaded to the blockchain with the creation of a new block for the specific booking for the whole period of staying. All the orders, suggestions and opinions made by the guest can now be checked through trusted terminals anytime throughout the hotel with the specific timestamp. This information could also be stored in the guest profile and be reused during

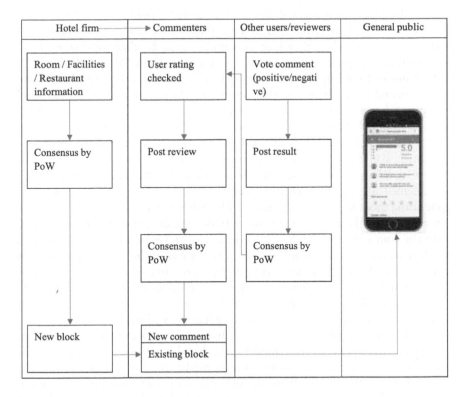

Figure 6.3 Framework for the reputation system.

their next stay. It helps to provide a full, immutable record for all the orders made by the guest within their stay and helps to reduce any dispute. During checkout, all the transactions stored in the specific block in the blockchain are retrieved and shown to the guest through the terminals in the room, and the guest can settle the payment by cryptocurrency or credit card through the payment system without going to the front desk. After that, the system-generated unlock key can be voided and the checkout process is completed.

6.3.2.6 Reputation system

Most of the users would check the reviews before they decide to dine in or accommodate a restaurant or hotel or before making a reservation, especially when they are unfamiliar with the place. Undoubtedly, trust is deemed to be the essential criteria for a reputation system. However, in most of the existing systems, it is hard to control the quality and truthiness of the reviews or comments the users post. In addition, some dishonest companies being reviewed may pay the reputation system platform providers to delete any negative comment about their products and services and make the reputation systems untrustworthy.

In order to achieve accessibility and security, a public blockchain using PoW will be used. A public blockchain allows users to view, generate and review comments when they join as a node in the blockchain system. PoW is chosen as it requires the attackers to gain more than 51% of all the computing power to manipulate the network, which is too costly to most of the attackers and make them lose their intention. As shown in Figure 6.3, hotel operators should create a block of every room, facilities or restaurants they have and upload some necessary information about the venue. Users can register a digital ID, which is only used in the reputation system, or returning customers could use their identity stored in the digital ID system to post a review or comment; a voting value is introduced and checked to see if they are deemed a good user or adversary before generating transactions and appending them to the specific block. The other registered users, who act as a reviewer, could have two-way voting to determine if they agree or disagree with the comments to decide if it is an honest and genuine review. This will result in increasing and decreasing the voting value of the author. The records of reviewing the other authors will also be stored in the blockchain ledger of their ID and are accessible to all other registered users at any time. Finally, the general public could read the verified comments stored in the blockchain system through the website or mobile application without registering.

Additionally, in order to encourage users to write comments after they experienced the services provided by the hotels, casinos or restaurants, a token will be issued to the author automatically as a reward after a specific amount of positive voting from the other users is met. Similarly, the token would also be given to the reviewers if they reviewed a specific number of comments. These tokens could be integrated into hotel loyalty programmes for items or services redemption. Due to the immutable and transparent nature of a blockchain network, all reviews and voting could be publicly verified and checked against alterations and deletions.

6.3.3 Comparison and evaluation

Implementing a blockchain system could bring some differences and challenges to the hotel firm.

6.3.3.1 SCM system

There is an increasing number of blockchain-based food traceability systems in the market. However, they are not widely implemented. Before implementing blockchain technology, although the restaurant operators and customers can access the origin of the ingredient of their cuisines through the webpages provided by the retailers, the records are stored on a centralised server that is controlled and can be manipulated by an administrator of the system [2,33,44]. This information may not include all trails to the records added. Moreover, consumers and restaurant operators have to trust the organisations or companies that the records are accurate. However, by using blockchain system similar to the platform provided by other vendors such as IBM Food Trust [23], supply chain events, transactions, master data and certificate data could be uploaded to the blockchain ledger. Different entities prove their identity through digital signatures; the transactions are immutable, publicly verifiable and stored forever. In the system, nutritional information and allergens could also be added to the distributed ledger; food manufacturers can also add that information to the specific product and consumers could be warned of food allergies. It also helps to shorten the time required for tracing to seconds as all the records are stored in various locations, which are highly available, accurate and complete.

6.3.3.2 Digital ID system

Ensuring the true identities of the customers is another critical concern regarding hotel security. In the existing self-check-in system used by Marriott [69], guests can check-in by themselves using a kiosk with facial recognition to prove the identity. Another software vendor, Clock Software [65], developed a system that identifies the guest by entering the booking number and the unique PIN without checking the identity. Both automatised solutions can allow keyless entries, but do not guarantee the truthiness of the identity of the users. By using the proposed blockchain system, the digital ID stored in the mobile application is checked instead of the real identity of the customers. As the digital identity is already verified by government authorities, their truthiness of identities can be ascertained. Besides that, staffs could also check if the guests fulfil the legal age requirement to consume alcohol and enter casino by the digital ID without asking for the customer's physical ID documents which include more information than required. In the blockchain system, users have to log in into the application with their credentials, biometrics or two-factor authentication. Therefore, a digital signature is used to ensure the digital identity belongs to the specific user account and identity which is linked to one or more government-approved identity documents without modification. Encryption will also be used to protect the user's privacy, other parties that are not authorised cannot view the sensitive information, and front desk staffs are allowed to access only limited information that is required rather than reading the whole profile of the users.

6.3.3.3 Booking system

Hilton Honors [30] allows guests to select rooms in its hotels. However, it is only available a day before the booked stay and is exclusive for members only. Agoda.com [5] is a popular online hotel booking platform available to the public and offers more than 2 million properties all over the world. However, users cannot choose the desired room they want to stay and need to enter their requirements every time they make a booking. By using the proposed blockchain system, the room statuses are uploaded to the public ledgers and can be accessible to the general public on a real-time basis. Customers can now view and book the room they want via the blockchain mobile application, settle the outstanding balance and check in immediately instead of booking via the original hotel reservation system and waiting for confirmation from the hotel, and in the existing mode of operation, most of the guests know in which room they will be staying only when they check in.

Apart from this, the system in use now is not capable of handling special requests automatically. In the proposed system, individual requests are linked to the specific user identity and will be retrieved once the guest is returning. Then the guests do not require to enter their requirements every time and their requests are always arranged. Moreover, the currently existing system focuses on providing innovative functions to hotel rooms only, but the blockchain system can also be extended to the restaurants and facilities offered by hotels.

6.3.3.4 Payment system

First and foremost, in the traditional credit card payment platform, most of the transaction fee is settled by the merchants (i.e. hotel firms), while the transaction fee is collected from the sender (i.e. customers) in the world of cryptocurrencies. Hotel firms should work out an incentive to compensate the customers for paying by cryptocurrencies, or they will continue to use the credit card for payment as it charges nothing for them (except transactions with foreign currencies).

The payment system will use Bitcoin as the infrastructure, and it sits on a public blockchain. However, the transaction fee is paid by the corresponding cryptocurrency. The average transaction fee for Bitcoin [11] is heavily affected by the market; it cost the highest (USD 36.78) on 21 December 2017 and the lowest (USD 0.04) on 1 January 2019, which is impossible to estimate in the coming years. Most of the customers are not attracted by the loyalty programmes that are running now because of the lack of variety of attractive redeemable items. For example, the loyalty programme by IHG [32] provides a limited number of items to redeem and most of them are discounted or free service or accommodation for night stay provided by the hotel participants in the same hotel group. It could be turned around by implementing the concept of cryptocurrency if the accumulated token can be used as a payment method to purchase items in different retailers.

6.3.3.5 Reputation system

Christopher Elliott pointed out some of the most trustable online reputation platforms for hotels. TripAdvisor is the winner according to the author as it is the most trustable. In that system, any public can register for a free account with a valid email address. They define a fake review as a review submitted by anyone who is biased or did not have any personal experience with the hotels they are reviewing. They developed a model to figure out any suspect paid review and send undercovers to verify the review in the hotels.

Moreover, they allow other users to report fraud from their user account and to report any blackmail. However, they try their best to get rid of fake reviews. In addition, they do not have any reward system. Thus, users are not motivated to leave comments or report any fake reviews. By using the proposed blockchain system, users in the system can post any comment on the reputation system about the facilities, rooms and restaurants in the hotels. First of all, the user rating is checked to ensure the user had not posted too much inaccurate, biased or fake review before. The other users can vote it positive and negative if they think the review is correct or not by their personal experiences during the stay in the hotel. Both the user posting the comment (after their comments are reviewed as positive) and the reviewer (if the reviews are reviewed as accurate) will get some token in the loyalty programme as a reward, which will encourage them to post comments and review comments actively. By implementing this mechanism, everyone will be motivated to post and review comments as the token earned can be used to redeem or buy other items directly through the payment system.

6.3.4 Comparative analysis on availability, privacy and costs

6.3.4.1 Availability

In most of the current hospitality systems, the systems were designed using the client and server architecture. These systems could be brought down due to various reasons; for example, the data centre of Opera System (used by Hyatt and Marriott) went down for an entire day in Germany due to severe weather. During the system outage, all check-in and check-out processes in their Europe hotels were processed manually and the staff manually re-processed all the transactions into computer systems again when the system was back online. With the unpredictable cases described above, it is clear that system availability is crucial to daily operations and could cost an enormous amount of money and manpower to restore the operations and compensate the customers for retaining the company reputation for hotel firm as well as other industries. For the hotel system itself, there are many vulnerabilities that will bring down the services, such as ransomware, which is an attack that encrypts the important files of a system and makes the system unable to function. Moreover, the DoS (denial of service) attack in which overwhelming requests beyond the server computing power were sent to the servers makes them become occupied and irresponsive and bring down the services. A hotel chain owned by the US president, Donald Trump, experienced a DDoS attack in 2017. When users wanted to access the system, an error showed that the website has concurrent visitors exceeding the maximum number set in the system, although Cloudflare, a computer service vendor providing Internet security service, was used to look after the site after two other attacks in 2016 and 2017.

In the proposed framework, consortium blockchain and public blockchain are used. They both consist of several nodes, which consist of different business partners (consortium blockchain) and public computers (public blockchain). We need to ensure all the nodes are well distributed all over the world in different geolocations and thus help to mitigate the risk of a system outage that affects a specific location, such as power outage and severe weather conditions. In a blockchain design, every node has the entire copy of the database and there will be no chance for the attackers to ransom any single copy of the data. Moreover, the blocks in the blockchain are immutable and it is impossible to alter the data even with the permission as the system or database administrator. In addition, the fact that every node has the entire copy of the database also helps to mitigate the risk of DDoS attack (DoS attack comes from distributed sources) as it does not have a single point of failure. When some of the nodes are down during the attack, the access to data will fall on other available nodes. Bitcoin itself did not experience any significant outage since its establishment in 2008. However, there were some interruptions in the operation of some exchange platforms, such as buying and selling bitcoins and other cryptocurrencies, and some of them were caused by the overwhelming number of transactions that exceeded the handling capacity that the exchange platforms provide. Besides that, the unconfirmed transactions are more than 15 MB all over the whole network, and it keeps accumulating. With the limitation by the design of Bitcoin (only 1 MB of data is being confirmed every 10 min), it always takes hours to finish the confirmation or the sender (customers) and prevents the transactions from being completed promptly. So, in conclusion, decentralised network and distribution network are still more secure against attacks such as DDoS than the other client and server architectures because there is no single target for the attackers to launch attacks.

6.3.4.2 Privacy

Privacy of an individual is crucial as it is valuable to different organisations, marketers and other individuals. Nowadays, most of the systems rely on the server and client architecture. Once the personal information is stored in the organisation's database, the access is controlled by the organisation and users have no option to decide which and how much information they are willing to share in different circumstances. In reality, most of the data breaches are unnoticed and unreported. Lodging industry systems mostly rely on the network to communicate because they are spread in different locations and the systems are interconnected by networks, particularly large hotel chains. However, there are existing problems that hackers break into the systems and intercept and retrieve the sensitive personal information of their customers, such as credit card information, phone numbers, email addresses, bank account numbers and booking details, which can be linked to other attacks such as phishing to retrieve more sensitive information such as username and password of some financial institutes. Moreover, this information can also be used in scams and fraud in cheating money. In addition, it is hard to detect the leaking of customer information in the system as attackers replicate the data and don't leave any trail of their break-in. As far as 2016, Hyatt found and announced there is a breach of payment cards information affecting more than 250 hotels across around 50 countries. In 2017, a data breach happened to a third-party hotel system "Sabre" leaking personal information of some major hotel brands, such as Four Seasons Hotels and Resorts.

In the past years, more hotels had suffered and announced they were attacked by hackers and lots of records were stolen, such as Radisson Hotel Group, Huazhu Hotels Group and Trump Hotels. Moreover, lastly, Marriott reveals that they suffered from an attack and 500 million of personal data of guests had been exposed in the late 2018 and, after investigation, it was realised that the unauthorised access had occurred as early as in 2014. It also shows the fact that it is hard to realise when the break-in occurs and how much data have been leaked during the attacks. The increasing trend of attacks alarms the industries to enhance the information security in their system to maintain the trust among customers.

In the proposed system, all the data saved to the blockchain system are first encrypted. Data should be encrypted with a symmetric key shared between the specific users and the hotel systems. Therefore, the encrypted cipher data can only be decrypted by both parties involved. Nowadays, AES encryption with a 192 bit key length is considered secure and used in most of the systems as it is regarded as the state-of-the-art encryption algorithm. There is size limitation to store data into a block, which limits the amount of data that can be fit into a block, and it makes the cost of storing a large file on the blockchain high, especially due to the enormous records of an individual profile for digital ID system. Therefore, the off-chain database could be used. Jonas Bentke suggested that a distributed database could be used; every node in the network has an identical database. That only the reference to the encrypted data in the database is stored on the distributed ledger instead of the full set of data also helps to save the transaction cost and makes the blockchain system more effective. From the users' perspective, they can use some applications that hold the digital wallet, which stores all the personal information securely. The wallet is accessible only when the user authenticates themselves by means of login credentials, biometric information or both. The users now have complete autonomy on how to use any of their data and what data to be shared by different organisations or companies in different circumstances as long as they can prove their identities by digital signatures or wallets. They can always modify the access rights through the application instead of the organisation administrator who manages the database held in the current server and client architecture. They can authorise another party to access the specific data in a specific period. For example, when the users want to enter the casino or consume alcohol, they can set the access right for the authority to access their age or just provide a "yes/no" answer as a zero-knowledge proof to check whether they have fulfilled the specific age requirement. After the verification, the users can revoke the access and make the information private again. Using the above mechanism, privacy autonomy is given back to the owner, that is the users, and it also helps to mitigate the risk of data breaches by sharing the required data only. If the cryptographic key has been compromised, there is another barrier to make the attack happen. The attacker still needs to access the reference of the sensitive information in the database of the specific user and read the database with the credentials set in the database system. On the other hand, if the database system is compromised, the attacker still cannot read the ciphertext unless they have the corresponding shared key for decryption.

6.3.4.3 Relatively high implementation and development cost

Blockchain is a relatively new technology compared to the existing client-server architecture. Sophisticated programmers are required to code bug-free smart contracts, and it is clear that there is a shortage in this kind of personnel, so the hiring cost could be high. Although there could be some ready-made blockchain platform in the market, the functionalities provided could not perfectly fit what the users require. Thus, the cost of customisation would also be high as the cost of hiring the team for the system development.

For example, a wallet application should be used to store and utilise the new tokens we use throughout the proposed system. However, initial coin offerings (ICO) may not apply as the new token used in the system is given by the hotelier and not bought from the public exchange market. Service providers are already in the market to help businesses build and implement their own blockchain. One of the service providers, Techcronus, reported that the cost of implementing a wallet app could be from around USD 5,000 USD up to USD 20,000 depending on the application scope and the blockchain platform that needs to be supported. Also, another service provider, Polygant, suggested that the total cost including the implementation cost of some of the blockchain applications may range from USD 37,500 to USD 53,500.

On the other hand, if a hotel firm wants to hire its team for blockchain development to maximise the suitability through customisations, the cost could be enormous depending on the application scope and the man-hour needed for the development. According to Shilov, the average annual salary for a blockchain engineer or developer is around USD 95,541. Although oversea freelance development may cost lower from around USD 50 to USD

70 per hour, there may be a risk that the quality of the work may not be guaranteed and monitored closely. Furthermore, it is hard to estimate the exact amount of the total cost for the talent pool as it will be heavily dependent on the scale of the blockchain system, which affects the team size and the project duration.

However, the cost could be lower as the increasing maturity of blockchain technology and more professional developers working in this field as the technology evolves. Moreover, the development and implementation cost could be shared by any other application of the software that needs to be upgraded or replaced simultaneously.

6.3.4.4 Increasing transaction cost

The transaction cost is charged not only for the payment handled by the payment system, but also for all other systems that require consensus in the public blockchain network. According to Jenkinson, it is noteworthy that the reward for the miner who generates a new block successfully as of now is 12.5 bitcoins. While Bitcoin is designed to have a maximum 21 million of bitcoins to be mined (without changing the protocol) and the reward halved every 210,000 blocks generated, it is predicted that all the bitcoins will be mined in 2140 with the current increasing trend, which is 122 years. It is inevitable that when all the bitcoins are mined, and no more reward is given to miner to create blocks, the transaction will dramatically be higher than now as it will be only the incentives for the miner to compensate for the mining cost and make profit. Besides that, a block for Bitcoin is capped at 1 MB and the transaction time of a block is performed once at 10 min. It is clearly not enough for the current increasing volume of transaction. The users now are facing the problem of slow confirmations and high transaction fee as the number of transactions confirmation per block is scarce.

SegWit helps to lower the transaction size by dividing the signature data and non-signature data and increasing the number of transactions in a block and provides hope to increase the overall efficiency and prolongs the mining lifecycle for Bitcoin. However, it is unfavourable for the miners as they get lesser rewards of unlocking blocks with the same number of transactions. In fact, other cryptocurrencies will face the same problem as they have a similar reward system and a cap of the mining capacity.

In order to address the problem, possible considerations could be taken. With the advancement of technology, the mining chips and machines will become handier and more effective. This could help to relieve the high cost of the miners in running the mining machines. In addition, with the nature of transaction fee is in an open market, there will still be sufficient incentive for the miners if they could ask for a higher transaction fee to compensate for their cost and eventually make a profit. However, this could cause an unstable transaction fee, which becomes an unforeseeable cost to hotel firms.

6.4 CONCLUSIONS

It is concluded that the blockchain technology is still in its infancy. Similar to the other emerging technologies, it has its benefits together with its drawbacks. Undoubtedly, plenty of researchers are trying to unground the potential of this technology in streamlining the business processes as well as lowering the operation cost at the same time. It is also considered as the solution to data breaches by providing a reference to the encrypted data stored in a distributed database. In this chapter, we first give an overview of blockchain technology and some details of its consensus algorithms and types of blockchain networks. Then some of the blockchain applications in different industries and how blockchain technology is linked to the hospitality industry are discussed. After that, some system frameworks of how blockchain technology can be applied to the critical systems running in lodging industries are discussed, together with the comparison between the existing platforms and the proposed idea. Finally, there is a discussion about how the blockchain technology can bring benefits and its drawbacks, security concerns and barriers in adapting the technology for the whole lodging industry.

The development of blockchain technology is still in very early stage. Researchers are still focusing on many aspects of blockchain technology, such as consensus algorithms and different applications in different industry sectors. However, most of the researches are focused on using blockchain in the finance sector or cryptocurrencies. In this chapter, the proposed idea is still an abstract. Therefore, in the next step, the suggested framework could be implemented and provide a practical reference to the interested hotel firms.

Moreover, all consensus algorithms have their drawbacks. More researches can be done to develop a better algorithm, particularly for the lodging industry. Finally, we can study the potential to integrate with other technologies, such as IoT, to provide extraordinary experiences to the guests, and big data analysis, to design hotel facilities and fulfil some common requirements that suit most of the general public in advance before the guests arrive.

BIBLIOGRAPHY

1. Timeline: The growing number of hotel data breaches, Nov 2018.
2. LM Abenavoli, F Cuzzupoli, V Chiaravalloti, AR Proto, et al. Traceability system of olive oil: a case study based on the performance of a new software cloud. *Agronomy Research*, 14(4): 1247–1256, 2016.
3. Saveen A Abeyratne and Radmehr P Monfared. Blockchain ready manufacturing supply chain using distributed ledger. *International Journal of Research in Engineering and Technology*, 5(9):1–10, 2016.
4. Noelle Acheson. What is segwit? Feb 2018.
5. Agoda. Hotels, resorts, hostels & more, Feb 2019.

6. Tareq Ahram, Arman Sargolzaei, Saman Sargolzaei, Jeff Daniels, and Ben Amaba. Blockchain technology innovations. In *2017 IEEE technology & engineering management conference (TEMSCON)*, pages 137–141. IEEE, 2017.

7. Abdullah Al Hasib and Abul Ahsan Md Mahmudul Haque. A comparative study of the performance and security issues of AES and RSA cryptography. In *2008 Third International Conference on Convergence and Hybrid Information Technology*, volume 2, pages 505–510. IEEE, 2008.

8. ALYSSA.NEWCOMB. Hyatt reveals data breach impacted about 250 hotels: What you need to know, Jan 2016.

9. Roman Beck, Jacob Stenum Czepluch, Nikolaj Lollike, and Simon Malone. Blockchain–the gateway to trust-free cryptographic transactions. 2016.

10. Jonas Bentke. On-chain vs off-chain, Apr 2019.

11. bitcoinfees.earn.com. Bitcoin transaction fees, Feb 2019.

12. Stéphane Blemus. Law and blockchain: A legal perspective on current regulatory trends worldwide. *Revue Trimestrielle de Droit Financier (Corporate Finance and Capital Markets Law Review)*, (4–2017), 2017.

13. BLOCKCHAIN.LUXEMBOURG.S.A. Blockchain charts, Apr 2019.

14. Christian Cachin et al. Architecture of the hyperledger blockchain fabric. In *Workshop on distributed cryptocurrencies and consensus ledgers*, volume 310. Chicago, IL, 2016.

15. Davide Calvaresi, Maxine Leis, Alevtina Dubovitskaya, Roland Schegg, and Michael Schumacher. Trust in tourism via blockchain technology: results from a systematic review. *Information and Communication Technologies in Tourism 2019*, pages 304–317, 2019.

16. CERTNZ. Phishing | cert nz, Apr 2019.

17. CERTNZ. Scams and fraud | cert nz, Apr 2019.

18. Prakash K Chathoth. The impact of information technology on hotel operations, service management and transaction costs: A conceptual framework for full-service hotel firms. *International Journal of Hospitality Management*, 26(2):395–408, 2007.

19. Gertrude Chavez-Dreyfuss. Coinbase exchange has outage due to high trading volume, Apr 2019.

20. Jaewon Choi. Modeling the intergrated customer loyalty program on blockchain technology by using credit card. *International Journal on Future Revolution in Computer Science & Communication Engineering*, 4(2):388–391, 2018.

21. Luisanna Cocco, Andrea Pinna, and Michele Marchesi. Banking on blockchain: Costs savings thanks to the blockchain technology. *Future Internet*, 9(3):25, 2017.

22. Mitel Networks Corp. Top 10 communication trends in hotel technology for 2018, Jan 2018.

23. IBM Corporation. About ibm food trust, Mar 2019.

24. Samburaj Das. World's largest crypto exchange suffers outage amid bitcoin cash craze, Nov 2017.

25. Tarik Dogru, Makarand Mody, and Christie Leonardi. Blockchain technology & its implications for the hospitality industry. *Boston University*, 2018.

26. Christopher Elliott. These are the best hotel review sites in the world, Feb 2019.

27. Valentina Gatteschi, Fabrizio Lamberti, Claudio Demartini, Chiara Pranteda, and Victor Santamaria. To blockchain or not to blockchain: That is the question. *IT Professional*, 20(2):62–74, 2018.

28. Stuart Haber and W Scott Stornetta. How to time-stamp a digital document. In *Conference on the Theory and Application of Cryptography*, pages 437–455. Springer, 1990.

29. Alex Hern. Marriott hotels: data of 500m guests may have been exposed, Nov 2018.

30. Hilton. Digital check-in and room selection faq, Mar 2019.

31. Nan Hua, Cristian Morosan, and Agnes DeFranco. The other side of technology adoption: examining the relationships between e-commerce expenses and hotel performance. *International Journal of Hospitality Management*, 45:109–120, 2015.

32. IHG. Ihg reward club homepage, Mar 2019.

33. Wherefour. Inc. Food, beverage, natural product traceability erp production software: Lot tracking and inventory control, Mar 2019.

34. Ori Jacobovitz. Blockchain for identity management. *The Lynne and William Frankel Center for Computer Science Department of Computer Science.* Ben-Gurion University, Beer Sheva, 2016.

35. Gareth Jenkinson. A glimpse into the future - what happens when there are no more bitcoin to mine? Mar 2019.

36. Reshma Kamath. Food traceability on blockchain: Walmart's pork and mango pilots with ibm. *The Journal of the British Blockchain Association*, 1(1): 3712, 2018.

37. Thomas P Keenan. Alice in blockchains: surprising security pitfalls in pow and pos blockchain systems. In *2017 15th Annual Conference on Privacy, Security and Trust (PST)*, pages 400–4002. IEEE, 2017.

38. Kari Korpela, Jukka Hallikas, and Tomi Dahlberg. Digital supply chain transformation toward blockchain integration. *In Proceedings of the 50th Hawaii International Conference on System Sciences*, 2017.

39. Kristián Košt'ál, Tomáš Krupa, Martin Gembec, Igor Vereš, Michal Ries, and Ivan Kotuliak. On transition between pow and pos. In *2018 International Symposium ELMAR*, pages 207–210. IEEE, 2018.

40. Nir Kshetri. Blockchain's roles in strengthening cybersecurity and protecting privacy. *Telecommunications Policy*, 41(10):1027–1038, 2017.

41. Chelsea Lam. Applying blockchain technology to online reviews. *LES Business Review Blog*, 2017.

42. Rob Law, Daniel Leung, Norman Au, and Hee Andy Lee. Progress and development of information technology in the hospitality industry: Evidence from cornell hospitality quarterly. *Cornell Hospitality Quarterly*, 54(1):10–24, 2013.

43. Iuon-Chang Lin and Tzu-Chun Liao. A survey of blockchain security issues and challenges. International Journal of Network Security, 19(5):653–659, 2017.

44. Emydex Technology Ltd. Complete flexibility - emydex - factory floor software for food processors, Mar 2019.

45. B Marr. 30 real examples of blockchain technology in practice. *Alıntıtarihi*, 11(14): 2018, 2018.

46. Lee Mathews. Travel giant sabre confirms its reservation system was hacked. Apr 2019.

47. Rene Millman. Trump hotels website appears to be under ddos attack by hackers. Feb 2019.

48. Christopher Muller. Hospitality technology: A review and reflection. *Worldwide Hospitality and Tourism Themes*, 2(1):9–19, 2010.

49. Netsurion. The top five cyber threats hotel brands and franchisees need to know about, Mar 2019.

50. Takeshi Ogawa, Hayato Kima, and Noriharu Miyaho. Proposal of proof-of-lucky-id (pol) to solve the problems of pow and pos. In *2018 IEEE International Conference on Internet of Things (iThings) and IEEE Green Computing and Communications (GreenCom) and IEEE Cyber, Physical and Social Computing (CPSCom) and IEEE Smart Data (SmartData)*, pages 1212–1218. IEEE, 2018.

51. John Ollila. Opera hotel management system outage in western Europe on Sunday. Mar 2019.

52. Georgios Papadopoulos. Blockchain and digital payments: an institutionalist analysis of cryptocurrencies. In *Handbook of Digital Currency*, pages 153–172. Elsevier, 2015.

53. Polygant. The cost of blockchain projects, Feb 2019.

54. Deepak Puthal, Nisha Malik, Saraju P Mohanty, Elias Kougianos, and Gautam Das. Everything you wanted to know about the blockchain: Its promise, components, processes, and problems. *IEEE Consumer Electronics Magazine*, 7(4):6–14, 2018.

55. Rogelio Rivera, José G Robledo, Víctor M Larios, and Juan Manuel Avalos. How digital identity on blockchain can contribute in a smart city environment. In *2017 International smart cities conference (ISC2)*, pages 1–4. IEEE, 2017.

56. J. ROETS. Dragonchain business summary, Jun 2016.

57. Renato P dos Santos and Melanie Swan. Pow, pos, & hybrid protocols: A matter of complexity? *arXiv preprint arXiv*, 2018.

58. Markus Schuckert, Xianwei Liu, and Rob Law. Hospitality and tourism online reviews: Recent trends and future directions. *Journal of Travel &Tourism Marketing*, 32(5):608–621, 2015.

59. Maja Šerić, Irene Gil-Saura, and María Eugenia Ruiz-Molina. How can integrated marketing communications and advanced technology influence the creation of customer-based brand equity? evidence from the hospitality industry. *International Journal of Hospitality Management*, 39:144–156, 2014.

60. Kirill Shilov. Blockchain jobs and salaries—2018 report, Feb 2019.

61. Ajay Kumar Shrestha, Ralph Deters, and Julita Vassileva. User-controlled privacy-preserving user profile data sharing based on blockchain. *arXiv preprint arXiv*:1909.05028, 2019.

62. Arjun J Singh and Michael L Kasavana. The impact of information technology on future management of lodging operations: A delphi study to predict key technological events in 2007 and 2027. *Tourism and Hospitality Research*, 6(1):24–37, 2005.

63. SOEGJOBS. Hotel industry analysis and market statistics for 2018, Jan 2019.

64. SOEGJOBS. Overview of the hospitality and tourism industry today- and projections for future, Aug 2021.

65. Clock Software. Hotel check in/out and self service kiosk, Mar 2019.

66. Jianjun Sun, Jiaqi Yan, and Kem ZK Zhang. Blockchain-based sharing services: What blockchain technology can contribute to smart cities. *Financial Innovation*, 2(1):1–9, 2016.

67. D. Taylor. 6 ways technology can improve the hotel guest experience, Feb 2018.

68. Techcronus. How much does it cost to develop blockchain wallet app? Feb 2019.

69. Hospitality Technology. Marriott to trial facial recognition check-in technology in China, Mar 2019.
70. TripAdvisor.LLC. About tripadvisor reviews | tripadvisor insights, Mar 2019.
71. Mark Wolfskehl. Why and how blockchain? *The Journal of The British Blockchain Association*, 1(1): 3562, 2018.
72. Karl Wüst and Arthur Gervais. Do you need a blockchain? In *2018 Crypto Valley Conference on Blockchain Technology (CVCBT)*, pages 45–54. IEEE, 2018.
73. Xiwei Xu, Ingo Weber, Mark Staples, Liming Zhu, Jan Bosch, Len Bass, Cesare Pautasso, and Paul Rimba. A taxonomy of blockchain-based systems for architecture design. In *2017 IEEE international conference on software architecture (ICSA)*, pages 243–252. IEEE, 2017.
74. Affan Yasin and Lin Liu. An online identity and smart contract management system. In *2016 IEEE 40th Annual Computer Software and Applications Conference (COMPSAC)*, volume 2, pages 192–198. IEEE, 2016.
75. Zibin Zheng, Shaoan Xie, Hongning Dai, Xiangping Chen, and Huaimin Wang. An overview of blockchain technology: Architecture, consensus, and future trends. In *2017 IEEE international congress on big data (BigData congress)*, pages 557–564. IEEE, 2017.
76. Hengyu Zhou, Yukun Niu, Jianqing Liu, Chi Zhang, Lingbo Wei, and Yuguang Fang. A privacy-preserving networked hospitality service with the bitcoin blockchain. In *International Conference on Wireless Algorithms, Systems, and Applications*, pages 696–708. Springer, 2018.

Chapter 7

Hardware security considerations and challenges in IoT architectures

Mohammad S. Khan
East Tennessee State University

Sherali Zeadally
University of Kentucky

Nathan Eggers
East Tennessee State University

CONTENTS

ABSTRACT

The Internet of things is a transformational technology for society. IoT offers a wide variety of applications as computing devices shrink and become embedded in virtually everything. Smart devices can be used in home appliances, infrastructure, and even medical technologies. Smart homes, smart factories, and autonomous vehicles will eventually give rise to entirely automated cities. As IoT grows and advances, it becomes more critical that existing security concerns will be addressed.

DOI: 10.1201/9781003304203-7

Embedded systems are small and are cheap by necessity. It is important that effective, inexpensive, and low-cost solutions for security are found for IoT devices. While it is not yet clear whether the best solutions will be provided by software or hardware, it is clear that regulation must be part of the solution. Effective policies and procedures for the Internet of things should mirror effective security solutions for existing cloud infrastructure. The primary differences will be that IoT solutions should be scalable to low-memory application, of low cost, standardized, or even open source and should be efficient in their use of processing power. As such, the security needs for IoT will require greater commitment and research. Research avenues which include blockchain and improved algorithms, encoded within both hardware and software systems, will make a more secure and resilient IoT infrastructure possible. Secure IoT networks will be crucial as distributed computing applications gain importance in society. Distributed security can be as transformational as the applications which it enables.

7.1 INTRODUCTION

The Internet of things has unlimited potential. The unfortunate problem is that this potential also carries with it a certain level of risk. Connected devices can vary in scale and in the type of operating system that they can employ [56,88], if they employ an operating system at all. Some specialized low-resource devices may be designed to utilize programs which are boot-loaded on device start-up, a well-known technique in embedded systems design. Mobile devices often connect to and control IoT systems [58,71], which are typically small embedded systems [56,58,68] which vary from the scale of the Raspberry Pi system to smaller devices which are also typically based on RISC instruction set architecture [88] and are similar to the processing chip found in Arduino microcontroller systems.

The things featured in the Internet of things typically have a minimal operating system [88] and connect to the external control of Internet cloud applications in order to provide advanced features [58]. Because it may be challenging to providing strong security mechanisms within these devices, the most obvious way to protect these devices is through continuous monitoring and intervention [87]. This may become a particularly problematic approach as these devices increase in number, however. The need to reduce the vulnerability of these devices can now be approached by the use of minimalized versions of decentralized secure technologies, such as blockchain, which are being adapted by companies such as IBM in their ADEPT system [56]. Until now, this may have been impractical due to the traditionally high processing demands of decentralized technologies such as blockchain [70]. Efforts to reduce the need for excessive processing for blockchain have led to the development of IPFS, an interplanetary file system based on block-chain technology which utilizes an alternative consensus system which is less demanding of processing resources [36]. This technology alone is unlikely to work to secure the minimal systems, which comprise the Internet of things, but such a technology does act as a good model for how such a system's architecture may be designed when applied to identifiers [52].

7.2 BACKGROUND

7.2.1 IoT hardware

IoT devices can be built around ARM architecture [88], AVR architecture [88], and specialized architectures such as FPGA devices [73]. ARM architectures for IoT tend to utilize ARM Cortex series processors [16,56], which include the M4 or M7 processors [48]. More recent Raspberry Pi systems now use alternative ARM Cortex processors with more processing power than the ARM Cortex M4 or M7. The Raspberry Pi 4 uses a quad-core 64-bit ARM Cortex A72 processor [22], while the Raspberry Pi 3b+ uses a quad-core 64-bit ARM Cortex A53 processor [21]. The low cost and high availability of Raspberry Pi platform mean that systems based on Raspberry Pi have a high likelihood of being implemented in IoT environments [51]. AVR architectures are of wide range, but full IoT devices typically use the ATmega series [16] such as ATmega328, which is widely available in Arduino kits. Although FPGA devices are not found in most kits for IoT, the programmable hardware has been used for research in hardware-based security and in optimizing processing efficiency for specialized applications [16,59,62,83]. FPGAs, such as ASICs, can be used for specialized devices in which the physical logic of the chip can be programmed using a hardware description language such as Verilog [44]. FPGAs are more cost-effective than ASICs for most applications due to the requirements for a high initial investment for ASIC development [44].

Security considerations for AVR architecture as seen in Figure 7.1 may be the hardest to accomplish, due to the minimal nature of microcontroller units. MCUs are slower than processors [2,17,29] and may have less internal memory [88] depending on the model. AVR development requires a different toolchain than ARM development and relies on manufacturer-provided development environments rather than open-source development environments, such as those available for Raspberry Pi, for deploying software to the hardware system. Security approaches designed for operating systems and software which run on processors may not be implementable for microcontrollers [56]. MCUs, due to their low processing speed and low memory [17,19], are likely to be less capable of encryption or the maintenance of secure user accounts. Role-based access and authentication are critical issues in IoT security [66].

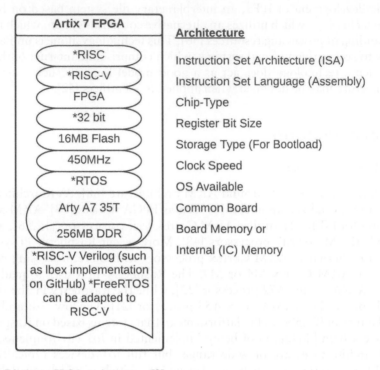

Figure 7.1 Artix FPGA architecture [3].

ARM Cortex M4 and higher processors seem to be the standard for IoT applications [48]. Security approaches that are minimal enough to be used in AVR systems should be applicable to most other systems, however. Considering the addition of security features to even more lightweight systems, it may be possible to produce a system that is both lightweight and secure. AVR architectures such as Atmel's ATtiny RISC chips are one example of what kind of systems may be used for this type of experimental setup. By using the lightweight Femto OS and adding the necessary features for security and IoT within the limits of one of the ATtiny chips, a security-focused operating system may be produced. The limits of this microcontroller are very challenging for development, with only 8KB of flash program memory and 512 bytes of RAM [27]. The Femto OS stress test program, which is named Remember, is intended to replicate the system running near its limits and runs at 2.6KB and with 368 bytes of RAM [11]. The results of adding appropriate security measures to Femto OS are likely to be similarly within the limits of the operating system. The suggested experimental system would have value as an example of what minimal security measures should be within IoT systems, both in policy and in practice. In this system, IoT communication features would be expected to be provided within another more computationally robust system which would be integrated with this minimal secure system, or be controlled by another such microcontroller as ATtiny MCUs are very inexpensive.

A RISC architecture is also available for programmable hardware devices, such as FPGA [23,24]. This open-source architecture is referred to as RISC-V [23,24], with V representing the Roman numeral for five. Security is already a built-in concern with FPGA devices, so RISC-V provides an additional layer of security within its design [24]. Another RISC architecture that is popular is the ESP8266 and ESP32, which use Xtensa assembly language [15,19]. The combination of 32-bit architecture with a low-cost single chip, which combines Wi-Fi with processing [19], has contributed to the success of the ESP8266 in IoT projects.

7.2.2 IoT operating systems and software

Because FreeRTOS is compatible with both AVR and ARM architectures [12], it would be possible to adapt this work into a secure operating system that is adaptable to most IoT devices as seen in Figures 7.2 and 7.3. Being built on a more minimized device, however, should make the operating system even more capable of additional security features once it is on a slightly more robust platform. If the chip is kept in a minimal form and if it is possible to add monitoring features, which update a remote server to potential intrusion, it would be an embedded intrusion detection system.

Keeping this type of system within the constraints of the limited hardware would be very challenging. Programs on these devices are flashed or stored in a semi-permanent memory known as EEPROM. These programs must be designed to work within the specific constraints of the chip being used. The programming tools are sometimes provided by the manufacturer, as they are with Microchip's Atmel Studio for AVR architecture [4]. Similar toolchains are provided by FPGA manufacturers for development on the FPGA boards. Xilinx provides the Vivado and ISE suites to support FPGA development on the boards which they manufacture [7].

Most available programs for security have been developed with the X86 architecture in mind due to the prevalence of the x86 in laptops and desktop computers, as well as servers. These security suites are not easily adapted to ARM or AVR architectures due to lower processing and memory resources within these systems [56]. The company SEGGER has developed an operating system with security features for embedded systems, however [9]. Transport layer security is one feature that is part of embOS [9]. Transport layer security, which takes the place of SSL, is incorporated in the open-source wolfSSL library [26]. Alongside the FreeRTOS library and several adapted libraries for web protocols, such as HTTPS, which can be found on the FreeRTOS.org website, a fully secure IoT-compatible operating system could be produced with these considerations. Security can be added to AVR systems using an additional hardware unit as well, which Microchip sells under the trade name

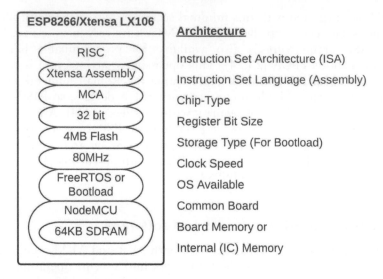

Figure 7.2 ESP8266 architecture [19].

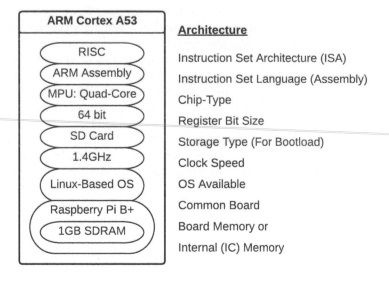

Figure 7.3 ARM architecture [21].

of CryptoAuthentication or as the Trust Platform [28]. The units with the widest feature set are sold as Trust&GO, TrustFLEX, and TrustCUSTOM [28].

The use of transport layer security does not justify the development of additional operating system functionalities by itself, however. If deeper security concerns than encryption, security certificates, and secure HTTP are addressed, that would make the development process worthwhile. This security concern could be a low-level trust protocol. There are many considerations for a trust protocol, but many of these would bear some level of similarity to blockchain consensus.

7.2.3 Cyberthreats and security breaches

Common types of security breaches include DDOS, MiM, and various injection attacks [63]. For IoT devices, man-in-the-middle attacks are a particular vulnerability [35,38,39,46,54]. The connected nature of the device and its reliance on particular cloud applications for functionality introduces a scenario for attack as seen in Figure 7.4. The scenario would be that some intercepted communication to or from the cloud server is intercepted and changed [63].

An attack on the server would be detrimental enough, but a server requires more resources to compromise than an IoT device [49]. The most likely target for these attacks is the IoT device itself if this IoT device can be made a profitable target [35,57]. An IoT device is a connected device like a computer on the Internet, but it is less secure. The vulnerable situation of unencrypted communication involving IoT devices [35,75] creates an ideal target for individuals who wish to create a botnet of compromised devices. If one device could be compromised by a man-in-the-middle attack, such a compromised device could be used to automate further man-in-the-middle attacks on other IoT devices. Compromised devices in a botnet could, in fact, be used to do almost anything within the collective ability of the devices that are compromised. This may lead to a chain reaction. A number of IoT devices may be breached, one after another. The compromised devices could reach staggering numbers if no successful intervention is carried out, but it is unknown whether such attacks currently target IoT devices over mobile devices such as smartphones and tablets. Mobile devices have been compromised in this fashion before, and this may form the largest botnet traffic currently.

IoT devices often lack authentication or trust features [56]. One solution to this problem is to use a dedicated security device for authentication. Microchip produces such devices; ATECC508A or TrustFLEX is one such device that is uniquely suited for IoT [28]. This device is MCU, or processor, agnostic [28]. A C library grants the ability to authenticate transactions using the device. Additionally, there are cryptographic hashing features for encoding communication. Because Microchip requires a minimum order quantity of 2,000 units, however, it would be difficult to order these units in amounts which are appropriate for research and testing. Additionally, each unit must be used with a development board, which is likely to be paired with a form factor of MCU available from Microchip [25].

For the development of secure devices in this way, the cost for such measures is not extravagant in terms of per unit pricing. The ATECC508A itself is priced by the manufacturer at about 0.80 cents per unit. The MCU itself

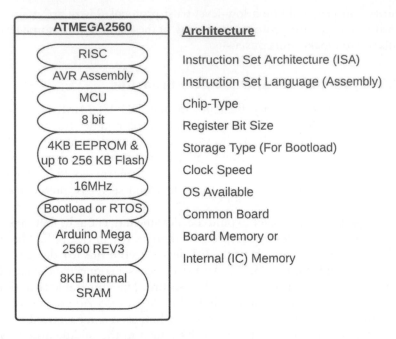

ATMEGA2560	Architecture
RISC	Instruction Set Architecture (ISA)
AVR Assembly	Instruction Set Language (Assembly)
MCU	Chip-Type
8 bit	Register Bit Size
4KB EEPROM & up to 256 KB Flash	Storage Type (For Bootload)
	Clock Speed
16MHz	OS Available
Bootload or RTOS	Common Board
Arduino Mega 2560 REV3	Board Memory or
	Internal (IC) Memory
8KB Internal SRAM	

Figure 7.4 AVR/ATmega architecture [17].

is much higher, at about 8 dollars per unit depending on the order quantity. This only amounts to 10% of the price of the MCU, if the price of the development board were not included. It is unclear whether the boards that support these features will be competitive with similar boards at this point. If providing similar features requires the addition of more circuit boards, hardware-based security may be expensive on the per unit basis depending on the details of implementation.

7.2.4 IoT web portals

IoT web portals are the cloud technology that drives IoT. Some of these technologies are more secure than others, and much of the challenge in choosing an adequately secure service lies in the protocol options used. The AWS IoT portal platform allows for the use of three different protocols for communication packets. MQTT with TLS encryption is possibly more secure than WebSocket communication or a non-encrypted HTTP packet [45]. MQTT is standardized by both ISO and open OASIS [45]. Because MQTT is designed for a small footprint and uses TLS for encryption, it is a very good option for IoT [18].

Another IoT web portal platform service is Microsoft Azure for IoT. Azure IoT also supports MQTT, but for multiple device connections, also supports the open OASIS standard AMQP (Advanced Message Queuing Protocol) [6]. HTTPS is also available, but is less efficient than the other standards available due to larger packet size and limitations in how cloud server to IoT device must be addressed in HTTPS. AMQP is also limited to use with devices with RAM over 1MB, which is over the SRAM specification for ARM Cortex M4 for any microchip manufacturers which provide RAM with their ARM MCUs [30]. Azure allows for the use of MQTT and AMQP over a WebSocket connection [6].

Both Watson IoT and Google Cloud IoT core support the use of MQTT [8]. Google Cloud IoT core may also use a HTTP 1.1 bridge [20]. Google Cloud IoT uses JSON to create Web Tokens and a public key for authentication [20]. Watson IoT also has some use for JSON in cloud device management [8].

7.2.5 IoT protocols

MQTT is an application layer protocol that runs on top of TCP/IP, which is the Internet standard transport layer protocol [45]. MQTT is being used by the most popular IoT platform services currently [5,6,8,18] and, with small improvements to the standard, could become the primary application protocol of IoT due to its prevalent use among platform providers. An overwhelming amount of options for datalink layer services exist currently, however. Bluetooth is for short-range applications only [25], LoRaWAN is able to send data at low power over a few miles [25], but Wi-Fi has several advantages, which may cause it to prevail over the others in the long term. Other competing technologies to Wi-Fi in IoT include Z-Wave and Zigbee, which are used in smart home applications. There are hybrid gateways, nodes, and hubs available, which utilize Wi-Fi alongside other protocols.

Many kits are available for IoT at this time, and these include many considerations. Kits for LoRaWAN are relatively expensive when compared to Wi-Fi-enabled kits, which include Raspberry Pi, or other conventional kits which are built around the ARM Cortex M4 or extension kits for Arduino based around the ESP8266 chip. While Zigbee is often presented as a good overall solution to IoT, it is interesting that options for Zigbee or Z-Wave must be found using smart home-related search terms. After doing so, it is possible to find development kits in online marketplaces for electronics, including Amazon.

7.3 ANALYSIS OF CURRENT AND FUTURE SECURITY STANDARDS AND METHODS

Ubiquitous standards tend to win out over time, unless there is a clear advantage. The low power and long range of LoRaWAN devices may justify their use in certain applications, such as smart farm and smart grid applications. The wide coverage of 4G and 3G networks and the widespread use of 3G or 4G in mobile devices encourages future interest in cellular IoT. Another suitable option is to simply convert cellular signals to Wi-Fi utilizing a hotspot device. Various protocols are being adapted to become more secure because of the need for specialty devices needing additional security, such as home healthcare devices or smart grid appliances. It is still unclear which data link technology will succeed in capturing this market.

Many devices in IoT, whether connected by Wi-Fi or some other network data link layer technology, have failed to implement available security options in previous years of manufacture [35,75]. Higher-end IoT devices, such as those with ARM cortex M4 processors or higher, should have options such as TLS available to them [26]. Many such devices have not been developed with these options fully implemented, however [75]. The failure to encrypt data makes it far easier for bad actors to execute a man-in-the-middle attack.

Interfaces, such as mobile apps, which are used to access IoT devices may also be insecure. Two or more factor authentication should be used to prevent unauthorized access to devices by malicious individuals. In addition, efforts to validate user data should be made to prevent injection attacks and other such exploits. It is advisable that home Wi-Fi settings utilize WPA2 security measures, as well.

The MQTT protocol is often used with TLS for encryption. Because MQTT sends binary files for data rather than human-readable text, it should be somewhat more secure than similar HTTP applications. The use of a secure protocol as well as recommended security measures is very important in preventing cyberattacks. Authentication and the principle of non-repudiation [56], which connects users to their actions (presumably through time-addressed logging of actions performed), is very important as the foundation of other measures to protect users, their devices, and their data from potential harm from cyberattacks.

Cyberattacks occur much more frequently than most people realize. In the industrial environment, physical access to systems may expose such systems to attack by Trojan horse or virus, or by creating a backdoor to systems, which could be utilized by hackers or botnets. IoT systems in a SCADA environment, which utilizes a complex layered architecture of control, may be particularly vulnerable due to the inherent security weaknesses of legacy devices which are often found in this environment [40,65,72,79]. Compromising either the control system computers, or the IoT device itself, or both, could cause immense financial harm to a company. The use of external USB thumb drives by employees can heighten this risk immensely. Banning the use of USB storage devices that haven't been fully scanned by the company is one policy which could address this weakness. The use of blockchain to secure normally insecure legacy devices may be an important measure of security which could find use in industry as IoT starts becoming more prevalent in industrial cyberphysical systems [86].

RFID devices lack the internal complexity of higher-end IoT devices, but give stores and warehouses the ability to log and track events in an item's history. Because trackability is critical in ISO quality management standards, using RFID devices may be appealing due to the low cost of passive RFID and the ability to automate tracking. Security by obscurity may not be an option to prevent access if bad actors possess an RFID reader writer device themselves. Reader impersonation is a known vulnerability of RFID systems. Modifications to the security authentication standards in use can make these systems more secure to such attacks. Zero-knowledge proofs could potentially add further security to these systems, a solution which would require further inquiry. With RFID having several known vulnerabilities, GPS tracking RFID systems should make some attempt to anonymize location data in the case of a breach through the use of internal proprietary schema as well as standard encryption.

7.3.1 Security algorithms and methodologies

Using ECC (a discrete logarithm problem on elliptical curves), it is possible to use low memory and low execution time with secure results [32,61]. There does seem to be a threshold of tolerance, however, for the size of the message that can be encoded using this technique [61]. Fragmented messages resulting from the use of these protocols will overload the systems that must communicate using them [61]. This is by no means the only available answer to the problem of keeping vital information secure.

Anonymity is one of the three requirements for the goal of maintaining privacy [42,56], with unlinkability and untraceability being the others. Anonymity is the inability of an outside entity to recognize an individual identity in a system [42,56]. Unlinkability is related to anonymity as an outside entity should not be able to surmise what a person's identity is from the information they produce [88]. Untraceability is the difficulty of tracking a particular entity's behavior within the system [88]. For healthcare-related IoT, the maintenance of privacy within the system is a mission-critical concern.

The security concern of non-repudiation is, on the surface, contradictory to being untraceable. The interactions of these requirements may lead to some complexity in implementing a secure yet private system. The key is to be sensitive to the legal requirements of the system and to avoid sharing any information with any individual who does not absolutely need that information. This may lead to some data being held in confidential trust rather than being completely private, but as long as the access is within the constraints of the law, this is appropriate.

Distributed identification (DID) is one measure to anonymize users within a system [52,56] and could be used to identify devices in an IoT environment. This technique is similar in some ways to a cryptographic hash used by blockchain to access cryptocurrency [52]. By using the hash, which is generated by the system at the time of use, a user may access the data generated during use. This could be a way to secure transactions in IoT.

Alternatively, a hidden identification system could be used. If a hidden ID was created using a testable algorithm, but no longer directly referenced, but data generated from it were tested against algorithmically, this would be a secure usage of IDs. Because these data would only be available to the machines that are part of the system transaction, either as client or as server, it would be unlikely for a bad actor to compromise the communication with a man-in-the-middle attack. This hidden ID system would create and share an ID one time only. No other entity should have received it, and only data which suggest that the ID is known would be given to the server.

No system is perfect, and every system may be vulnerable in some way. The key to IoT security is to use the available resources to make each device as secure as it can possibly be within its own individual constraints. Security is a moving target and requires continuous effort to achieve. IoT devices can be engineered with security in mind, but until recently, security has not been given enough thought by the companies that were producing these devices [35,50].

The continuous nature of cyberthreats and the potential to upend competitors on a global scale using hackers for hire to command and conquer rives is too large a concern to be ignored any longer. IoT devices are widely known to have vulnerabilities [35,75]. These vulnerabilities can be addressed one by one and engineered to be less relevant to reduce the ability of bad actors to target these devices. This is akin to patching software to mitigate security risks. These updates have to be applied universally to be effective, however. With IoT security, the primary option for the universal application of secure practices will likely be regulation.

IoT, like many other technological frontiers, is rapidly changing. Programmable hardware such as FPGAs creates new opportunities and risks for IoT development [73]. Securing devices with efficient hardware-driven algorithms could be a worthwhile challenge for future research. FPGAs have a wide variation in price, but some are becoming affordable enough to allow academic experimentation in optimizing hardware for use in IoT [44]. Secure IoT platforms may require specialized hardware to efficiently calculate zero-knowledge proofs or cryptographic hashes [59].

There are many other algorithms, from the field of AI or swarm intelligence, which also may have security application [59]. Those algorithms that are minimal enough to be created in a programmatic manner within a hardware development language, such as Verilog, may prove essential to the security of power-constrained system architectures like those in IoT [23]. Evolutionary computing provides the ability to respond to threats in a more adaptable way. Currently, it is unclear whether the best method would be to obscure targeting or to find effective counter-solutions to attack, but cybersecurity is mainly driven by human intervention [57] currently or by large and complex software systems such as current intrusion prevention systems [49].

Interventions may be distributed in IoT systems driven by swarm intelligence or artificially intelligent agents. Such systems may be empowered by creating application-specific, hardware-driven algorithms for intelligent security.

Privacy is one of the key issues for IoT devices [31,42,47,60,76,80]. Until very recently, unencrypted communication has still been common for many IoT services [66]. Because poor privacy practices continue in IoT development, there could be public resistance to adopting the technology along with all of the myriad benefits that the advancements in technology bring. Lack of a strongly supported standard for security, privacy issues, and encryption in IoT will cause legal, social, and political issues related to the use of these devices.

7.3.2 Legal, political, and social rationale for security in IoT

Legally, European companies already have strict privacy laws, and in the USA, strict standards exist for the exchange of health-related information [37,76]. Biometric devices, which also handle personal information, may cause breaches of the law relating to health privacy. This could be a legal gray area due to IoT device manufacturers rarely selling such devices as actual medical diagnostic equipment, and perhaps falling into some loophole by not being a health-related company. Historically, legal gaps in the regulation of new technology happen quickly after a few landmark cases.

Socially, IoT devices allow for a new form of social media, which is automated. Automated devices may generate a huge amount of data, and there may be implications for society which are similar in nature to the initial impact of social media. Social media extends the reach of the individual, but in some respects, isolates and anonymizes existing social networks and relationships. Unintended complexities, which have been prevalently negative, have arose from the immersive nature of social networks. With IoT devices being able to constantly monitor our behaviors and actions, social applications, which connect to these data and share them, risk exposing a person to social shaming, micromanagement, and cyberbullying. IoT-enabled cyberbullying would be far worse than through current social media, because IoT devices may be everywhere in a smart home, smart car, or smart city.

Politically, IoT is both dangerous and promising. Connected devices may be able to democratize information and may aid in current struggles for social equality and prevention of injustices. The danger comes from the motivation of repressive governments to monitor individuals and suppress political rivals or humanitarians. Aside from the misuse of IoT technology from repressive governments, there may also be misuse of IoT to perform acts of corporate espionage or use by cyberterrorists groups to infiltrate previously secure systems.

Clear laws and standards for what IoT devices should and should not be able to do are the primary way to prevent the misuse of these technologies to breach personal privacy, or to damage the financial security of corporations. IoT devices create the ability to automate services at deeper and deeper levels. This can create a lucrative opportunity for companies to streamline and mobilize assets. Such opportunities are rarely risk-free. Risk management is an important security concern for IoT.

Redundancy and self-healing networks would be important considerations for future development in IoT. Backup systems are commonly used to minimize threats in standard cloud technologies. For IoT, the need to automate the mobilization of backup systems would be incredibly important. Policies and procedures to ensure that backups are in place should be part of the risk management approach to IoT.

7.4 FUTURE CONSIDERATIONS FOR IoT SECURITY

Critical infrastructure is often a significant investment. For IoT, this infrastructure would include servers that act as portals to cloud platforms and services. Additionally, the data represented and exchanged between devices could be critical transactions to secure. The loss or tampering with such transactions could create a significant cost to companies that sustain such losses. Secure transactions thus represent a loss prevention program, which can be established within the risk management policies and procedures of an organization.

Another aspect of loss prevention that should be considered is trade secrets and intellectual property. With continuous transactions occurring on a minute-by-minute basis, a lot of data could be leaked, which would allow a bad actor to infer the workings of a system. Knowledge of the internal workings of an IoT system are twofold, allowing both the reverse engineering of the system by competitors and effective attacks by cyberthreats such as hackers and botnets.

Leakage of such data is difficult to prevent as communication must be preserved. One method would be to use short-range communication, which is encrypted to keep too much of the network from being exposed. Obviously, this is not an option for all components in an IoT system, but for some components of a system, this would be a good approach to prevent loss. Considerations for loss prevention such as intellectual property, reverse engineering, and trade secrets should be included in a risk management plan.

To be truly effective, any risk management plan must include a risk assessment. Risk management and risk assessment are essential practices in cybersecurity [40,41,64,82]. Each system and each organization utilizing it are unique, and this implies unique risks and threats. Effective policy and procedure create guidelines for the development of secure systems within each unique organizational environment. This allows for the advancement of IoT security even without the additional guidelines, which would be created by international standards for security in IoT.

The formal risk assessment for an organization should include both the risks and suggestions to prevent such risks. Legal issues should be considered, from privacy to risk of lawsuit or risk of loss of intellectual property. Any government standards or existing organizational policies should be considered and adhered to. Any replacement systems should, at a minimum, accomplish every necessary task that previous systems were able to do. Wireless systems should include more security considerations than wired systems due to the fact that wireless systems may be more easily penetrated.

The opportunities for IoT systems include smart factories, smart appliances, smart homes, autonomous vehicles, product tracking, smart cities, and smart energy grids [56,68,77]. Additionally, there are uses for IoT for home healthcare automation and for medical devices, which could simplify remote healthcare [37]. Even though many of these devices will not be deployed within an organizational environment, there is still risk of cyber-attacks and there are definite privacy issues and concerns [42,85].

Cloud-enabled devices, such as consumer robotics, may create security concerns. Consumer IoT devices, which can respond to human voice commands, may create opportunity for consumer privacy breaches. Voice-controlled smart hubs and voice-controlled robots could leak information related to political preference, lifestyle choices, and health issues. Social implications for such breached data are still unknown, but it is likely that public outcry would result following major breaches of privacy.

In some ways, IoT devices allow an individual more control over their own lives. Accessing services over the Internet could be streamlined; refrigerators could order more groceries to be delivered when certain grocery supplies run low or run out, for instance. In other ways, IoT devices represent a lack of control; privacy breaches and loss of control over personal data will increase in poorly implemented IoT systems. Balancing risk with opportunity through the creation of secure devices will allow consumers to have more control without being at significantly increased risk of loss of privacy or personal data.

Smart factories increase the organizational financial risks. When smart factories are tampered with, or hacked into, these systems could incur significant costs from a single attack [40,41]. Efficient manufacturing systems may produce thousands or tens of thousands of products a day. If the manufacturing system is compromised, resources will be used, but errors in the manufacturing process could make the products unusable. This may be a risk consisting of millions of dollars a day. Efficiently coupling ordering to manufacturing may also save millions of dollars a day, as well. Utilizing blockchain smart contracts together with IoT could be one technological framework for such coupling to occur. The implication is that smart factories utilizing IoT technology must create secure technology, which reduces the likelihood that such losses will be incurred. One route to achieve this is to integrate blockchain into IoT to add another layer of security [86].

Autonomous vehicles are another device that requires more complete security concerns. Vehicular networks should be more robust than home networks, but data will still be exchanged between the vehicle and the Internet inevitably. This implies that autonomous vehicles will be IoT devices. Loss of control of vehicular applications, which could occur during a man-in-the-middle attack, virus, or botnet, could result in loss of life. International cyberterrorist attacks on vehicular networks will become more of a concern when autonomous vehicles are widely available to consumers. Since autonomous vehicles are in an active development stage, it should be possible to prevent such risks before they actually arise.

Autonomous shipment vehicles, which are unmanned, may also be at risk of tampering from competitors or from bad actors that wish to take advantage of criminal opportunities for redirecting shipments. Unmanned shipment vehicles are also larger than consumer vehicles and may incur greater damage if they are compromised. The additional risk of targeting implies that such vehicles must be made to be more secure than consumer vehicles. Virtual private networks may be one way to increase security for IoT devices [10] such as unmanned vehicles, but other measures should be taken as well. Invasion detection and prevention are critical [33,34,74,78,87], and hardware-level security [16,28,59] could add another layer of security for at-risk devices such as autonomous shipment vehicles.

Product tracking could also be utilized by bad actors to anticipate and tamper with shipments of products. Increased risk of stolen product in route may arise from insecure systems for product tracking. RFID is often sent as plain text and may contain product information, which would allow targeting [43]. This is a particular risk for high value products, such as electronics, which may be resold online fairly easily.

Smart homes with electronic locks may be another particular risk of loss. Electronic door locks, which can be unlocked over the Internet, could allow a robber to invade your home. These systems also may increase the risk of other types of home invasion, such as murderers or kidnappers. This level of risk certainly implies a high level of security, such as requiring authentication for the operation of any lock at the time of use. Facial recognition or voice recognition technology within the mobile application could aid in security measures to prevent infiltration of the system and the resulting home invasions.

Smart energy grids also represent a risk of attack [39,49,53]. Infrastructure, which could be disrupted, is a potential target for cyberterrorists. Power plants, hospitals, and manufacturing could all be affected by disruption to the energy grid. Denial of power service by redirecting power, affecting power production, or directly shutting down service could be potential attacks to a smart energy grid. Attempts to overwhelm the system to cause permanent damage may also occur, similarly to the damaging of equipment noted in a 2016 Z-Wave exploit experiment [75].

Smart cities would also include other infrastructures that could compromised. Water systems, sewage, and coordination of city services could all be affected by cyberattacks. These attacks could occur for many reasons, from cyberterrorism to simple grudges. City services can be highly political, and the temptation to damage the reputation of city officials could result in a greater danger of attack.

7.5 DISCUSSION

The Internet of things is growing. People who travel or spend a lot of time away from home may see energy savings from a programmable smart home, which reduces energy usage while they are away. Smart appliances can customize our daily experiences, with smart refrigerators letting users know when they have run out of certain grocery items and smart thermostats providing temperature settings which coincide with our regular schedules.

As IoT grows, it is important that IoT devices and services are more secure than computers rather than less secure. The potential for harm is greatly increased by the power that these devices have over our lives. Smart ovens should only be programmable by their owners, not by children or by hackers, for instance. Such devices have potential for accidental or purposeful harm if security is not addressed.

When IoT is applied to infrastructure, the power of these devices only grows larger. Smart cities and smart grids could increase the ability to become energy efficient and the ability to provide services in a timely manner. The problem arises with the misuse and abuse of these abilities to cause harm to the underlying infrastructure, services, and the citizens which are being served by these.

Security has many aspects, and aside from potential harm to person or finances, there is potential for a person to be harmed by reputation or the violation of trust. Such emotional harm can and does damage lives and can also cause deaths. This is one reason why privacy is of such importance within the profession of cybersecurity. An additional consideration is that some information that is being kept private is financially important. Patents, copyrights, and trade secrets can all be violated by the leakage of information. It is important that privacy concerns are met.

Privacy is protected legally by many acts both in the USA and internationally. Youth in the USA are protected by COPPA, which includes IoT devices such as wearables [13,42]. Health information is protected by HIPAA, and health data used by IoT are included in the legal concerns of this act [14,42]. The right to privacy could be a constitutional concern as well and may be considered a basic human right. European laws in recent years has further restricted digital privacy violations and what customer contracts can or cannot dictate in terms of privacy [42]. The lack of security in IoT devices goes beyond being a practical concern for IoT companies and can cause expensive legal liabilities.

Many companies that are already making IoT devices, such as smart appliances, have failed to respect previous security standards such as SSL protocol [35]. Internet communications are now protected by the TSL protocol, and the same should be done for IoT devices. Encryption should be considered a minimal layer of security in modern Internet applications. Multi-factor authentication, voice recognition, and facial recognition are all additional security measures that should be used to prevent unauthorized access to IoT services.

As a relatively new technology, regulation has not yet caught up with IoT's security challenges and concerns. Additional international standards should be created to address this issue. Other regulatory actions will also be needed to further protect both the customer and the IoT industry from security breaches. The stakes are high, and security violations can cause significant financial and personal harm.

Vehicular networks, which may eventually utilize Internet technology, will also be a regulatory challenge. While it is important that autonomous vehicles are embraced by consumers and automotive producers, it is also important that autonomous vehicles are safe and error-free. Security concerns for autonomous vehicles should be addressed the same way as for other mission-critical applications, such as smart factories and home health devices. If done sensitively enough, these concerns should not be enough to have a chilling effect on the production of autonomous vehicles. Because additional regulation makes such vehicles safer, it should encourage the consumer market to embrace this new technology as well.

As IoT technology improves, we will see further uses for it. Smart farms will one day make food production more efficient. Sensor networks connected to the Internet could monitor potential risks of flooding, drought, earthquakes, tidal waves, and fires. Such an early warning network could improve the safety and well-being of everyone.

7.6 CONCLUSIONS

Security is an important concern in society. Trust in critical infrastructure has enabled free trade and free movement of people at an unprecedented scale. For IoT technology, increased security will create trusted distributed applications, which have the potential to create economic growth and increase the efficiency of vital services.

It is a harsh reality that vital technological infrastructure is under constant attack. Unfortunately, it has taken time to apply that lesson directly to IoT devices and many smart devices fail to be as secure as computers are. There are challenges to securing IoT devices, but the technology does exist to secure these devices in a more robust fashion than companies and other organizations are currently doing.

Standardization and regulation are the key to secure IoT. Despite legal, social, and political pressure to create secure IoT applications, many organizations have failed to properly implement basic encryption. Additionally, improper authentication can allow attackers access to private data or control over devices, which affect the daily routines of individuals.

Algorithms are being discovered, which can add greater security and protection to IoT devices. ECC and zero-knowledge proofs are capable of exchanging information both efficiently and securely [1,61,81,84]. It is worth noting that blockchain environments such as Ethereum have added zero-knowledge proofs as an additional security option recently [69]. If efficient ECC techniques and zero-knowledge proofs are applied to authentication, it may allow IoT devices to become a more secure environment. Efficient authentication is a necessary measure to prevent an attacker from having access to devices that are critically connected to our lifestyles as well. Authentication is becoming available at lower and lower levels within the architecture of IoT devices [28]. FPGAs and dedicated security ICs will enable efficient hardware-based security [16,59]. It is likely that hardware-based security will supplement rather than replace software-based security practices. In particular, combining a hardware technique utilizing manufacturing variance known as PUFs and blockchain has recently been proposed as a framework for secure authentication [67].

There is no question of whether IoT devices should have increased security. The lack of security within IoT continues to be a potential threat as IoT grows in scale and ability to be used in applications, which affects society on a large scale. IoT security must be faced differently than computer-based security, but must meet the same challenges. The threat of cyberattacks and of the particular vulnerabilities is known by both industry and researchers in the field of IoT. Designing IoT solutions to this challenge will likely require an integrated approach, combining software and hardware security methods to address the widespread threat of attack. IoT devices must be secured, and to this effect, there must be effective policies and regulations that standardize secure practices in IoT.

BIBLIOGRAPHY

1. Advanced Encryption Standard - Tutorialspoint. AES 256 Standard Encryption.
2. ® Cortex®-R8 MPCore Processor Technical Reference Manual.
3. Arty A7· Artix-7 FPGA Development Board for Makers and Hobbyists.
4. Atmel Studio 7 Microchip Technology.
5. AWS IoT Core Features Amazon Web Services.
6. Azure IoT protocol gateway Microsoft Docs.
7. Developer Tools.
8. Developing gateways.
9. embOS - RTOS, Real-Time Operating System SEGGER.

10. Enhance IoT Security & Optimize Data with a VPN.

11. Femto OS.

12. FreeRTOS Plus IO -a POSIX style peripheral driver library extension for FreeRTOS.

13. FTC Reaffirms that IoT Devices Must Comply with COPPA Mintz.

14. HIPAA Compliance for IoT Security: What Devs Need to Know.

15. Insight Into ESP8266 NodeMCU Features & Using It With Arduino IDE (Easy Steps).

16. IoT Hardware Guide | 2019 Prototyping Boards & Development Kit Options.

17. Mega 2560 Rev. 3 Microcontroller Board - Arduino Mouser.

18. MQTT connectivity for devices.

19. NodeMCU v3 — Zerynth Docs documentation.

20. Protocols Cloud IoT Core Documentation.

21. Raspberry Pi 3b+ Specs and Benchmarks.

22. Raspberry Pi 4 Model B specifications – Raspberry Pi.

23. -RISC-V Assembler Reference.

24. Running a RISC-V Processor on the Arty A7 [Reference.Digilentinc].

25. Wireless Connectivity Microchip Technology.

26. wolfSSL Embedded SSL/TLS Library Now Supporting TLS 1.3.

27. Atmel 8-bit AVR Microcontroller with 2/4/8k Bytes In-System Programmable Flash, 2013. 8kb 512 bytes 512 bytes.

28. ATECC608a-TFLXTLS CryptoAuthentication Data Sheet, 2019. ISBN: 978-1-5224-5051-1.

29. Atmel SMART ARM-based Flash MCU, January 2019.

30. SAME54 Curiosity Ultra Users Guide, 2019.

31. EPIC Internet of Things (IoT), 2020.

32. Shajina Anand and Varalakshmi Perumal. To prevent MITM attack in cloud computing. *Digital Communications and Networks*, 5(4):276–287, November 2019.

33. Faisal Arafsha, Fedwa Laamarti, and Abdulmotaleb El Saddik. Cyber-physical system framework for measurement and analysis of physical activities. *Electronics*, 8(2):248, February 2019.

34. Amin Azmoodeh, Ali Dehghantanha, Mauro Conti, and Kim-Kwang Raymond Choo. Detecting crypto-ransomware in IoT networks based on energy consumption footprint. *Journal of Ambient Intelligence and Humanized Computing*, 9(4):1141–1152, August 2018.

35. Mario Ballano Barcena and Candid Wueest. Insecurity in the Internet of Things. *Security Response, Symantec*, 2015. researchgate.net.

36. Juan Benet. Ipfs - content addressed, versioned, p2p file system, 2014.

37. Rihab Boussada, Balkis Hamdane, Mohamed Elhoucine Elhdhili, and Leila Azouz Saidane. Privacy-preserving aware data transmission for IoT-based e-health. *Computer Networks*, 162:106866, October 2019.

38. Gustavo Rovelo, Peter Quax, and Wim Lamotte. Insecure network, unknown connection: Understanding Wi-Fi privacy assumptions of mobile device users. *Information*, 8(3):76, July 2017.

39. Lipi Chhaya, Paawan Sharma, Govind Bhagwatikar, and Adesh Kumar. Wireless sensor network based smart grid communications: Cyber attacks, intrusion detection system and topology control. *Electronics*, 6(1):5, January 2017.

40. Angelo Corallo, Mariangela Lazoi, and Marianna Lezzi. Cybersecurity in the context of industry 4.0: A structured classification of critical assets and business impacts. *Computers in Industry*, 114:103165, January 2020.

41. Addie Cormier and Christopher Ng. Integrating cybersecurity in hazard and risk analyses. *Journal of Loss Prevention in the Process Industries*, page 104044, January 2020.

42. Ashutosh Dwivedi, Gautam Srivastava, Shalini Dhar, and Rajani Singh. A decentralized privacy-preserving healthcare blockchain for IoT. *Sensors*, 19(2):326, January 2019.

43. Imran Erguler. A potential weakness in RFID-based Internet-of-things systems. *Pervasive and Mobile Computing*, 20:115–126, July 2015.

44. Umer Farooq, Zied Marrakchi, and Habib Mehrez. An overview. In *Tree-based Heterogeneous FPGA Architectures*, pages 7–48. Springer, New York, 2012.

45. Iván Froiz-Míguez, Tiago M. Fernández-Caramés, Paula Fraga-Lamas, and Luis Castedo. Design, implementation and practical evaluation of an IoT home automation system for fog computing applications based on MQTT and ZigBee-WiFi sensor nodes. *Sensors*, 18(8):2660, August 2018.

46. Yulong Fu, Zheng Yan, Jin Cao, Ousmane Koné, and Xuefei Cao. An automata based intrusion detection method for internet of things. *Mobile Information Systems*, 2017:1–13, 2017.

47. Grant Gross. Potential impact of two IoT security and privacy laws on tech industry HPE, December 2018.

48. Jovan Ivković and Jelena Lužija Ivković. Analysis of the Performance of the New Generation of 32-bit Microcontrollers for IoT and Big Data Application, 2017.

49. Swapna Iyer. Cyber security for smart grid, cryptography, and privacy. *International Journal of Digital Multimedia Broadcasting*, 2011:1–8, 2011.

50. Yier Jin. Introduction to hardware security. *Electronics*, 4(4):763–784, October 2015.

51. Steven Johnston and Simon Cox. The raspberry Pi: A technology disrupter, and the enabler of dreams. *Electronics*, 6(3):51, July 2017.

52. Jonnycrunch, A Ronning, K Duffy, and C Lundkvist. as a General Pattern for DID Documents and Verifiable Claims.

53. Yasin Kabalci, Ersan Kabalci, Sanjeevikumar Padmanaban, Jens Bo Holm-Nielsen, and Frede Blaabjerg. Internet of things applications as energy internet in smart grids and smart environments. *Electronics*, 8(9):972, September 2019.

54. Md Tanzim Khorshed, A B M Shawkat Ali, and Saleh A. Wasimi. Classifying different denial-of-service attacks in cloud computing using rule-based learning: Classifying different DoS attacks in cloud computing. *Security and Communication Networks*, pages n/a–n/a, September 2012.

55. Yki Kortesniemi, Dmitrij Lagutin, Tommi Elo, and Nikos Fotiou. Improving the privacy of IoT with decentralised identifiers (DIDs). *Journal of Computer Networks and Communications*, 2019:1–10, March 2019.

56. Djamel Eddine Kouiçem, Abdelmadjid Bouabdallah, and Hicham Lakhlef. Internet of things security: A top-down survey. *Computer Networks*, 141:199–221, August 2018.

57. Nir Kshetri. Reliability, validity, comparability and practical utility of cyber-crime-related data, metrics, and information. *Information*, 4(1):117–123, February 2013.

58. Engin Leloglu. A review of security concerns in internet of things. *Journal of Computer and Communications*, 05(01):121–136, 2017.

59. Régis Leveugle, Asma Mkhinini, and Paolo Maistri. Hardware support for security in the internet of things: From lightweight countermeasures to accelerated homomorphic encryption. *Information*, 9(5):114, May 2018.

60. Nicole Lindsey. New IoT security laws seek to protect consumers from hacks of internet-connected devices. *CPO Magazine*, 2019.

61. Ankur Lohachab and Karambir. based inter-device authentication and authorization scheme using MQTT for IoT networks. *Journal of Information Security and Applications*, 46:1–12, June 2019.

62. Mehrdad Majzoobi, Farinaz Koushanfar, and Miodrag Potkonjak. Oriented Security.

63. Jeff Melnick. Top 10 most common types of cyber attacks, May 2018.

64. Jan Meszaros and Alena Buchalcevova. Introducing OSSF: A framework for online service cybersecurity risk management. *Computers & Security*, 65:300–313, March 2017.

65. Sajid Nazir, Shushma Patel, and Dilip Patel. Assessing and augmenting SCADA cyber security: A survey of techniques. *Computers & Security*, 70:436–454, September 2017.

66. Bruce Ndibanje, Hoon-Jae Lee, and Sang-Gon Lee. Security analysis and improvements of authentication and access control in the internet of things. *Sensors*, 14(8):14786–14805, August 2014.

67. Lydia Negka, Georgios Gketsios, Nikolaos A. Anagnostopoulos, Georgios Spathoulas, Athanasios Kakarountas, and Stefan Katzenbeisser. Employing Blockchain and Physical Unclonable Functions for Counterfeit IoT Devices Detection. In *Proceedings of the International Conference on Omni-Layer Intelligent Systems - COINS '19*, pages 172–178, Crete, Greece, 2019. ACM Press.

68. Razvan Nicolescu and Petar Radanliev. State of the art in IoT beyond economic value.

69. Mike Orcutt. A mind-bending cryptographic trick promises to take blockchains mainstream.

70. Chao Qu, Ming Tao, Jie Zhang, Xiaoyu Hong, and Ruifen Yuan. Blockchain based credibility verification method for IoT entities. *Security and Communication Networks*, 2018:1–11, June 2018.

71. P. P. Ray. A survey on Internet of Things architectures. *Journal of King Saud University - Computer and Information Sciences*, 30(3):291–319, July 2018.

72. Nicholas R. Rodofile, Kenneth Radke, and Ernest Foo. Extending the cyberattack landscape for SCADA-based critical infrastructure. *International Journal of Critical Infrastructure Protection*, 25:14–35, June 2019.

73. Alfonso Rodríguez, Juan Valverde, Jorge Portilla, Andrés Otero, Teresa Riesgo, and Eduardo de la Torre. Based high-performance embedded systems for adaptive edge computing in cyber-physical systems: The ARTICo3 framework. *Sensors*, 18(6):1877, June 2018.

74. Nikolaos Serketzis, Vasilios Katos, Christos Ilioudis, Dimitrios Baltatzis, and Georgios Pangalos. Improving forensic triage efficiency through cyber threat intelligence. *Future Internet*, 11(7):162, July 2019.

75. Ms. Smith. Wave: A Z-Wave hacking tool capable of breaking bulbs, abusing Z-Wave devices CSO Online, January 2016.

76. Amy Talbott. Privacy Laws: How the US, EU and others protect IoT data (or don't) ZDNet, March 2016.

77. Klervie Toczé and Simin Nadjm-Tehrani. A Taxonomy for Management and Optimization of Multiple Resources in Edge Computing, 2018.

78. Nguyen Binh Truong, Hyunwoo Lee, Bob Askwith, and Gyu Myoung Lee. Toward a trust evaluation mechanism in the social internet of things. *Sensors*, 17(6):1346, June 2017.

79. Darshana Upadhyay and Srinivas Sampalli. (Supervisory Control and Data Acquisition) systems: Vulnerability assessment and security recommendations. *Computers & Security*, 89:101666, February 2020.

80. Chris Usatenko. The IoT, Privacy Laws, and Your Clients - Law Technology Today, November 2019.

81. Marcus Walshe, Gregory Epiphaniou, Haider Al-Khateeb, Mohammad Hammoudeh, Vasilios Katos, and Ali Dehghantanha. Non-interactive zero knowledge proofs for the authentication of IoT devices in reduced connectivity environments. *Ad Hoc Networks*, 95:101988, December 2019.

82. Jiali Wang, Martin Neil, and Norman Fenton. A Bayesian network approach for cybersecurity risk assessment implementing and extending the FAIR model. *Computers & Security*, 89:101659, February 2020.

83. Maciej Wielgosz and Michał Karwatowski. Mapping neural networks to FPGA-based IoT devices for ultra-low latency processing. *Sensors*, 19(13):2981, July 2019.

84. Huixin Wu and Feng Wang. A survey of noninteractive zero knowledge proof system and its applications. *The Scientific World Journal*, 2014:1–7, 2014.

85. Hongyang Yan, Xuan Li, Yu Wang, and Chunfu Jia. Centralized duplicate removal video storage system with privacy preservation in IoT. *Sensors*, 18(6):1814, June 2018.

86. Shiyong Yin, Jinsong Bao, Yiming Zhang, and Xiaodi Huang. M2m security technology of CPS based on blockchains. *Symmetry*, 9(9):193, September 2017.

87. Xuyun Zhang, Yuan Yuan, Zhili Zhou, Shancang Li, Lianyong Qi, and Deepak Puthal. Intrusion detection and prevention in cloud, fog, and internet of things. *Security and Communication Networks*, 2019:1–4, May 2019.

88. Yousaf Bin Zikria, Sung Won Kim, Oliver Hahm, Muhammad Khalil Afzal, and Mohammed Y. Aalsalem. Internet of Things (IoT) operating systems management: Opportunities, challenges, and solution. *Sensors*, 19(8):1793, April 2019.

Chapter 8

Virtualization using Docker container

Brijesh Pandey

Goel Institute of Technology and Management

Ashish Kumar Mishra

Rajkiya Engineering College Ambedkar Nagar

Arun Yadav

Goel Institute of Higher Studies Mahavidyalaya

Durgesh Tiwari

Goel Institute of Technology and Management

Mahima Shanker Pandey

Institute of Engineering and Technology, Lucknow

CONTENTS

DOI: 10.1201/9781003304203-8

ABSTRACT

Many developers are having software packages for supplying them to other different users. These software packages are provided in the environment where all the required settings and dependencies are already available. This scenario gives the opportunity to all users to execute the applications in a similar environment. All the requirements of such users who are in need of providing their software can be fulfilled by Docker. At the same time, it provides the implementation of least level isolation (also known as process sandboxing) to other different processes that are running over the system in which Docker is hosted by utilizing features of Linux's kernel. Such types of containers can be utilized as an alternative in some scenarios to conventional virtual machines because the overhead involved is negligible in most of the cases. The objective of this chapter is to present an overview of different methods of virtualization keeping in focus the Docker containers with a case study. This virtualization platform is different from the conventional approaches of virtualization, which are based on virtual machines. Docker-based projects are emerging from a single command-line tool to the entire operating system. Describing Dockers' internal mechanism is the focus of this chapter with a demonstration of Docker API.

8.1 INTRODUCTION

Virtualization is the process of executing multiple user applications and operating systems (OSs) in isolation to each other on the same hardware [1]. Virtualization is used all over the world in almost all information systems. Many companies such as Amazon, Google, and Facebook use it on their several infrastructure layers. The methodology is not restricted to several clusters of servers, but is used by millions of users on their personal computers. There can be an enormous number of use cases for virtualization. Some of them can be like executing an instance for resource-intensive applications such as MATLAB. Utilizing the virtualized environment, the system's computational power and memory can be restricted from being exhausted; testing is an integral part of the software development life cycle. Running large multiplatform software or projects on different system configurations could be a tedious task without a virtualized environment; emulation is just like adding another feather to the virtualization cap. Software written for different architecture can run on entirely different machines.

8.2 BACKGROUND

This section provides some background concepts related to Docker-based virtualization.

8.2.1 Virtual machine-based virtualization

Some of the approaches for virtual machine-based virtualization are as follows.

8.2.1.1 Virtual machine monitors (VMMs)

Virtual machine monitors (VMMs) are often known as hypervisors. They enable creating and running virtual machines (VMs), and they have been distinguished into two different types, namely Hypervisor type 1 which runs directly on the hardware and Hypervisor type 2 which acts as an application in another OS. The OS that can directly access hardware is known as a host, although the OS which is in a virtualized environment is known as guests. Microsoft Hyper-V, Oracle VM Server, etc., are an example of Hypervisor type 1, whereas VMware workstations and Virtual Box are examples of Hypervisor type 2.

8.2.1.2 Software-based virtualization

The guest OS runs over the top of the hypervisor, and it is not given direct access to hardware as it can get control over it or corrupt the host. Nowadays, CPUs often use resource protection schemes, where various privileged rings are generated with different trust levels. A paravirtualization compile time technique can be used to replace the instruction statically if it fails to execute in a virtualized environment. On the other hand, modern processors utilize the virtual memory concept in which every application has the false belief that the whole memory is being utilized by it only.

8.2.1.3 Hardware-assisted virtualization

A Virtual Machine Control Block (VMCB) was introduced, representing a VM, which is inside the CPU. When it gets executed, the host state is saved in memory. The state of the guest is unloaded from the memory area, and the guest code starts to execute. Intel and AMD also came up with a methodology that eliminates the requirement of page tables shadowing. In the model, the hardware does transformation from guest's physical address space to virtual address space and vice versa.

8.2.1.4 Virtual Box

Virtual Box is a Hypervisor type 2 branded by Oracle and is termed as Oracle VM Virtual Box. It mainly supports all the operating systems as a guest or host. Both hardware- and software-based virtualizations are implemented in it. Shared folders, clipboards, and the cloning of virtual machines are some of its added features.

8.2.1.5 VMware Player

It is a type of virtualization software, which is generated by VMware Company. It can be utilized for free, and it can provide better performance in comparison with Docker.

8.2.2 Containers-based virtualization

The container provides an execution environment that is self-contained. This environment also shares kernel of host system. It is (optionally) isolated from other different containers that are in the same system [11]. Development of Linux brought into the idea of keeping processes isolated form the host file system and for the same purpose "*chroot*" command was created. Chroot, which stands for root change, is both a system and utility call. This command allows specifying new commands other than /. The program, along with its children, cannot access files that are above the newly created root directory. But the programs that are placed at any other place can still look inside the newly created root. It becomes critical that inside processes could not get privilege of root. As it could permit them to divide the specific directories, the procedure is termed as *Jailbreak*. Chroot is often employed to provide an isolated environment for testing unstable applications and to discover unwanted dependencies.

Namespaces are also the key feature of Linux for helping in the light-weight virtualization. Its objective is to bind a resource which is global in an abstraction like the process within the namespace feels to have its iso-lated global instance. There are about six namespaces currently available in Linux. They are as follows:

- Mount Namespace: This is the first one to be implemented, and all mount/unmount from the global space is visible.
- UNIX Timestamp Sharing (UTS): It allows to isolate gethostname () and getdomainname () identifiers. The alterations done by calling the routines sethostname () and setdomainname () are visible in the namespace which is the caller.
- Interprocess Communication (IPC): This namespace gives isolation of memory that is shared along with semaphores.
- Process ID (PID): This namespace is an isolated list of process IDs.
- Network Namespace: It allows each namespace to have its network stack.
- User Namespace: It is the last to get implemented and provides means to process different user and group IDs inside user namespaces.

The use of namespaces could isolate the process from each other; however; it is still far from the fundamental definition of virtualization. Then, control groups came into the scene in 2006, abbreviated as cgroups. It is a kernel fea-ture that enables the administrator to limit or restrict system resource usage for a group of processes. Moreover, a control group provides a subsystem that can freeze a non-root group of processes and monitor each relevant subsystem.

8.2.3 Various container architectures and their management

In order to achieve the expansion of large allocated resources, the virtualiza-tion process is implemented in the cloud [12]. Virtual machines (VMs) are the backbone of the infrastructure. Separate segregation allows for easy identifi-cation with bespoke use of containers as program packages from individual images (usually found in the archive), which are small and time consuming resources. They also provide in-house support for the required application of portable, cloud-based software applications [13]. Containerization is depen-dent on the ability to test, develop, and deploy systems on numerous servers and to connect these containers accordingly. The address of containers is concerned at the cloud level of PaaS. If the significance of the whole cloud is given, an inclusive view in recent activities is very much important.

8.2.3.1 Basis of container technology

The container contains the components of custom applications, ready to be shipped, and, if required, it also contains the business logic (in binaries and libraries) and the middleware for making applications. Tools such as Docker are prepared around engines of container when they are served like portable ways for packing apps. It creates the requirement for managing interdependence among containers that are present in many applications. The orchestration system can define the components with their dependencies along with the life cycle into a systematic process. The PaaS cloud then enables workflow from system through several agents (such as container engine). Submission of requests from containers can be supported by PaaS. The orchestration [10] here includes its formal construction, dispatch, and continuous management.

Many solutions of container are dependent on the techniques of Linux LXC. Part of the latest Linux allocation for the Linux LXC container project provides channel processes such as namespaces and batch separation processes in the shared application. Docker is the most famous solution of container at the present time, and it can be utilized for illustrating integration. The image of Docker is made from the systems of files that are separated from each other, such as a Linux stack, using LXC methods. Docker also uses the mountain of the union to install a file system above the file system which is read-only, and it allows these systems of file to be placed on the top of one other. This area is utilized for creating novel images by creating more than just basic images. There is no other layer than the top layer that can be written, which is the container itself.

The container installation process facilitates the transition from single container usage to container clusters that can run applications that contain all cluster centers. This is the benefit of containers that are built-in. Individual-type containers are then collected into linked containers. Each collection contains multiple nodes (hosting). App services are the containers of logical groups from an image. The application allows scaling of system at various hosting locations. The volumes are methods utilized by the applications that need data persistence. The containers load these different rolls for storing afterward. The links permit the connection and connection feature of two or more containers. The setting and management of these containers also needs support of orchestration for internal communication, service meetings, and links [13].

8.2.3.2 Cloud-based container architectures

The container configuration does not work by opening or closing only applications (i.e., starting or stopping containers) and transferring them between servers. The orchestration is defined as the creation and continuous management of potentially distributed clusters. These clusters are made of applications that are container based. The container setup process permits users for specifying the way containers are linked to the cloud at the time of installing a multi-container system. Container configuration means not only the starting flow of containers, but also managing multiple containers as a single business. It is responsible for taking care of the measurement, availability, and communication of containers. Basically, the construction of a cloud-based container is an orchestration method within a distributed cloud space. The cloud may be considered as a territorial and distributed structure with a tiers of basic infrastructure platform and application that are distributed in cloudy areas [1]. The technology of the vessel is very helpful. As such, vessel technology plays a major character in future in the management of application and especially in the context of PaaS.

Recently, the construction of facilities for small services has been seen in the framework of the cloud with the help of containers [8,9]. The API compatibility, PaaS, automation, and orchestration as shown in Figure 8.1 highlight the procedure in which management server works in accordance with REST API, Plugin API, and Resources API.

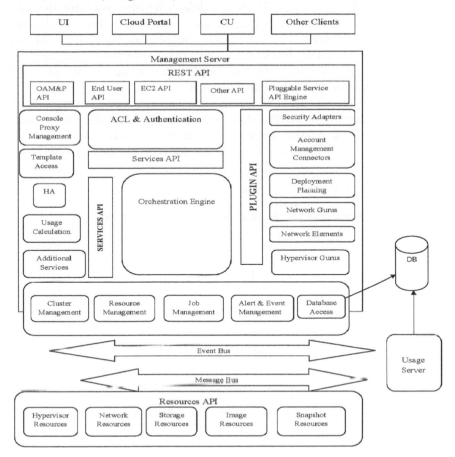

Figure 8.1 API compatibility, PaaS, automation, and orchestration.

8.3 DOCKER

The ultimate goal set up by the development team of the Docker project was to "Build a button which entitle any application which is to be developed and also deployed over a server, any place." Docker is a platform that is an open source and permits applications to be deployed in the containers of software [5]. Google, Microsoft, Amazon, and many others have added assistance for Dockers to the platforms along with the contribution to the development of the project [6].

The Docker infrastructure is shown in Figure 8.2, where it can be seen that Docker engine is layered upon operating system which itself is layered upon physical server or virtual machine. The container application is run on Docker engine. To run an application on any platform, the first step is to bring out its binaries, scripts, and data [7]. The entire application is packaged inside the pack in Docker, which is known as image. These images, in turn, are stored in registries. There is a default registry available that can be explored using a browser or Docker search command. The search command returns repositories containing many images, but one is distinguished as "latest." An ID uniquely identifies every image in Docker. An image is executed to bring out the virtualization; Docker creates a container and puts the application from the image inside it.

To run an image, the user can specify the image ID, repository name with tag, or repository name with default tag "latest." A number of optional parameters can be passed, including the option to name the container and specify the port mapping from the container to the host. *Docker pull*

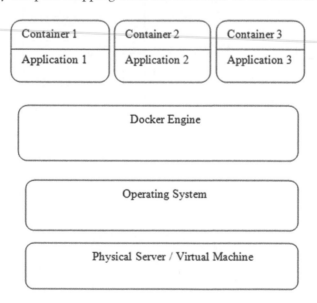

Figure 8.2 Docker infrastructure.

command can be utilized in downloading the image, and Docker create command can be used to make a container out of an image without running it.

On the host, Docker provides all the essential features to the containers, such as listing the running containers, stopping them from running, or removing them. Some interesting capabilities can also be added, such as *docker logs* for examining logs, *docker top* for viewing processes inside containers, or *Docker attach* for connecting to a running container. The daemon mode with -d switch can be used to execute the container in the background. Restriction can be also possible while starting on the usage of a number of resources. To impose a maximum memory limit -m can be used. Similarly, to set CPU priority level -c parameter can be used.

The Docker environment contains applications in the form of read-only images. A layered architecture is created, as the application image contains a reference of its parent image. An image is called a base or root image if it does not have any parent image. For building a customized image, there are two possible methods. An existing image can be executed as a container, and changes can be made to it. Then the *docker commit* command will save the changes, and *the docker push* command will save the changes in the repository. The other method is to take advantage of the automated building of images. It is handled by the docker *build command*, which needs the instructions to be provided in a Docker file. Instructions may include copying files, downloading files, excluding scripts, specifying parent or root image, exposing ports, or anything, etc.

If a developer wants to publish his image, then it can be uploaded to a Docker registry. A public registry at the Docker hub or a private registry can be used for this purpose. Docker hub registry contains three types of repositories: official, private, and public. The public and private repositories can be used to share public and non-public images, whereas the official repository contains images from vendors and Docker contributors.

8.3.1 History of Docker

Preliminarily, an interior project on dotCloud was published as an open source in the month of March 2013. Then, after two months later, the public register of Docker was infused. In the second part of the year 2013, Baidu, Yandex, and Google (the most widely used search engines in Russia and China) included Docker in their services of cloud. Docker enters in the year 2014 by reaching a fund of $ 15 million [15], which allows it for investing mostly in open-source-type projects and organized support of business along with its expansion into the public domain.

In the month of April, LXC was downgraded as default location for making the Dockers' lib container. The very next month, Ubuntu 14.04 was a first-class distribution of Linux traditional Docker shipping integrated, coming together millions of servers of Ubuntu. These are at most three commands far from the use of such container. Its first version, i.e., 1.0, was ultimately published in the month of June in the first conference, which is Docker-centric. This conference is known as Docker Con. In September, it was announced that another large $ 40 million fund had been raised [17], in the announcement of the project of approximately $ 400 million. After 1 month, Microsoft and Docker announced their co-partnership along with the idea of building a Docker Engine of Windows Server and a model of container, which is multi-Docker. It includes the favor for applications containing both Windows and Linux Docker containers.

In the month of December, the first conference of Docker was held at Amsterdam in Europe, where new projects which are concerned to Docker and Enterprise of Docker Hub were announced. Another version of it, i.e., 1.4, was published in the year 2014, becoming a 24-star project on the GitHub. In the month of February 2015, another version 1.5 was published, which provided support of IPv6. It is read-only container and provides support for many Docker increased per project. After that, orchestration tools, namely Docker compose, Docker Machine, and Docker Swarm [8], were declared. The recent stable version 1.6 was published in the month of April. It comes along with long-awaited Windows client and the capability to use defined labels on containers and photos.

8.3.2 Docker daemon

Docker utilizes a model that is a client-server model. In this model, the server is a daemon that can work with a completely different system in comparison with the client. This daemon can be initiated by giving the Docker command during the transfer of -d flag, or start the application with the program ctl start docker or service docker start. The use of a privileged account is needed for using a Docker in the mode of daemon, or a concerted effort is done to eliminate this problem, so that even ordinary users can use them. The server only hears to the UNIX socket by default. It makes itself unavailable via network. It threatens security because anyone with the right of access to these daemons can easily control every administrator [2]. Minor attacks can be made using a container with hosts/directory installed. The container will then can easily rewrite any file of host. It is hence very important to use Docker only on public IP via TLS, where every client is certified through a trusted authority of certification.

8.3.3 Libcontainer

In the Docker version 0.9, the notion of execution drivers was proposed. It was supported by two drivers, namely the LXC driver and traditional driver. The LXC driver was utilized previously, and it needs a lib lxc with a traditional driver using the library of Dockers, a Libcontainer. Written only on Go, it is handled by container management, by utilizing the kernel powers. In the past, it was known as control groups and word spaces. Libcontainer is anticipated to be exported to other different languages with support applications, eliminating the requirement of extra tools such as Boot2Docker when the Docker was being used on the platform of Windows.

8.3.4 Layering file system in Docker

At the time of introduction of the container, Docker utilizes a process known as union mount – systems. These systems are not installed in multiple locations but in more than one location, so the contents of the guide may be made up of files and references from various programs. In Docker, apps probably mean an image of parent. One example can be if a web application may be dependent on a particular web server, which is, on the contrary, dependent on the operating system (OS) only. That is to say, the whole picture adds a new layer of reading only to the system on the top of its origin layer. When the application starts in the form of a container, one extra writing layer is placed on top. When dough from a layer, which is read only, requires to be adjusted or replaced, this insert is imitated to a written layer and then a change or adjustment is done. It is also vital that the alteration made for the upper layer continues after the container becomes out and so operates at its next stage.

The only exceptions to the existing union are the data volumes [9]. They offer a way to share information among containers, doing direct alteration to this system, and these alterations are not present at the time of updating of a utilized image. The user can construct a blank volume of data or install a directory or host. These data volumes can be included to a particular container, or a container of devoted data volume can be constructed. This created container not only is being allocated to containers, but also enhances different functions such as Docker migration, retrieval, and backup.

8.3.5 Security in Docker

The current requirements for Dockers is root rights, in case of violation, the manager or host is exposed. One illustration of such a condition in this chapter is concerned with Docker daemon. Due to these security threats, one of Dockers' goals is its capability in which non-root-type users use containers. The Docker has declared that it is working and is varying the structure into more than one daemon. The recent daemon is to be created in the space of user; however, the functions of privileged type are to be transferred to the novel service in the space of kernel. In the month of December 2014, Docker introduced one novel feature known as photo signing. It has been expected by users since long that images contain a cryptographic signature, to be verified before processing. However, a detailed implementation check reveals that "Dockers' claimed that the verification of the downloaded image is dependent only on the existence of a manifest which is signed, and it has nevermore confirmed the checksum of image which is from the manifest. The attacker may render an image next to the manifest which is signed. Some moreover problems were searched. These problems can be poorly created bitumen utilized to secure the image, manifest processing after capturing the photo, or the statement that if this manifest was not correct solely an alert message was issued and this image was so far valid." It will update Dockers' security.

Another probable fear for container-based visibility is with the issues of security in the use of Linux usernames. That is, the bugs are found in the namespace of user, which has not been properly tested in producing as it has been used presently. One example of a presently found risk is that the procedure may result in systemic intrusion, and the user's access to such intrusion is not allowed. It can be achieved by the probability of dumping additional groups inside the user namespace. It can be accessed by calling preset groups, which could have happened before the guide map was available (thus you only have root rights in the namespace). There are many other weaknesses recorded and mixed in the later months. Presently, during fixation of security in the month of December 2014, another kernel engineer warned that "while it may appear to contain a right within the username space, there is ever probability of such surprises of concealing in the nook of system. There may be chance of occurrence, before it can be truly assured that unfair construction of user spaces is a safe bet" [24].

8.3.6 Performance using Docker

A detailed Docker performance test was conducted by IBM in January 2014. Tests compared Docker with visual devices that hide access of memory; blocking of I/O, connect and measure MySQL and Redis instances. Given the distinction between the two technologies of simplification, the outcomes were anticipated: "Both containers and VMs have grown technologically advanced from the decade of hardware development and software development. By standard comparison, the performance of Docker is equals or supersedes in comparison to KVM in all the tested cases. The outcomes prove that both Docker and KVM present high-performance CPU as well as memory (excluding the extreme cases)." The overhead moves slowly at the time when data are collected in a volume which is shared and not in the union system.

8.3.7 Future technologies related to Docker

Docker tool encouraged the construction of several different projects, taking benefit of their opportunities. While the development of these projects, novel ones have also emerged, as everyone wishes to close the recess in the market very quickly. It is always a difficult question as to who will emerge as the winner in this competition, but below are the comments of those who seem to be showing a good place.

8.3.7.1 Kubernetes

The Google is indeed one of the biggest data center providers and has also accepted all of its services work within a container of Linux [26]. However, they did not share their interior work plans – Omega, and they hired other managers of corporate vessel Kubernetes, as a project which is open. At present, containers are operated within Docker, even if supported by rkt, which will be included in the next chapter.

Kubernetes introduced the concept of pods – groups of containers that are tightly packed and the smallest unit that can be used. A typical usage case can be a key tool that uses a web application and uses many other different containers with their auxiliary services. It can be made sense for these different containers to start and stop at a time and work in the similar host. Pods ordinarily attach tags (pair of key and value) with them, enabling queries for cluster nodes that run a specific pods group.

Another release is the service which is a group of different ports made by label, which produces the same hole and performs the same program. The pod may stop working at one node and can be duplicated in other, so that with the utilization of the service, some pods do not require to identify which pod is executing on any node, but they can utilize the visible service IP address. For supporting the measurement, Kubernetes introduced duplicate controllers. The duplicate controller utilizes a template, depending on how the pods are structured, and it also permits setting the number of replicas of pod to work. It may help to enhance or easily reduce the count of active application conditions. Another use case would be an app update; when you use one repetition controller in the version which is old and another in the novel version, continued downtime can be found.

8.3.7.2 Mesos

Apache Mesos, published in the year 2013, incorporates the resources present in the collection, placing you as one big computer. The design of it defines the notion of a framework – an app which is written for Mesos includes a scheduler program that manages application functions. Kubernetes can be used as one of the frameworks and therefore potential tasks for pod implementation. The cycle among the collection, framework, and Mesos can be described as below:

- Mesos slaved daemon that works over all nodes in the collection.
- A master daemon is utilized to control different slaves.
- The slaves bring present resources from node to master.

- The master node chooses a framework and assigns a portion of present resources and node recognizers – a policy document for determining what framework determines which unreliable resources.
- The framework editor determines what functions will be applied to the nodes and specifies resource allocation.
- Master node requests a framework provider for chosen nodes, along with the resources which are requested.

Mesos speedily obtained fame in the companies, which used large collections. The companies, namely Airbnb, Vimeo, Netflix, PayPal, and Twitter, all use Mesos. The company Apple has declared that Siri, which is a human subsidiary on iOS, is using Mesos behind it. The Mesosphere database is presently built on Mesos, which focuses on growth, tolerance, and self-healing. It is anticipated to be published in the year 2015.

8.3.7.3 CoreOS

CoreOS is an operating system (OS) dependent on the Google Chrome Operating System. Along with its very first release in the fall of year 2013, it began to further its objective of an OS that is container-centric. The meaning of it is that CoreOS excludes a package manager, but applications are offered in the form of containers. The Docker is presently being utilized as a container manager. CoreOS attempts to aim infrastructure for cloud along with two essential resources, fleet and etcd. The etcd is a compilation of integration management, which provides the API for the integration of integration changes across a collection of etcd situations. On the other hand, a daemon is included in the control of the level of the collection. It allows the shipping of containers either worldwide (to all equipment in the collection) or to a single failover-supported machine.

8.3.7.4 Snappy Ubuntu Core and LXD

Another app, aimed at using applications installed in containers is Canonicals' Snappy. This project attempts to provide the minimum application required to use container-based applications, although very few applications are installed. Multi-container providers are supported (including Docker), called frames. Renewals occur in a transactional manner; therefore, it is always probable to reverse an unsuccessful/unwanted update. Snappy maintains basic versions of all the different packages inside, and updates are just sent with the distinction from the past version. Ubuntu also created Linux Contained Daemon (LXD), which aims to "receive all the skills and speeds of the Docker, and also turn it into a complete sense of visibility" [29]. The LXD should be an enhanced version of LXC, provide the API of REST, and in particular, support live transfer with the ability to re-contain containers.

8.3.7.5 Project Atomic

Project Atomic (PA) is a collection of materials that give solutions for delivering installed systems. The main results of PA are Project Atomic Organizations (PAOs), which are applications of lightweight. These applications are dependent on Fedora, Red Hat Enterprise Linux, or CentOS. The features mainly include Kubernetes, Docker, SE Linux, Project Cockpit, and rpm-ostree. The past version is reserved for retrieval motives, as it performs by fixing an upgraded version on the newly structured system roots. This system also deviates from the novel system, by maintaining the past version stable. Project Cockpit (PC) is a distant server manager of Linux. It also includes a GUI which is web based. Its prime advantage is to provide a clear view for the status of the server, which is very useful for administrators of novel system. PC is anticipated to be shipped also with Fedora Server 21.

8.3.7.6 Rkt

In the month of December 2014, the team of CoreOS had articulated its care for the direction taken by the project Docker. It published a blog post, which instantly grabbed attention. The dissent with the increase in the wideness of the Docker's scope has been expressed. "In the early of the year 2013, when the Docker was first published, the thought of standardized container was shaped and soon becomes tempting, a normal component part namely composable unit, which can be utilized in several different types of systems. The repository of Docker contains a declaration what should be the standard of a container. The declaration of standard container was then removed. The discussion about Docker container should be stopped instead the discussion about Docker platform should be started. The imagination of normal composable building block is not come into existence." This criticism was probably targeted at the trio of projects, Docker Machine, Docker Swarm, and Docker Compose, which were released in 2015. They also claimed that the architectural model of Docker, where all things are executed through a daemon which is central, is "fundamentally flawed" from the security's perspective. Such arguments immediately spawned discussions whether or not Docker is trying to do too much and becoming a large monolithic platform, without providing reasonable modularity, or has only stepped into the business area of other projects/start-ups, and this blog is an example of an attempted defense.

Furthermore, the post contained an announcement of Rocket – a new container runtime and a direct competitor to Docker. CoreOS vision is to center it on specifications for containers and the "App Container executor," which they included and encouraged developers to submit feedback. Later, it was renamed to rkt – "rockit." The rkt is currently under heavy development, with very little documentation or examples, but it already allows running of native Docker images. The team has also expressed that it is possible for Docker to implement their App Container Specifications, making the two projects interoperable. A statement that CentOS will continue to ship Docker was included, too.

8.3.8 Docker orchestration tools and APIs

Some Docker orchestration tools are available, such as Docker Swarm, also known as a clustering tool for Docker. It takes several Docker Engines and exposes them as a single instance. The most dynamic solution to add the individual machine to the cluster is to generate a cluster ID and then send it to the swarm to join each node's command. Once the swarm is made, a *swarm manage* command will start the swarm manager, and all the Docker commands can now be issued for the whole swarm. While using the Docker Swarm, some additional parameters can be passed to the Docker run command, which imposes the restriction for selecting the node to run the image. Such restrictions can also be named as filters and may be used to exclude the selection of specific nodes based on name, available ports, operating system, etc.

Docker Machine is another tool that is not only available in Linux, but also available in Windows. It is an example of how a classical and container-based virtualization can coexist. The basic idea for having a Docker Machine was to have a dedicated virtual machine whose main function would be to run Docker daemons. It also creates a cluster with Docker swarms. It runs all the basic commands of creating, stopping, restarting, etc. It also upgrades the Docker daemon into the virtual machine. The Docker Machine can work with local virtual machines created by the virtual box or cloud solutions as Microsoft Azure.

In most cases, complex software is composed of several components as, for example, a database or a web server. Therefore, it became a repetitive and error-prone task to install every single component manually. A project called fig came into existence, which was later deprecated as Docker Compose. The main idea behind it was making the ability to link several containers, which allowed composing a complex application using several images. It used *the YAML* configuration that allowed specifying the settings for exposing ports, mounting data volumes, and passing environment variables. Docker Compose works well with Docker Swarm as well, where linked containers can be shared on the same host.

The Docker platform uses three separate APIs to allow interaction with third-party applications: Docker Hub API, Docker Registry API, and Docker Remote API. All API work over HTTP and conform to the REST style. Docker Hub provides services to users, such as registering, updating, logging, and creating and deleting repositories. Docker Registry API is responsible for handling putting and getting images with exposure to the search function. And, to establish a remote connection with containers, Docker Remote API is utilized.

8.3.9 Docker on Linux

Ubuntu 16.04 is being chosen to install Docker Engine in it since this is a version of long-term support for 5 years and provides greater stability. The privileges of sudo are assumed to be with users, which allows the user to execute commands as a superuser, also called as root. Internet connectivity is thought of as permanent and stable. The dollar symbol in front of every line depicts it as a terminal command, and the user shall omit it while typing the command.

- For updating the packages and for making the system up to date, the below command is used:
  $ "sudo apt-get update && sudo apt-get upgrade"
- For ensuring that apt-transport-https and ca-certificates packages are to be installed in the system, the below command is used:
  $ "sudo apt-get install apt-transport-https ca-certificates"
- For adding GNU Privacy Guard Key from Advanced Packaging Tool repository, the following command is used. This command verifies that packages are not manipulated.
  $ sudo apt-key adv –keyserver hkp://p80.pool.sks-keyservers.net:80– recv-keys 58118E89F3A912897C070ADBF76221572C52609D
- Docker APT repository is then added to the system repository list by utilizing the below command:
  $ echo "deb https://apt.dockerproject.org/repo ubuntu-xenial main" *| sudo tee/etc/apt/sources.list.d/docker.list*
- For updating index of the local APT package, the below command is used:
  $ "sudo apt-get update"
- For installing the requisite packages of Docker, the driver of default storage AUFS (advanced multilayered unification filesystem) can be utilized with the below command:
  $ "sudo apt-get install linux-image-extra-$(uname -r) linux-image-extra-virtual"
- The Docker Engine can be installed in system using the following command:
  $ "sudo apt-get install docker-engine"

8.3.10 Implementation of Docker use case: WordPress

This use case exhibits a WordPress appliance using Docker and the container images from WordPress with the supported database MySQL. For setting up the complete WordPress LAMP, i.e., Linux+Apache+MySQL+PHP stack in other environment not in Docker, the following things need to be accomplished:

- Installing and configuring Apache.
- Installing and configuring MySQL.

- Installing PHP (Hypertext Preprocessor) and modules of PHP (Apache, MySQL, and GD support).
- Downloading WordPress and keeping it in the proper directory of the web server.
- Setting up permission of a file.
- Editing file of WordPress configuration for matching settings of MySQL.
- Resetting of Apache as well as MySQL for applying changes.

With the advent of Docker Compose, the above-said things can be easily done. The Docker Compose tool gets into the system as soon as installation of Docker is finished. It can be called by the command:

$ *docker-compose*

There is a requirement of *the docker-compose.yaml* file for this command, which is available in the directory when it gets executed. Docker Compose takes two containers and performs linking in between two, but allows the user to maintain and organize the resources better. The first step in writing the definition of Docker Compose is to choose the images of containers and their versions that are going to be utilized.

8.4 DOCKER APPLICATIONS IN INTERNET OF THINGS (IoT)

Here, we will explore the usage of Docker containers in the IoT applications based on the current research. Here, we briefly describe the usage of Docker for the IoT. These findings are based on the journals and conferences published in the IEEE digital library from 2014 to 2018.

8.4.1 Message Queuing Telemetry Transport (MQTT) broker cluster

MQTT broker is used to exchange measurement data and other data between IoT devices in the IoT environment. Researchers in [15] proposed the implementation of MQTT broker that is of low cost and scalable by using Docker containers. The MQTT cluster is implemented by using Raspberry Pi clusters with the Linux operating system. The MQTT broker is running in the Docker container within the Raspberry Pi. By using Raspberry Pi cluster rather than normal server for MQTT broker, better message broker throughput is achieved at a fraction of cost of normal server implementation.

8.4.2 Edge/Fog computing

In the article [4], Docker resided in the node of IoT edge. The BeagleBone Black is used for edge nodes [20]. Due to being lightweight and consuming less memory, Docker is chosen for the project to provide low-latency real-time applications in the IoT edge computing.

In the paper [19], the authors proposed an emulation framework called EmuFog for Fog computing. This emulation framework uses Docker to build emulation platform that can simulate real Fog computing environment based on user-defined requirement scripts [21]. With the EmuFog [42], workloads and performance of the currently studied Fog computing environment can be evaluated and can be adjusted to suit the requirement of the users for the deployment of Fog computing infrastructure.

Foggy [25,38] is a workload orchestration and resources management platform based on open-source software to support IoT in Fog infrastructure. Docker Containers are used to Implement Foggy Negotiator, Foggy Orchestrator, and Foggy Inventory within clustering environment for Fog computing infrastructure. With Docker and Kubernetes cluster, workload orchestration and resource negotiation can be implemented in Foggy platform.

Researchers experiment containerization of an IoT/M2M platform called one M2M. Fog Manager, Fog Workers, and Fog Nodes are implemented in the Docker environment. They have also used Docker Swarm to manage container clusters in the platform.

8.4.3 IoT analytics

IoT systems may be located in a distant place between each other [22]. Data analysis latency is expected to be at low latency between the user and the IoT application. Researchers in [3] designed GeeLytics, a platform of analytics type which does analytics in real time at the network edge in cloud using Docker environment. With GeeLytics, they can achieve outcomes of low-latency analytics and are able to decrease the consumption of bandwidth consumption between IoT cloud and IoT edges [34,35].

Docker containers are also used in the analytics application as in the article [12] to analyze greenhouse environmental data. The greenhouse environmental data are supplied to analytics applications that are running in Docker containers. Docker containers are used in this analytics application due to easy deployment.

8.4.4 Smart healthcare monitoring system

Docker containers can also be used in IoT applications in healthcare areas [13]. Patients' data collection can be automated with the function of the Raspberry Pi as edge devices, and Docker is installed in the Raspberry Pi. This will assist doctors to diagnose patients easily disregarding the patient's location. Vital data of a patient will automatically be collected and processed within Docker containers in Raspberry Pi. Patient's current statuses are viewed by using a web browser or with a mobile application. This so-called IoT-cloud healthcare model enables up-to-date patient data and improves doctor response toward the patients.

8.4.5 Vehicle-to-everything (V2X) applications

Researchers proposed that by using Docker, V2X applications [23] be easily deployed and monitored through DevOps methodology [36]. DevOps methodology enables software developer team and operation team to work together to achieve better software development and deployment lifecycle. The Docker containers are used as self-contained applications for V2X applications. Clustering of applications is done with the help of Docker Swarm. Thus, the real-time monitoring of V2X applications can be done.

8.4.6 Aquaculture

Docker containers and Docker Swarm are used in intelligent turtle breeding [40]. A few of the Raspberry Pi are located at each turtle breeding station to monitor environmental data. Each of them is installed with the Docker platform. Docker Swarm is used to cluster all Raspberry Pi within a breeding station. Therefore, the Docker implementation in the turtle's breeding base not only reduces the operating cost of the turtle breeding station, but also improves the turtle's survival rate.

8.4.7 Precision agriculture

Containerized applications are used in the precision agriculture graduate project. This project implements Docker for the data collector framework in more than 8,000 hectares of precision agriculture site in Hungary. Docker Swarm is also to manage the cluster of Docker. With Docker virtual machines, it is able to create a knowledge center for precision agriculture.

8.4.8 Smart homes

Researchers in [17] showcased a "Smart Bell in a Collaborative Neighbourhood," an application of IoT. They used Docker to deploy applications for smart homes using Fog computing. Their application lifecycle for Fog computing [27] is based on Docker technologies.

Some researchers are working on a DeCy Mo architecture for the use of blockchain for cyber-physical systems for home and industry [10]. In DeCy Mo, IoT gateway not only acts as MQTT broker, but also acts as a blockchain node. The Raspberry Pi is used to implement IoT gateway in the DeCy Mo.

8.4.9 Energy management

Docker containers and Docker Swarm are used to implement a prototype of IoT-cloud services for smart energy [16]. In the cloud-based environment, the services provided users with a web interface called "Control Room" to maintain a proper temperature for server rooms and lower operational costs.

8.4.10 Industrial IoT (IIoT)

A modular and scalable architecture based on Docker is proposed for industrial IoT (IIoT) applications [37]. Docker Environment is used in the Raspberry Pi [31] for cyber-physical and border gateway. Docker is also used in the enterprise systems of the proposed architecture. With the Docker orchestration, reliability can be achieved for the IIoT.

Cyber-physical systems are a combination of the mechanical components such as programmable logic controllers (PLCs) and software components tightly integrated to form a single entity. The authors in paper [18] proposed an architecture to modularize control applications in real time [41] by utilizing Docker containers in the pre-emptive real-time Linux kernel [28]. Linux kernel patched with pre-emptive real-time function is necessary to enable real-time control in the Linux environment. By doing this, it is possible to run real-time applications into the Docker containers [43].

In paper [11], the researchers proposed an industrial robot control platform by using Docker because of its lightweight and flexible characteristics. Consistency is achieved through different development and production releases with this architecture.

8.4.11 Smart cities

Researchers in [14] described the use of Docker containers in the application of video analysis to guarantee public safety. They designed IoT cameras by using Raspberry Pi [44] and Raspberry Pi Camera module. Docker installed the Raspberry Pi and containerized IoT camera application in wireless connection [30].

8.5 CONCLUSIONS

This chapter introduced the virtualization using Docker containers in IoT. It is possible to run Docker containers in the IoT environment, especially in the edge/Fog computing [32] since the devices have more capabilities in computing power and Docker platform requires Linux-based operating system to be operational. Lightweight, consistency, and easy orchestration of application containers in Docker are an attraction for researchers and developers to explore the possibility of integrating the Docker platform into their IoT applications. The IoT, which is currently in rapid advancement, sparks new ideas on how to implement IoT applications. With the narrowing gap between IoT, cloud computing, and Fog/edge computing, IoT applications are designed for improved lifecycle development, robust application orchestration, fast deployment, and tolerance of failures [33]. Docker environment is still considered to be large and limited in the IoT environment due to the lack of computing power and low memory capacity of the IoT devices. However, with the rapid development and advancement in the IoT technologies, this gap will be narrowed in the future [39] and Docker containers can be widely utilized in the environment of IoT.

REFERENCES

1. Al-Fuqaha, A., Guizani, M., Mohammadi, M., Aledhari, M., & Ayyash, M. (2015). Internet of things: A survey on enabling technologies, protocols, and applications. *IEEE Communications Surveys & Tutorials*, 17(4), 2347–2376. https://doi.org/10.1109/COMST.2015.2444095.
2. Center for Internet Security. (2017). CIS Docker Benchmarks. Retrieved November 3, 2018, from https://www.cisecurity.org/benchmark/docker/.
3. Cheng, B., Papageorgiou, A., Cirillo, F., & Kovacs, E. (2015). GeeLytics: Geo-distributed edge analytics for large scale IoT systems based on dynamic topology. *2015 IEEE 2nd World Forum on Internet of Things (WF-IoT)*, 565–570. https://doi.org/10.1109/WF-IoT.2015.7389116.
4. Deshpande, L., & Liu, K. (2017). Edge computing embedded platform with container migration. 2017 IEEE Smart World, Ubiquitous Intelligence & Computing, Advanced & Trusted Computed, Scalable Computing & Communications, Cloud & Big Data Computing, Internet of People and Smart City Innovation (Smart World/SCALCOM/UIC/ATC/CBDCom/IOP/SCI), 1–6. https://doi.org/10.1109/UIC-ATC.2017.8397578.
5. Docker. (2018a). About Docker. Retrieved October 17, 2018, from https://www.docker.com/company.
6. Docker. (2018b). Docker Hub. Retrieved October 17, 2018, from https://hub.docker.com.
7. Docker. (2018c). Future proof your Windows apps and drive continuous innovation. Retrieved October 14, 2018, from https://www.docker.com/.
8. Docker. (2018d). Swarm mode overview - Docker Documentation. Retrieved October 18, 2018, from https://docs.docker.com/engine/swarm/.
9. Docker. (2018e). Use volumes - Docker Documentation. Retrieved October 18, 2018, from https://docs.docker.com/storage/volumes/.
10. Gallo, P., Nguyen, U. Q., Barone, G., & van Hien, P. (2018). DeCyMo: Decentralized Cyber-Physical System for Monitoring and Controlling Industries and Homes. *2018 IEEE 4th International Forum on Research and Technology for Society and Industry (RTSI)*, 1–4. https://doi.org/10.1109/RTSI.2018.8548507

11. Garcia, C. A., Garcia, M. V., Irisarri, E., Perez, F., Marcos, M., & Estevez, E. (2018). Flexible Container Platform Architecture for Industrial Robot Control. *2018 IEEE 23rd International Conference on Emerging Technologies and Factory Automation (ETFA)*, 1, 1056–1059. https://doi.org/10.1109/ETFA.2018.8502496.

12. Hyun, W., Huh, M. Y., & Park, J. (2018). Implementation of docker-based smart greenhouse data analysis platform. *2018 International Conference on Information and Communication Technology Convergence (ICTC)*, 1103–1106. https://doi.org/10.1109/ICTC.2018.8539551.

13. Jaiswal, K., Sobhanayak, S., Turuk, A. K., Bibhudatta, S. L., Mohanta, B. K., & Jena, D. (2018). An IoT-Cloud Based Smart Healthcare Monitoring System Using Container Based Virtual Environment in Edge Device. *2018 International Conference on Emerging Trends and Innovations In Engineering And Technological Research (ICETIETR)*, 1–7. https://doi.org/10.1109/ICETIETR.2018.8529141.

14. Jang, S. Y., Lee, Y., Shin, B., & Lee, D. (2018). Application-Aware IoT Camera Virtualization for Video Analytics Edge Computing. *2018 IEEE/ACM Symposium on Edge Computing (SEC)*, 132–144. https://doi.org/10.1109/SEC.2018.00017.

15. Jutadhamakorn, P., Pillavas, T., Visoottiviseth, V., Takano, R., Haga, J., & Kobayashi, D. (2017). A scalable and low-cost MQTT broker clustering system. *2017 2nd International Conference on Information Technology (INCIT)*, 1–5. https://doi.org/10.1109/INCIT.2017.8257870.

16. Kim, S., Kim, C., & Kim, J. (2017). Reliable smart energy IoT-cloud service operation with container orchestration. *2017 19th Asia-Pacific Network Operations and Management Symposium (APNOMS)*, 378–381. https://doi.org/10.1109/APNOMS.2017.8094152.

17. Letondeur, L., Ottogalli, F. G., & Coupaye, T. (2018). A demo of application lifecycle management for IoT collaborative neighborhood in the Fog: Practical experiments and lessons learned around docker. *2017 IEEE Fog World Congress, FWC 2017*, 1–6. https://doi.org/10.1109/FWC.2017.8368526.

18. Marosi, A. C., Farkas, A., & Lovas, R. (2018). An Adaptive Cloud-Based IoT Back-end Architecture and Its Applications. *2018 26th Euromicro International Conference on Parallel, Distributed and Network-Based Processing (PDP)*, 513–520. https://doi.org/10.1109/PDP2018.2018.00087.

19. Mayer, R., Graser, L., Gupta, H., Saurez, E., & Ramachandran, U. (2017). EmuFog: Extensible and scalable emulation of large-scale fog computing infrastructures. *2017 IEEE FogWorld Congress (FWC)*, 1–6. https://doi.org/10.1109/FWC.2017.8368525.

20. Morabito, R. (2017). Virtualization on internet of things edge devices with container technologies: A performance evaluation. *IEEE Access*, 5, 8835–8850. https://doi.org/10.1109/ACCESS.2017.2704444.

21. Nastic, S., Sehic, S., Le, D.-H., Truong, H.-L., & Dustdar, S. (2014). Provisioning Software-Defined IoT Cloud Systems. *2014 International Conference on Future Internet of Things and Cloud*, 288–295. https://doi.org/10.1109/FiCloud.2014.52.

22. Paul, P. V., & Saraswathi, R. (2017). The Internet of Things — A comprehensive survey. *2017 International Conference on Computation of Power, Energy Information and Commuincation (ICCPEIC)*, 421–426. https://doi.org/10.1109/ICCPEIC.2017.8290405.

23. Rufino, J., Alam, M., & Ferreira, J. (2017). Monitoring V2X Applications using DevOps and Docker. *2017 International Smart Cities Conference (ISC2)*, 1–5. https://doi.org/10.1109/ISC2.2017.8090868.

24. Rufino, J., Alam, M., Ferreira, J., Rehman, A., & Tsang, K. F. (2017). Orchestration of containerized microservices for IIoT using Docker. *2017 IEEE International Conference on Industrial Technology (ICIT)*, 1532–1536. https://doi.org/10.1109/ICIT.2017.7915594.

25. Santoro, D., Zozin, D., Pizzolli, D., Pellegrini, F. De, &Cretti, S. (2017).Foggy: A Platform for Workload Orchestration in a Fog Computing Environment. *2017 IEEE International Conference on Cloud Computing Technology and Science (CloudCom)*, 231–234. https://doi.org/10.1109/CloudCom.2017.62.

26. Singh, D., Tripathi, G., & Jara, A.J. (2014). A survey of Internet-of-Things: Future vision, architecture, challenges and services. *2014 IEEE World Forum on Internet of Things (WF-IoT)*, 287–292. https://doi.org/10.1109/WF-IoT.2014.6803174.

27. Song, Y., Xie, J., Huang, Q., Wang, M., & Yu, J. (2018). Design and Implementation of Turtle Breeding System Based on Embedded Container Cloud. *2018 2nd IEEE Advanced Information Management, Communicates, Electronic and Automation Control Conference (IMCEC)*, 2531–2534. https://doi.org/10.1109/IMCEC.2018.8469537.

28. Tasci, T., Melcher, J., & Verl, A. (2018). A Container-based Architecture for Real-Time Control Applications. *2018 IEEE International Conference on Engineering, Technology and Innovation (ICE/ITMC)*, 1–9. https://doi.org/10.1109/ICE.2018.8436369.

29. Tseng, C.-L., & Lin, F. J. (2018). Extending scalability of IoT/M2M platforms with Fog computing. *2018 IEEE 4th World Forum on Internet of Things (WF-IoT)*, 825–830.https://doi.org/10.1109/WF-IoT.2018.8355143.

30. Tyagi, V., & Kumar, A. (2017). Internet of Things and social networks: A survey. *2017 International Conference on Computing, Communication and Automation (ICCCA)*, 1268–1270. https://doi.org/10.1109/CCAA.2017.8230013.

31. VictorColsne. (2015). Update: Raspberry Pi Docker Con Challenge-Docker Blog. Retrieved November 5, 2018, from https://blog.docker.com/2015/09/update-raspberry-pi-dockercon-challenge/.

32. Mayer, R., Graser, L., Gupta, H., Saurez, E., & Ramachandran, U. (2017). EmuFog: Extensible and scalable emulation of large-scale fog computing infrastructures. *2017 IEEE Fog World Congress (FWC)*, 1–6. https://doi.org/10.1109/FWC.2017.8368525.

33. Morabito, R. (2017). Virtualization on internet of things edge devices with container technologies: A performance evaluation. *IEEE Access*, 5, 8835–8850. https://doi.org/10.1109/ACCESS.2017.2704444.

34. Nastic, S., Sehic, S., Le, D.-H., Truong, H.-L., & Dustdar, S. (2014). Provisioning Software-Defined IoT Cloud Systems. *2014 International Conference on Future Internet of Things and Cloud*, 288–295. https://doi.org/10.1109/FiCloud.2014.52.

35. Paul, P. V., & Saraswathi, R. (2017). The Internet of Things — A comprehensive survey. *2017 International Conference on Computation of Power, Energy Information and Communication (ICCPEIC)*, 421–426. https://doi.org/10.1109/ICCPEIC.2017.8290405.

36. Rufino, J., Alam, M., & Ferreira, J. (2017). Monitoring V2X Applications using DevOps and Docker. *2017 International Smart Cities Conference (ISC2)*, 1–5. https://doi.org/10.1109/ISC2.2017.8090868.

37. Rufino, J., Alam, M., Ferreira, J., Rehman, A., & Tsang, K. F. (2017). Orchestration of containerized microservices for IIoT using Docker. *2017 IEEE International Conference on Industrial Technology (ICIT)*, 1532–1536. https://doi.org/10.1109/ICIT.2017.7915594.

38. Santoro, D., Zozin, D., Pizzolli, D., Pellegrini, F. De, & Cretti, S. (2017). Foggy: A Platform for Workload Orchestration in a Fog Computing Environment. *2017 IEEE International Conference on Cloud Computing Technology and Science (CloudCom)*, 231–234. https://doi.org/10.1109/CloudCom.2017.62.

39. Singh, D., Tripathi, G., & Jara, A. J. (2014). A survey of Internet-of-Things: Future vision, architecture, challenges and services. *2014 IEEE World Forum on Internet of Things (WF-IoT)*, 287–292. https://doi.org/10.1109/WF-IoT.2014.6803174.

40. Song, Y., Xie, J., Huang, Q., Wang, M., & Yu, J. (2018). Design and Implementation of Turtle Breeding System Based on Embedded Container Cloud. *2018 2nd IEEE Advanced Information Management, Communicates, Electronic and Automation Control Conference (IMCEC)*, 2531–2534. https://doi.org/10.1109/IMCEC.2018.8469537.

41. Tasci, T., Melcher, J., & Verl, A. (2018). A Container-based Architecture for Real-Time Control Applications. *2018 IEEE International Conference on Engineering, Technology and Innovation (ICE/ITMC)*, 1–9. https://doi.org/10.1109/ICE.2018.8436369.

42. Tseng, C.-L., & Lin, F. J. (2018). Extending scalability of IoT/M2M platforms with Fog computing. *2018 IEEE 4th World Forum on Internet of Things (WF-IoT)*, 825–830. https://doi.org/10.1109/WF-IoT.2018.8355143.

43. Tyagi, V., & Kumar, A. (2017). Internet of Things and social networks: A survey. *2017 International Conference on Computing, Communication and Automation (ICCCA)*, 1268–1270. https://doi.org/10.1109/CCAA.2017.8230013.

44. Victor Colsne. (2015). Update: Raspberry Pi DockerCon Challenge - Docker Blog. Retrieved November 5, 2018, from https://blog.docker.com/2015/09/update-raspberry-pi-dockercon-challenge/.

Chapter 9

IoT-enabled smart street light control for demand response applications

Aroshana Hettiarachchi and Shama Naz Islam
Deakin University

CONTENTS

ABSTRACT

The ubiquitous connectivity and decision-making capabilities of intelligent devices have paved the way for the integration of Internet of things (IoT) to numerous applications, especially in a smart city. Intelligent control of street lights using real-time information of weather and traffic data is an emerging application of IoT in smart cities. In addition, the sustainability goals of modern smart cities necessitate effective strategies to achieve energy-efficient operation. Integrating IoT-enabled street light control technologies with demand response applications can help in reducing electricity consumption. In this regard, the proposed research develops a framework for intelligent control of smart street lights based on weather data, traffic density and demand response signals. The framework optimises the number of street lights in a certain area that should be turned off or dimmed to reduce energy consumption according to the demand response signal. The developed algorithm considers the cloud cover and visibility and defines priority thresholds for individual streets based on traffic density data. The proposed technique is evaluated numerically in terms of reduction in energy consumption

DOI: 10.1201/9781003304203-9   183 under different weather condition scenarios for a real-life case study in Victoria, Australia, which demonstrates the effectiveness of the proposed framework in IoT-enabled demand response applications.

9.1 INTRODUCTION

The advancement of information and communication technologies enables the adoption of intelligent devices in almost every possible application in today's world. These intelligent devices or "things" with the ability to connect with each other for sharing information can solve the optimal decision-making problem even in complex scenarios. Thus, Internet of things (IoT) has emerged as an indispensable component of the modern smart cities. The smart city ecosystem enables a common platform for integrating intelligent applications with sustainability objectives [1]. In this essence, demand response (DR) applications have attracted significant attention from researchers, industry and government for their ability to achieve sustainable energy systems.

DR refers to technologies that can control electricity consumption when and where requested by the electricity utility. These technologies often aim to curtail loads when the overall electricity consumption is beyond the safe operating limits of the electricity distribution networks. IoT-enabled DR applications involve sending DR requests to intelligent controllable devices that can reduce their consumption accordingly while electricity is available to other critical applications [2]. On the other hand, smart city applications promote better controllability through the integration of information and intelligence from a multitude of platforms [3]. One such application can be smart street lighting enabled by light-emitting diode (LED) technologies, different sensors and lighting control circuits that can control light levels based on weather or traffic conditions [4]. Utilising street light control to reduce electricity consumption of street lights to match the amount requested from the utility can be an effective mechanism to satisfy DR requirements [5].

Existing research on smart street lights has focussed on the energy-saving benefits of street light control technologies. To improve the energy saving from existing lighting systems rather than installing LED lamps, a part-night lighting scheme has been investigated for Coventry, which dims lights by 100% in residential areas from midnight until 5 a.m. Although the proposed method has a lower energy saving, its deployment is less expensive as compared to LED installations [6]. To facilitate technologies that promote energy-efficient and environment-friendly street lighting systems, the authors in [7] developed a decision support system based on environmental and energy performance criteria. The tool helps to rank lighting systems using power density and annual electricity consumption as well as environmental factors such as colour temperature and light distribution.

Replacing existing street lights with smart street lights will incur capital investment, and so an economic analysis will be necessary to deem the feasibility of such initiatives. In this essence, the authors in [8] performed an economic analysis for street light replacement project in Pontedera, Italy, and investigated the sensitivity with respect to electricity prices. A case study for controlling the lighting levels for the typical routes taken by pedestrians and cyclists in Helsinki has been considered in [4], where passive infrared (PIR) sensors are used for tracking motions. The approach has a limitation of recording false movements due to strong wind conditions. The authors in [9] developed a real-time adaptive street light control algorithm, which obtains information on pedestrian and vehicle movement using wireless mesh networks and controls the light level accordingly. The energy efficiency of the proposed approach is evaluated based on a street utility model.

Recently, a number of research papers have investigated IoT technologies for advanced street light control applications. The smart street lighting applications such as asset management, energy monitoring and maintenance that can be integrated in the smart city platforms have been elaborated in [10]. The authors in [11] proposed Fog computing-based street light control mechanisms comprising of dynamic dimming and autonomous alarm systems, where street lights can communicate using narrowband IoT (NB-IoT) technologies. A smart lamppost integrated with sensors for environmental parameters monitoring and light and image sensing, which can communicate using Long Range Wide Area Network (LoRaWAN) technologies, is proposed in [12]. When smart street lights are connected to the IoT network, they often become vulnerable to cyber-threats such as denial of service, eavesdropping and session hijacking. As a result, cyber-security assessment of the IoT-enabled smart street lighting system has been conducted in [13]. The authors in [14] presented a street light control approach using a remote web server communicating with local sensors enabled with Zigbee communication as well as video processing features for motion detection.

Although the aforementioned research papers have considered the energy-saving aspects of smart street lights, the integration with demand response strategies has been an open research problem. Although a DR strategy for street lights integrated with energy storages are proposed, the integration of motion detection or traffic parameters to dynamically dim the lights has not been considered. Given that smart street lights with dimming features can act like an adaptive controllable load, these lights can be controlled to reduce electricity consumption based on the DR requested from the utility. As a result, this research addresses the problem of developing an IoT-enabled smart street light systems for supporting DR requests by dimming or turning off lights. To be specific, the following contributions are made:

- An IoT-enabled street light control algorithm has been developed, which monitors the weather conditions using weather service application programming interface (API) and turns off or dims the light levels when sufficient visibility is present.

- The proposed algorithm also uses traffic data API to obtain real-time traffic conditions and, based on DR request from utility, dims or turns off street lights on roads with smaller amount of traffic.
- The IoT-enabled street light control algorithm is evaluated for a real street light network in Belmont, Victoria, Australia, for different DR values and different days for 1 hour before sunrise and 1 hour after sunset. The evaluation shows that the considered street light network is able to achieve the requested DR when external weather conditions have sufficient light levels.

The rest of the chapter is organised in the following manner: Section 9.2 elaborates on existing smart street light control technologies. Section 9.3 outlines enabling IoT technologies for controlling smart street lights. Section 9.4 discusses the DR opportunities from street light control. Section 9.5 presents the proposed street light control approach. Section 9.6 defines the case study considered in this research, while Section 9.7 incorporates the numerical results and discussion. Finally, Section 9.8 concludes the chapter.

9.2 SMART STREET LIGHT CONTROL TECHNOLOGIES

Traditionally, street lights have been hard-wired to distribution boxes as a group and integrated with some automation equipment such as programmable logic controllers for remote operation. However, these deployments were far from the concept of smart street lighting technologies, which heavily rely on information and communication technologies for more sophisticated and intelligent controllability features. One of the key enablers of smart street lighting technologies is the LED street lights, which can be integrated with intelligent control mechanisms. Such intelligent control techniques allow monitoring of energy consumption of individual smart street lights. In addition, the lights can be dimmed based on weather conditions or traffic density [15].

Smart street light control incorporates a central management system, communication network and electronic devices that can connect with the central management system using the communication network. The central management system can integrate advanced monitoring and control features such as dimming of the lights. Moreover, the status of individual smart street lights can be monitored through visualisation platforms. The communication technologies that enable interaction between the street lights and the central control can encompass cellular technologies as well as IoT technologies such as LoRaWAN and Sigfox, which are relatively cheaper to deploy [15].

An energy-efficient street lighting control that adapts depending on traffic density has been proposed in [16]. The approach utilises Zigbee mesh network to control the smart street lights incorporated with sensors to measure temperature, light level and power consumption. The optimal scheduling of dimming operation of the LED lights is coordinated through an energy management system. The approach allows controllability of individual or predefined group of street lights. For traffic density monitoring, vehicular communication networks are deployed and traffic pattern is modelled based on vehicle speed and distances among vehicles [16].

A smart street lighting control based on artificial neural networks and fuzzy logic controller has been developed in [17] to improve the energy efficiency of the street lighting application. The developed approach utilises street lights based on the lighting requirement for pedestrian movements. The street lights are integrated with motion sensors and PIR sensors, which help in detecting the movement of pedestrians or vehicles. Accordingly, the lighting levels of the street lights are adjusted. For controlling the lighting level based on the natural light available in the streets, fuzzy logic controllers are used. To improve the efficiency of the decision-making process, ANN is utilised, which can make inferences based on the lighting conditions from the training process [17].

A quadratic integer programming-based optimisation problem to select optimal action for improving energy saving while satisfying cost constraints is formulated in [18]. The solution considers distributing the optimal actions over the subsets of street lights. The actions considered include replacing 150 W or 250 W high-pressure sodium (HPS) lamps or installing energy-harvesting modules [18]. Although the aforementioned approach achieves energy saving, it does not consider low-cost smart control features, which can further reduce energy consumption.

An autonomous street lighting control mechanism based on solar generation forecasting and then adjusting the lighting level according to the available solar generation is proposed in [19]. The street lighting system is powered by solar cells and batteries to operate as a stand-alone system without depending on the utility grid. Long short-term memory (LSTM)-based deep learning techniques are utilised to generate weather and irradiance forecasts from which solar generation for the next 5 days is predicted. The street lights form a cluster and communicate the information from light and motion sensors to the routers that forward the signals to the network coordinator [19]. Although the developed approach ensures grid-independent operation resulting in significant energy saving, the integration of demand response applications has not been considered.

Although the aforementioned approaches developed a number of intelligent techniques to achieve energy-efficient operation of the street lights, they often rely on separate sensors for individual street lights, which can add to the installation cost of such smart street lighting systems. Often, these intelligent techniques operate on their own and cannot exploit information from the network of connected things. Moreover, the focus is either energy consumption saving, or grid-independent operation. However, coordinating with the energy network to reduce energy consumption when the energy is required by higher-priority applications is not explored in these research.

9.3 IoT FOR STREET LIGHT CONTROL

IoT technologies can offer ubiquitous connectivity among the smart street lights as well as other sensors and intelligent devices connected to the network. Such connectivity can allow for coordination of weather and traffic data from global databases to generate optimal control actions for the street lights. Enabling IoT for smart street lights can help street lighting systems to form an integral part of the smart city ecosystem. As a result, smart street lights can act like a common sensor platform for a range of applications such as air quality monitoring, traffic pattern analysis and surveillance systems [20].

IoT-enabled street light systems will need to utilise low-power wireless communication technologies such as NB-IoT, LoRaWAN and Sigfox. NB-IoT can exploit the benefits of the widespread cellular infrastructure, but offers an expensive solution to IoT devices as cellular connection costs are involved. LoRaWAN and Sigfox are cheaper and have good receiver sensitivity although the coverage can be an issue. Apart from these, there are wireless mesh network technologies such as IEEE802.15.4 and Bluetooth mesh networks, which are short-range techniques and utilise multi-hop communication to relay the messages across the nodes [21].

A number of control strategies for IoT-enabled smart street lights have been evaluated in [22] using an open-source street light simulator StreetlightSim. These control strategies are simulated for Phillips Luma street lights, which are embedded with dynamic dimming options. The study compares Dynadimmer, Chronosense, part-night and adaptive schemes. The comparative analysis shows that dynamic dimming and part-night (turning off lights at night) have similar energy saving. However, the adaptive scheme which monitors traffic flow and turns on/off street lights accordingly demonstrates significantly lower energy consumption.

The authors in [14] considered an IoT-enabled street light configuration where street lights incorporated with smart cameras communicate with each other and gateway devices using Zigbee protocol. On the other hand, the weather and traffic data as well as control commands are communicated using cellular networks. The lights are controlled based on the video processed by smart cameras, which can detect motion and send this information to lighting boards. The lighting board then calculates the appropriate lighting levels for street lights based on the traffic density and weather conditions. In addition, a web application is developed to visualise street light status, energy consumption patterns and alarms.

To enable long-range communication with increased battery life, LoRaWAN communication is integrated among smart street lights and IoT gateways in [23]. Communication between the gateway and cloud storage is achieved using Wi-Fi connection. In this work, each street light is equipped with Arduino Nano microcontroller boards, current/voltage sensors, motion detectors and dimmers. Based on the detected motion and illumination levels in the streets (obtained from gateways), the microcontroller computes the required light level and operates the dimmer accordingly [23]. However, the approach does not consider utilising cloud databases for weather forecasts or traffic data.

The aforementioned research work has focussed on the communication network design aspects considering multiple sensors connected to individual street lights. Moreover, the day-ahead optimisation of lighting levels based on weather forecasts has not been considered. These papers highlighted the key objective of lighting control as reduction in energy consumption. However, the integration of demand response applications through IoT-enabled smart street lights has not been addressed.

9.4 DEMAND RESPONSE USING STREET LIGHT CONTROL

Controllable street lights (e.g. LED lamps with dimming feature) present an option for offering DR services when information on electricity demand and the system status of street light networks in a particular location can be integrated. In the existing research, the optimisation of smart street lights has often been performed to achieve energy consumption or cost saving. When the sustainability objectives of the smart street light systems are aligned with the reliability objectives of the electricity networks, the resulting benefits can be massive.

To achieve energy saving in existing HPS lamps, a dimming technology is proposed in [24] by controlling the voltage wave shape applied to the lamps. The authors demonstrate that a trapezoidal voltage supply can effectively address the dimming problem locally in the lamp, rather than centralised control where voltage drop across the network can cause issues. The authors also experimented using rectangular and sinusoidal voltages with regulated frequencies and found that these waveforms can also achieve similar effectiveness for dimming applications. Although it can achieve energy saving, it cannot offer the best outcomes without the integration of optimal dimming schedule.

An energy audit is performed in [25] for different cities in Indonesia to quantify the savings from street light systems. The audit recommends a number of energy efficiency improvement measures such as replacing old lamps, installing dimming ballasts, adding power meters, adding capacitor to individual lamps and renewable energy integration. The study demonstrated that installing power meters for individual panels can achieve the maximum benefits among the aforementioned energy efficiency measures. A similar study has been undertaken by the authors in [26] for South Italy, which considers economic assessments of dimming technologies and existing street light replacement. The study finds that when both of the aforementioned initiatives are adopted, the energy-saving strategies are economically feasible.

A hybrid renewable energy system integrated with street lights has been considered in [27] from the energy-saving perspectives. The system can suffer from uncertainties in renewable generation and load shapes, which can cause challenges in optimising the street light energy consumption. To address this problem, the authors utilise genetic algorithm to solve a multi-objective optimisation problem, which aims to reduce energy cost while ensuring energy supply quality. The method also integrates real weather and traffic model in the optimisation problem. However, the focus is energy consumption saving and the DR opportunities have not been considered.

The authors in [5] considered distributed energy storages with street light systems for reducing the dependence on grid. The approach can turn off street lights during peak demand conditions. However, the dimming options to satisfy variable DR requirements have not been considered. Moreover, the approach does not integrate traffic data or weather conditions. The following section elaborates the proposed approach, which combines the integration of weather and traffic data from web APIs with the optimisation algorithm to turn off or dim street lights for achieving the DR requirements.

9.5 PROPOSED APPROACH

The proposed approach for IoT-enabled street light control utilises the connectivity of the street lights with remote cloud servers, which coordinate demand response signals, weather and traffic data as well as the street light control applications. The demand response signals contain information on how much energy demand needs to be curtailed at what time instant. The proposed street lighting control algorithm is executed twice in a day, 1 hour before sunrise and 1 hour after sunset. The residential electricity demand is higher during these times, reflecting the operation of electric heaters and hot water systems in the early morning and cooking or air conditioner use in the evening when people come back home. Although the approach considers street light control for 2 hours, it can be readily extended to 24-hour time period.

The weather data are obtained from AccuWeather application programming interface (API) in the hourly format. The API returns weather data for specific location in the form of cloud ceiling, precipitation, pressure, temperature, visibility, wind gust and wind speed [28]. The traffic data are obtained from HERE API in the form of traffic flows and jams. It shows the positive and negative traffic flows (inward and outward traffic) for major intersections when specific GPS coordinates are given [29]. When a demand response signal is sent, the street light control application aims to dim or turn off street lights in a certain suburb to achieve the demand response. To determine whether natural light levels are sufficient or not, weather data are utilised. On the other hand, traffic data are used to prioritise roads in terms of traffic density. The roads with higher traffic are assigned a higher priority. The proposed approach optimises the number of street lights that need to dim or turn off, ensuring that street lights in the lower-priority roads are dimmed/turned off before the higher-priority roads. In the following part, the algorithm used for weather data and traffic data processing and the street light control algorithm are outlined.

9.5.1 Weather data collection

First, Location API is used to obtain location key of the suburb for which street light status will be optimised. From the daily forecasts, the sunrise and sunset times for a particular day are obtained. The natural light levels based on which street lights can be turned on or off are defined based on the cloud cover and visibility metrics. These metrics are extracted from the weather data API 1 hour before sunrise and 1 hour after sunset. The visibility is represented in kilometres (km), while the cloud cover is represented using percentage. To obtain these data, HTTP requests are sent to the weather API. The responses are then converted to JSON variables for further processing. The weather data collection process is illustrated in Figure 9.1.

9.5.2 Traffic data collection

The traffic data obtained from HERE API have the following format:

Traffic Data={"RWS": [ ], "MAP_VERSION": (), "CREATED_ TIMESTAMP": (), "VERSION": (), "UNITS": ()},

where "RWS" or list of roadway items is a dictionary containing the following elements:

"RWS": [{"RW": [ ], "TY": (), "MAP_VERSION": (), "EBU_COUNTRY_ CODE": (), "EXTENDED__COUNTRY_CODE": (), "TABLE_ID": (), "UNITS": ()}],

where "RW" contains a dictionary of traffic data for major road sections, "EBU_COUNTRY_CODE" represents single number country codes, "TY" represents type of information, and "TABLE_ID" is the table containing traffic message channels (TMCs).

Each major road element in "RW" has the following format:

{"FIS": [{"FI": [], "mid": (), "LI": (), "DE": (), "PBT": ()},

where "FIS" represents a list of traffic flow elements, "FI" contains a dictionary of the traffic intersection data, "DE" indicates the name of the road, "LI" is the location, and "PBT" is the local time.

The traffic data of each intersection are represented in the following format:

{"TMC": {"PC": (), "DE": (), "QD": (), "LE": ()}, "CF": [{"TY": (), "SP": (), "SU": (), "FF": (), "JF": (), "CN": ()}]}},

where "TMC" is a dictionary of traffic message channel locations, "DE" contains the name of the intersection, "PC" is the point location code of the traffic message channel, "LE" is the length of the road, and "QD" is the queuing direction, which can be positive or negative indicating the direction of traffic flow (inward or outward). "CF" indicates the current flow of traffic in the given location, "SP" is the average speed of the road, "SU" is the speed over the speed limit, "FF" denotes the free flow of speed, "JF"

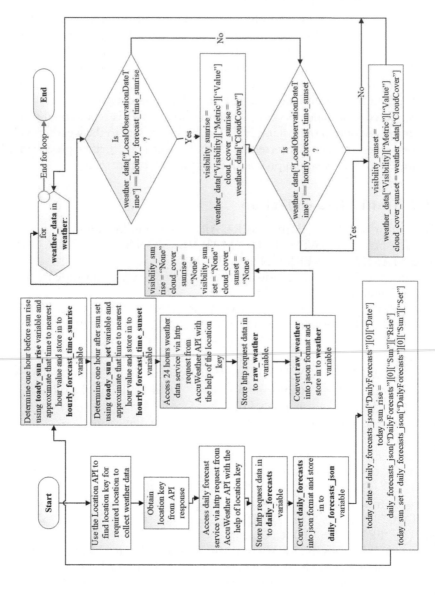

Figure 9.1 Flowchart for extracting weather data.

indicates the jam factor, which is a number between 0 and 10, and "CN" is a number between 0 and 1 representing the confidence attribute for using the percentage of real-time data in speed calculations.

In this proposed approach, the jam factor is used as an indicator of the traffic density in a certain intersection. Given that the roadway element contains traffic data for both positive and negative directions for each intersection, the jam factors for these two directions can be different. As a result, the jam factors for positive and negative directions are compared and the larger among the two is considered as an indicator of the amount of traffic in the specific intersection. The road elements with higher jam factor will be given higher priority. The traffic data are obtained using HTML request and then converted to JSON format. The traffic data collection and processing approach are shown in Figure 9.2.

9.5.3 Street light control algorithm

The proposed street light control algorithm takes user inputs for the wattage of lights, the number of lights and street names along with the requested DR value. The weather data are collected in the form of visibility and cloud cover for 1 hour before sunrise and 1 hour after sunset, which is detailed in Section 9.5.2. The traffic data are collected and processed as in Section 9.5.3 to extract the jam factors for the roads defined by the user input. Then jam factors of all the intersections in the major road are added together and divided by the total number of intersections of that road to calculate the average jam factor. The major roads are then categorised as high-priority, medium-priority and low-priority areas based on the average jam factors. If the major road has an average jam factor less or equal to 2.2, then that road is added to low-priority category. If the major road has a jam factor between 2.2 and 4.4, then that road is added to medium-priority category. If the major road has a jam factor between 4.4 and 10.0, then that road is added to high-priority category. After that, each of these categories are separately sorted from low to high jam factors to obtain major road names in each category in the order of low to high traffic. Jam factors and major roads in high-priority category are not considered since street lights in these major roads are too critical to be included in the optimisation algorithm.

The algorithm checks if the current time matches the hour before sunrise or the hour after sunset. If this condition is true, the DR value is checked. If no DR is requested at that time, then the algorithm checks the current visibility and cloud cover values. If visibility is less than 14 km and cloud cover is greater than 60%, all the lights in major roads will be turned on. If the visibility is greater than or equal to 14 km and cloud cover is less than or equal to 50%, all the lights in major roads will be turned off. If the visibility and cloud cover values are not in the aforementioned ranges, then all the lights will be turned on. If a certain DR is requested, and the visibility is between 14 and 16 km with cloud cover between 50% and 60%, then the

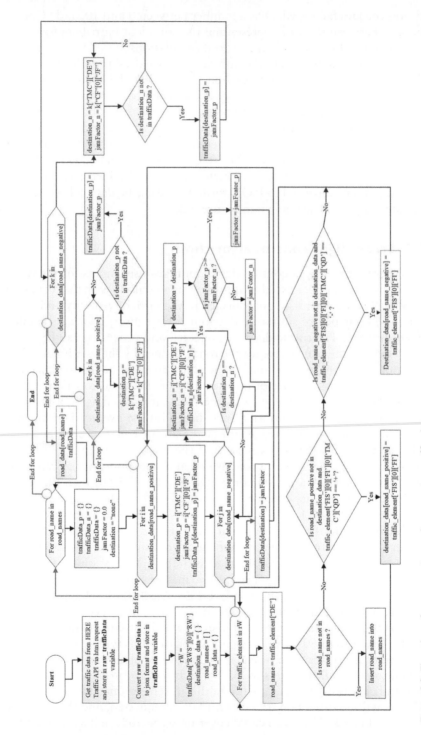

Figure 9.2 Flowchart for extracting and processing traffic data.

lights in low-priority area will be 50% dimmed in the order of low to high jam factors until DR request is satisfied. If DR is not satisfied even after dimming all lights in the low-priority areas, then lights will be turned off in these areas in the same order in which the lights were dimmed before. The aforementioned approach is illustrated through the flowchart in Figure 9.3.

9.6 CASE STUDY EVALUATION

The proposed approach elaborated in Section 9.5 has been evaluated for a real street light network in Belmont, Victoria, Australia. The case study considers 11 major roads in Belmont, which includes South Valley Road, Pioneer Road, Fellmongers Road, Barwon Heads Road, Torquay Road, Thompson Road, Settlement Road, Latrobe Terrace, High Street, Colac Road and Breakwater Road. The existing street light network in the afore-mentioned locations can be obtained from [30]. As an example, the map view of the street lights in Settlement Road is shown in Figure 9.4. The number of street lights considered for each of the roads is listed in Table 9.1.

According to VicRoads technical guideline for street lights [31], L1-type luminaires are used within the residential areas. L1 luminaires are a replace-ment for 150 W HPS lamps, and according to the VicRoads specification for LED road lighting luminaires [32], LED luminaire replacement for a partic-ular HPS lamp should provide a minimum of 30% reduction in total system watts compared to the equivalent HPS luminaire. According to this specifi-cation, typical wattage of a L1 street light will be $150\,W \times 70/100 = 105\,W$, which is considered in the case study.

The case study evaluates the proposed street light control approach for the hour before sunrise and the hour after sunset for three different days in terms of the number of lights turned off or dimmed due to a demand response signal. For the hour before sunrise, the required demand response is considered as 8,800 W, and for the hour after sunset, it is considered as 4,400 W. These values are considered based on the typical load demand of a Victorian house during early morning and evening time, respectively [33]. The visibility and cloud covers for the days under consideration are presented in Tables 9.2 and 9.3 for 1 hour before sunrise and 1 hour after sunset, respectively. The evaluation also considers how the street lights turn off at different roads in response to different levels of demand response sig-nals 1 hour before sunrise and 1 hour after sunset on 26 July 2021.

9.7 RESULTS AND DISCUSSION

Figure 9.5 illustrates the street light status as well as jam factors in the major roads for three different days during 1 hour before sunrise. The requested DR is 8,800 W. Since the cloud cover on 2nd August was 0%,

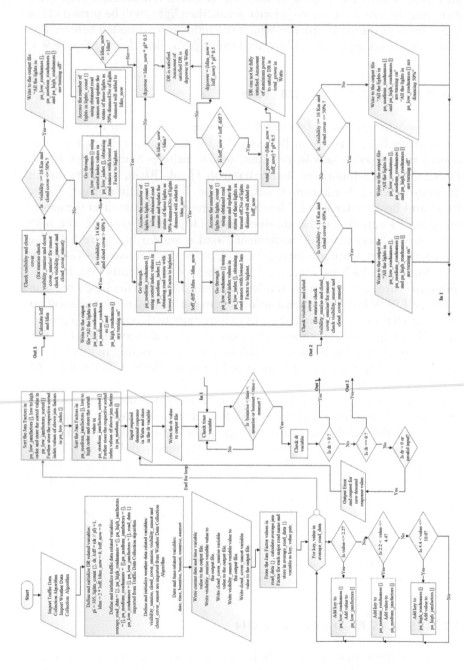

Figure 9.3 Flowchart for the proposed street light control algorithm.

Figure 9.4 Map view of the existing street lights in Settlement Road, Belmont, Victoria.

Table 9.1 Number of street lights in each major road evaluated in the case study

Name of the road	Acronym	Number of street lights
South Valley Road	SVR	60
Pioneer Road	PR	37
Fellmongers Road	FR	0
Barwon Heads Road	BHR	26
Torquay Road	TQR	99
Thompson Road	TR	64
Settlement Road	SR	82
Latrobe Terrace	LT	64
High Street	HS	36
Colac Road	CR	77
Breakwater Road	BR	2

Table 9.2 Visibility and cloud covers 1 hour before sunrise from AccuWeather API

Day	Visibility (km)	Cloud cover (%)
2 August 2021	16.1	0
3 August 2021	16.1	71
5 August 2021	16.1	66

Table 9.3 Visibility and cloud covers 1 hour after sunrise from AccuWeather API

Day	Visibility (km)	Cloud cover (%)
25 July 2021	16.1	93
26 July 2021	16.1	91
3 August 2021	17.7	66

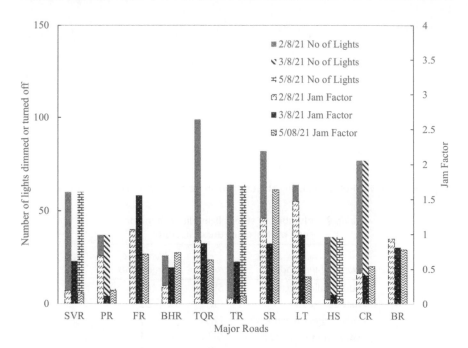

Figure 9.5 Number of lights that can be turned off/dimmed and jam factors 1 hour before sunrise.

all lights could be turned off to meet the requested DR. As a result, lights turned off from most of the roads except Fellmongers Road and Breakwater Road. The highest jam factor was recorded on Latrobe Terrace, and so a small number of lights turned off although there are 64 lights. On 3rd and 5th August, the cloud cover was more than 60%. As a result, lights could only be dimmed to maintain the required light levels in the streets. On 3rd August, lights could be dimmed from Pioneer Road, High Street and Colac Road only, as they have lower jam factors. On the other hand, Settlement Road, South Valley Road and Thompson Road have lower jam factors on 5th August, so lights are dimmed only from these roads.

The jam factors and the number of lights that can be turned off/dimmed during the hour after sunset on three different days are displayed in Figure 9.6. The DR requested from the street lights is 4,400 W. Due to the visibility and cloud cover conditions on 25th and 26th July and 3rd August, lights could only be dimmed in the major roads. Similar to the previous figure, it can be observed that lights are getting dimmed on roads with lowest jam factors.

Figure 9.7 shows the number of street lights that need to be dimmed on 26th July 1 hour after sunset for different DR requests. For a DR request of 5 kW, all lights in South Valley Road, Barwon Heads Road, High Street and Breakwater Road along with 12 lights from Torquay Road are

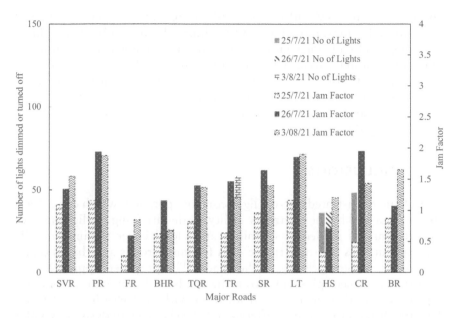

Figure 9.6 Number of lights that can be turned off/dimmed and jam factors 1 hour after sunset.

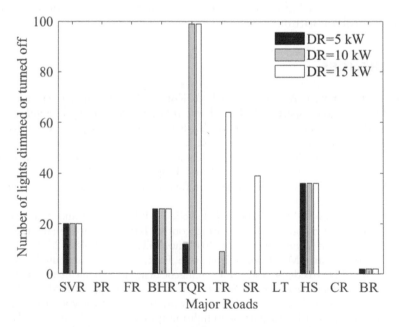

Figure 9.7 Number of traffic lights dimmed/turned off 1 hour after sunset for different DR values.

dimmed. When 10 kW DR is requested, all lights in Torquay Road and 8 lights from Thompson road need to be dimmed. For 15 kW DR, all lights in Thompson Road along with 39 lights in Settlement Road were dimmed. The aforementioned roads have low jam factors, and as a result, they have a lower priority for street lights meaning that lights will be dimmed in these streets before requesting from the higher jam factor streets. When all lights are dimmed, a maximum of 28.73 kW DR can be obtained from these street lights.

9.8 CONCLUSIONS

This chapter illustrated a street light control approach, which can achieve DR as requested by the electricity utility while satisfying the lighting level requirements as guided by visibility and cloud cover parameters. The approach utilises real-time traffic data for major roads and, based on the jam factor, assigns priority to the roads. The proposed approach dims or turns off street lights only from the roads with low jam factors. The approach is evaluated for a real location with real weather and traffic data for different days and different DR levels. The analysis shows that the proposed approach can successfully satisfy DR requirements when visibility and cloud cover conditions allow sufficient lights for street lights to dim or turn off. Future work will focus on developing a web API to monitor the street light status when optimised using the proposed street light control algorithm.

REFERENCES

1. T. D. Kumar, T. A. Samuel and T. A. Kumar, Transforming green cities with IoT a design perspective. In *Handbook of Green Engineering Technologies for Sustainable Smart Cities*, London, Taylor & Francis Group, 2021, pp. 16–33.
2. R. Deng, Z. Yang, M.-Y. Chow and J. Chen, "A survey on demand response in smart grids: Mathematical models and approaches," *IEEE Transactions on Industrial Informatics,* vol. 11, no. 3, pp. 570–582, 2015.
3. S. Smith, "Smart infrastructure for future urban mobility," *AI Magazine,* vol. 41, no. 5, 2020.
4. E. Juntunen, E.-M. Sarjanoja, J. Eskeli, H. Pihlajaniemi and T. Österlund, "Smart and dynamic route lighting control based on movement tracking," *Building and Environment,* vol. 2018, no. 142, pp. 472–483, 2018.
5. S. Park, B. Kang, M.-i. Choi, S. Jeon and S. Park, "A micro-distributed ESS-based smart LED streetlight system for intelligent demand management of the micro grid," *Sustainable Cities and Society,* vol. 2018, no. 39, pp. 801–813, 2018.
6. M. Pagden, K. Ngahane and M. R. Amin, "Changing the colour of night on urban streets - LED vs. part-night lighting system," *Socio-Economic Planning Sciences,* vol. 2020, no. 69, pp. 1–7, 2020.

7. L. Doulos, I. Sioutis, P. Kontaxis, G. Zissis and K. Faidas, "A decision support system for assessment of street lighting tenders based on energy performance indicators and environmental criteria: Overview, methodology and case study," *Sustainable Cities and Society,* vol. 2019, no. 51, pp. 1–17, 2019.

8. M. Beccali, M. Bonomolo, F. Leccese, D. Lista and G. Salvadori, "On the impact of safety requirements, energy prices and investment costs in street lighting refurbishment design," *Energy,* vol. 2018, no. 165, pp. 739–759, 2018.

9. S. P. Lau, G. V. Merrett, A. S. Weddell and N. M. White, "A traffic-aware street lighting scheme for Smart Cities using autonomous networked sensors," *Computers and Electrical Engineering,* vol. 2015, no. 45, pp. 192–207, 2015.

10. A. Pandharipande and P. Thijssen, "Connected street lighting infrastructure for smart city applications," *IEEE Internet of Things Magazine,* vol. 2019, no. June, pp. 32–36, 2019.

11. G. Jia, G. Han, A. Li and J. Du, "SSL: Smart street lamp based on fog computing for smarter cities," *IEEE Transactions on Industrial Informatics,* vol. 14, no. 11, pp. 4995–5004, 2018.

12. A. Gehlot, S. S. Alshamrani, R. Singh, M. Rashid, S. V. Akram, A. S. AlGhamdi and F. R. Albogamy, "Internet of things and long-range-based smart lampposts for illuminating smart cities," *Sustainability,* vol. 2021, no. 13, pp. 1–20, 2021.

13. D. Jin, C. Hannon, Z. Li, P. Cortes, S. Ramaraju, P. Burgess, N. Buch and M. Shahidehpour, "Smart street lighting system: A platform for innovative smart city applications and a new frontier for cyber-security," *The Electricity Journal,* vol. 2016, no. 29, pp. 28–35, 2016.

14. G. Gagliardi, M. Lupia, G. Cario, F. Tedesco, F. C. Gaccio, F. L. Scudo and A. Casavola, "Advanced adaptive street lighting systems for smart cities," *Smart Cities,* vol. 2020, no. 3, pp. 1495–1512, 2020.

15. IPWEA, "SLSC Briefing: Smart Street Lighting Controls '101'," 2019.

16. H. Y. A. W. A. a. C. L. Gul Shahzad, "Energy-efficient intelligent street lighting system using traffic-adaptive control," *IEEE Sensors Journal,* vol. 16, no. 13, pp. 5397–5405, 2016.

17. P. Mohandas, J. S. A. Dhanaraj and X.-Z. Gao, "Artificial neural network based smart and energy efficient street lighting: system: A case study for residential area in Hosur," *Sustainable Cities and Society,* vol. 48, pp. 1–13, 2019.

18. R. Carli, M. Dotoli and E. Cianci, "An optimization tool for energy efficiency of street lighting systems in smart cities," *IFAC Papers Online,* vol. 50, no. 1, pp. 14460–14464, 2017.

19. D. Tukymbekov, A. Saymbetov, M. Nurgaliyev, N. Kuttybay, G. Dosymbetova and Y. Svanbayev, "Intelligent autonomous street lighting system based on weather forecast using LSTM," *Energy,* vol. 2021, no. 231, pp. 1–13, 2021.

20. GSMA Internet of Things, "GSMA Smart Cities Guide Street Lighting," *GSMA,* 2017.

21. G. Pasolini, P. Toppan, F. Zabini, C. D. Castro and O. Andrisano, "Design, deployment and evolution of heterogeneous smart public lighting systems," *Applied Sciences,* vol. 2019, no. 9, pp. 1–25, 2019.

22. E. Dizon and B. Pranggono, "Smart streetlights in Smart City: A case study of Sheffield," *Journal of Ambient Intelligence and Humanized Computing,* pp. 1–16, 2021.

23. F. Sanchez-Sutil and A. Cano-Ortega, "Smart regulation and efficiency energy system for street lighting with LoRa LPWAN," *Sustainable Cities and Society,* vol. 2021, no. 70, pp. 1–16, 2021.

24. A. Burgio and D. Menniti, "A novel technique for energy savings by dimming high pressure sodium lamps mounted with magnetic ballasts using a centralized system," *Electric Power Systems Research,* vol. 2013, no. 96, pp. 16–22, 2013.

25. M. IndraalIrsyad and Rabindra Nepal, "A survey based approach to estimating the benefits of energy efficiency improvements in streetlighting systems in Indonesia," *Renewable and Sustainable Energy Reviews,* vol. 2016, no. 58, pp. 1569–1577, 2016.

26. M. Beccali, M. Bonomolo, G. Ciulla, A. Galatioto and V. L. Brano, "Improvement of energy efficiency and quality of street lighting in South Italy as an action of Sustainable Energy Action Plans. The case study of Comiso (RG)," *Energy,* vol. 2015, no. 92, pp. 394–408, 2015.

27. F. Ramadhani, K. A. Bakar, M. Hussain, O. Erixno and R. Nazir, "Optimization with traffic-based control for designing standalone streetlight system: A case study," *Renewable Energy,* vol. 2017, no. 105, pp. 149–159, 2017.

28. AccuWeather, "AccuWeather APIs," [Online]. Available: https://developer. accuweather.com/.

29. Here Developer, "Here Traffic API," [Online]. Available: https://developer. here.com/documentation/traffic/dev_guide/topics/what-is.html.

30. Powercor, "Outages Report a Streetlight Fault," [Online]. Available: https:// www.powercor.com.au/outages/report-a-streetlight-fault/.

31. Vicroads, "TCG 006: Guidelines to Street Lighting Design," Vicroads, Melbourne, 2016.

32. Vicroads, "The Supply of LED Road Lighting Luminaires," Vicroads, Melbourne, 2018.

33. Department of Industry, Science, Energy and Resources, "Electricity consumption benchmarks," 10 July 2014. [Online]. Available: https://data.gov. au/data/dataset/electricity-consumption-benchmarks.

Chapter 10

IoT in retail industry

The emergence of walkaway technology in business

Shivam Sakshi
Vellore Institute of Technology

Ramachandra Reddy Gadi
Ensar Solutions

CONTENTS

ABSTRACT

The past couple of decades is since when technology has started to play a vital role in business interactions, and many vertices of technology such as mobiles, websites and social media have been enormously influencing the interaction pattern between business and customers. IoT is one such pinnacle that is extensively being adopted by marketers across the retail industry to achieve excellence in delivering services to their customers. However, the extent of literature regarding the usage of IoT in the retail industry is very minimal to this point. The present chapter focuses on filling the gap of literature paucity and gives a comprehensive understanding of how IoT is gaining attraction in the retail industry.

10.1 INTRODUCTION

According to a report by McKinsey & Company [1], companies continue to enhance technology capabilities and are moving towards total digitalization and Industry 4.0 standards. Pertaining to various mobility regulations

DOI: 10.1201/9781003304203-10

administers across the globe, digitalization is rapidly increasing despite the market slowdown due to the pandemic which the world is going through as a result of the Coronavirus. For instance, the recent numbers show that 90% of manufacturing and supply chain professionals are planning to invest in talent, which is aimed at digitization.

According to BCC Research [2], IoT has emerged from an experiment conducted in 1999 in an attempt to link objects to the Internet through a radio-frequency identification (RFID) tag. IoT has ever since its inception been widely accepted, and it has now reached a point where researchers and practitioners argue that the IoT could be a game changer in the lives of consumers; for example, in his research in 2017, Kannan claimed that the IoT promises significant transformations in consumers' lives in the near future.

IoT essentially connects various physical items, which can be connected to Internet and can communicate through Internet. According to Khan et al. (2020) [3], the web of such connected devices communicating through Internet can develop an efficient system; for example, an entire system of household electronics such as air conditioning and lights can be controlled remotely by accessing them via Internet. IoT has influenced almost every sector of business activity ranging from food to apparel. The retail phenomenon in every sector is now rapidly witnessing IoT inclusion. Just like the usage of IoT in controlling and monitoring household devices as mentioned in the example above, IoT can be used to interconnect and interlink numerous technologies together, making it possible to monitor, trace, coordinate and take collaborative decisions remotely between the business allies [4]. The devices which connect with each other on the fabric of IoT can range from small devices like beacons connecting over Bluetooth which uses internet to transfer data to sophisticated industrial tools which needs to interact with each other to maintain accuracy in the production. Compared to the previous year (2021) when the number of global IoT connections were 12.2 billion endpoints, in 2022, the total number of global IoT connections is expected to escalate up to 14.4 billion endpoints.

The whole principle of market is pivoted on the social and economic frameworks. While the context of marketing is being defined, two objectives of business parts, i.e. social and business contexts, should become the backbone of technology that we adopt. According to Patel et al. [5], the technologies based on internet plays a virtual role in the real time markets to use the collected data. According to Kaspersky's recent report, "The State of Industrial Cybersecurity in the Era of Digitalization", 20% of organizations have already prioritized IoT-related incidents, but solutions effective against IoT threats are yet to become widespread. The evolving network of Internet penetration in the periphery of consumers' daily activities is skyrocketing, according to Atzori [6]. With the advancements in the collaboration of Internet and machine learning via smart gadgets they use, a transformation in the lifestyle of the consumers is being witnessed. Internet of things (IoT) is one such technological achievement in recent times. According to Pelino and Gillett [7], IoT is a fleet of connected devices consisting of wireless devices and sensors that can be remotely accessed through Internet or private networks. Connecting physical things with Internet to produce information, patterns, deep learning, etc., is the simplest way to explain what IoT is.

10.2 THE HISTORY AND EVOLUTION OF IoT

Though a similar mechanism of connecting two or more computers together as an experiment to transfer packets of information between them existed, Kevin Ashton a co-founder of Auto-ID Laboratory at MIT is considered as the inventor of Internet of Things (IoT). He has described a system where the internet is connected to the physical world via ubiquitous sensors which includes RFID (Radia Frequency identification). According to Gubbi et al. [8], RFID enables the design of microchips for wireless data communication. Tripathy and Anuradha [9] brought in focus that technology is revolutionizing life and it's not slowing down. An assistant brand manager at Procter & Gamble delivered a presentation about wireless connectivity with an intriguing title: "Internet of Things", sketching out a futuristic scenario where computers "knew everything there was to know about things as the network connected objects in the physical world to the Internet" [10]. Ashton predicted the IoT "has the potential to change the world, just as the Internet did. Maybe even more so".

With the advances made in wireless sensor technologies, Vermesan and Peter [11] in their paper asserted that with support in place, the nanotechnologies and other intelligent systems have brought about a turning point in communication methods we use. The IoT is representing our future of technologies. At the base of it, an Internet will consist of a connective tissue which combines reality together, that is where people have an easy access for living things and constitute even objects. The gain of IoT is enabling both inside the organization and in the production processes of companies, that is providing private and personal insights of the business to industry.

10.3 DEFINITION OF IoT

According to Pelino & Gillett [7], Internet of Things refers to a network of connected devices which includes networks OD sensors and wireless devices which can be remotely accessed through the internet or a private network. The entry of Internet has changed every technology boundary, that we scaled thus far, this stared to unfold a new shared economy, which is underscoring a fundamental change in the role of products and to human behaviour. It becomes apparent that the ownership of products is focused on ensuring the delivery of the product outcome rather than for the sake of ownership itself.

IoT is an emerging technology [1]. This is a new concept targeting the expansion of internet utility. A fast development is happening, and intelligent devices are being developed for various utilities, which are being used in households, factories, hospitals and many more fields [4,10]. From individuals to industries, everyone is streamed towards using a smart device such as a smart phone or a computer which is connected to internet to do day to day tasks enabling a smart environment improving the utilities functioning of our homes and factories.

According to Barnaghi [12], IoT is encapsulating a better vision in the world which is enabling billions of objects embedding the intelligence, communication means and sensing its capabilities by connecting with IP (Internet Protocol) networks. According to Carrez [13], IoT and its abilities to offer various kinds of services has made it the fastest growing technology of the present time. The Internet has gone through a fundamental radical shift from custom-driven hardware (computers, fibres and Ethernet) to market-driven application such as Facebook, Amazon, thus, creating many opportunities and challenges for the present times.

The IoT is for open environments and is an integrated open architecture of interoperable platforms [14]. These smart objects of cyber-physical systems the IoT entities which are connected with the objects of everyday life which are complimented with microcontrollers, sensors such as optical radio transceivers, and actuators, and are put on various protocol stacks, which are suitable for communicating in a constrained environments. It uses limited hardware resources and then allows them to collect data from various environments within the range. The devices that will make up the IoT usually have an IP address, on-board computing power, some kind of sensing devices that let them sense their environment and network connectivity (often wireless) [15]. A device can be anything from a consumer product to a giant industrial machine. IoT devices will run software programs that let the device "decide" when to take a specified action or to select among different actions. IoT devices may have vulnerabilities not present in a non-IoT device.

10.4 WHAT IS AN INTERNET OF THINGS?

IoT is a network of things which are sewn together using Internet. The things in the network shall possess the ability to interact with each. The things in IoT are usually embedded with sensors and software which enables them to transfer data across the fabric of IoT. IoT is essentially utilization of internet to establish a grid between two or more devices, things and in some cases living beings which are provided with a Unique Identifiers (UDs) and are capable of sending and receiving data with minimum to no human involvement.

The evolution of IoT has started in 1999 when Kevin Ashton coined the term "Internet of Things". The primary motive of connecting the things or

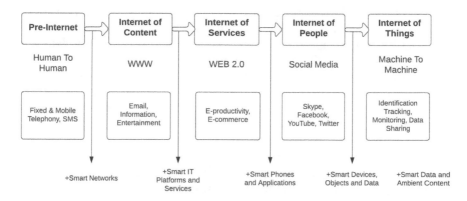

Figure 10.1 Evolution of IoT. (Source: BCC Research.)

devices and establishing a system of interaction between them is data which can be collected, stored, analysed and the results can be used for betterment.

Business needs that required to study is not rapidly expanding and this is where [16] of the IoT and its abilities to offer various kinds of services has made it the fastest growing technology of the present time (BCC Research LLC 2021, [2]) (Figure 10.1).

10.5 IoT AND SECURITY

Security is a lynchpin linchpin in the technology, although for outsider, it is just the same day as he was not aware of the nitty-gritty of the complex way technology is allied with [14,17]. For someone who lives with it day in day out it is just a cakewalk, in this IoT is not exception in fact as it is wired to millions of things out of its natural context, it is one of toughest challenge that folks involved or dealing with security as with new computing model or framework evolving, is currently one of hotbed for researchers and developers alike. Companies working in the security areas need an extensive ecosystem and infrastructure to evolve those interconnected devices. The operational tools are felicitated to holds much bigger data. This as much the technology is promised and people vouch for better security of their modelled system and infrastructure, as it is constantly is on data transfer.

The number of security issues is rising increasing on a huge amount of rate day- to- day because of the high accumulation of data that is getting piled on, and for now there is a concern for the security, as the number of attacks has been increased, but to alleviate it, the technologies are rapidly employed to counter these issues. In turn, it enormously improved in the, process to protect any object from physical damage, loss or theft, and unauthorized access, through high integrity of information, high confidentiality about the objects.

Ever since IoT devices are expected to generate large amounts of data, which will be aggregated using data management platforms on servers, the need for technologies that can index, store and process such data will has increased. Processing requirements may also be real- time in some instances, meaning that there would be windows, during which, the result must be presented. This additional demand for data processing (due to component devices constantly sending information to the cloud or data centre platforms) is the main connection between IoT and big data; the science of drawing valuable conclusions from massive data flows. In some IoT applications, big data analytics are an essential part of the system.

There are different actors in IT environment, they are typically for monetary gains, and, they range from miniscule to large ones, they are organized cybercriminals, whose attacks differ considerably in IT environments. There is no doubt that it is not inched into IoT environment [18]. IT is typically characterized by ever -evolving and intertwined technology stacks, which makes the attacks to suffer, the whole dynamics of the IT environment, primarily data traffic is hierarchical, north-sound bound. The cybersecurity is a main topic these days, as it is usually threat- based, constantly plugging holes with some malware or a virus.

When they are networked and where are processes studied to understand the current requirement to manage the assets in way, on that changing front to adopt technologies such as IoTs are impacting how people adopted. IoT is allowing everyone who get hooked on this technology, of where the companies are trying improve their style of livening;, in the end, it all depends on how data is are empowered [19]. There is a huge impact on the way we perceiving this these data -driven journey, which is taking us beyond our generation, the massive scales this these data that is generated is for analytics, look deep into that mined data and to find new insights, which is translating, the vast amounts of data that is collected, as it is this these raw data cannot be used, this needs to be cleaned and put some reliable algorithms to crunch that beast of data into an actionable intelligence, of it is in cities and metros, where this new in thing was created and as smart cities, and where these data getting generating, which are hyper in scales [10]. There is no doubt that the issues concerned with security is are of highest priority, on the one hand, accept the quality of data is at most important, and on the other hand, security cannot be compromising.

10.6 IoT IN BUSINESS APPLICATIONS

Innovation plays an exceptional role in the business arena. The fraternity of digitalization in business has blown the usage of internet enabled devices to control the key aspects of conducting business. Through IoT, a new fleet of machinery and devices capable of interacting among themselves as well as the other devices have brought about a new paradigm shift in the enterprises. For an instance, the machines are connected, through devices as part of deployment of IoT for accurately mapping the workloads on factory shop floor, companies are using employee IDs embedded with RFID, to manage and control physical access to their facilities, a farmer can use this IoT their land, by integrating with environmental monitors for an update information and their field equipment can also be automated and optimize their allocations of seeds and fertilizers, that scope is too vast it that new things need to concurred.

According to Lee & Lee [15], The IoT is recognized as one of the most important areas of future technology and is gaining a lot of attention from a wide range of industries. A rapid shift in the business is being witnessed in the recent times due to the integration of the network of machines and devices which are improving the business models [20]. The enterprise benefits of IoT are unlimited. Many organizations use IoT technology in connecting technologies which transcend vertically in scope. The most prominent benefits of deployment of IoT in business are as follows:

- Better understanding and visibility into real-world activities.
- Operational cost efficiency.
- Enhanced output.
- Improved productivity.
- Security.
- Better quality control.

IoT has gain traction in various industries in the recent times with the increase in the reliability on internet. One can claim with high reasoning that the IoTs utilizations would escalate in the coming years with betterment of connectivity. Below are some common areas where IoT utilization is being witnessed with high scope of increase in the same;

1. Smart homes: particularly in the urban set up, IoT based home set ups are becoming common. Mobile application controlled appliances are enabling a sophisticated lifestyle for many. Though there is a high scope of development in the area of smart homes, the present trend of it is highly appreciable.
2. Vehicles: the "self-driving cars" is a hot topic in the automobile industry. With giant companies like tesla introduction of consumer segment vehicles with highly reliable self-driving capabilities, many automobile companies are focusing on the technology to develop their produce in the area of self-driving cars.
3. Retail stores: IoT is extensively being used and studied in the area of retail management. Many IoT technologies can be used to keep the retail store processes smooth. Innovative IoT concepts like smart

shelves are helping organize the retail space in most efficient manner. We shall discuss the IoT in retail industry in detail in the coming parts of this chapter.

4. Managing traffic: Traffic poses a significant challenge for many countries. Many countries are using IoT to management such traffic challenges. The smart traffic management includes but not limited to smart signals, smart roads, smart parking solutions, etc. IoT is being used to analyse the real-time data of traffic congestions and the vehicles are diverted towards the best route with least traffic. IoT is also being used to identify the road accidents occurring at the remote location and sharing such data to the help centre enabling swift rescue actions.

10.7 IoT IN RETAIL INDUSTRY

With technological evolution, retail industry has witnessed a paradigm shift in the performance of the business itself like many other industries. With introduction and exponential growth in IoT, the retail space has seen many innovative concepts (one of it – smart shelves, is discussed in brief in the previous sub-chapter). IoT enables the conversion of simple devices to smart devices with capabilities to interact and share information, in this regard, retailers are using IoT to embed into their daily routine to organizing the activities with accuracy and efficiency.

The evolution in consumer's habits and dependence on swift delivery systems taking over the market place, the retailers are speculating the miracle of IoT help then catch up with the shift. Retail many times is interlinked with the far end of the business process when the business meets the customer/consumer. Given the position of retail in the business chain, it is imperative for the businesses to keep up with the technology adaption of the customers.

In the retail sector, there are two broad applications of IoT;

1. Gathering and sharing of data:

   Consumers are one of the most important entities of marketing process, maintaining consumer relations is of high importance to the managers. The data of such customers through interconnected devices which can gather and share information of customer preference, footfall details, shopping trends, etc. to the managers could be very helpful to the managers.

2. Utilization of data:

   The data collected by the smart devices can be automated to be shared among the devices which can in turn use the data to perform desired or designed tasks. With enormous potential that IoT retains in the retail industry, in this chapter we will look into the major spaces of retail industry where the IoT is being extensively utilized.

Retail many times has got to deal with the end customers and that's the sector where the actual revenue is generated, enhancement of sales and so the revenue is the major target of many retailers. The integration of IoT into the business of retail has evidentially given a boost to the retail sales. Countries like India are doing exceptionally well in integrating internet in the day-to-day tasks of their citizens and retail sector is witnessing enormous change in the dynamics of customer behaviour. The ability of IoT to get easily connected to many smart devices handled by many people on a daily basis is making it the most favourable technology.

It is expected that IoT in retail industry will escalate to a net worth of USD 30 billion by 2024, which indicated what future has to hold for IoT in the retail industry and one can estimate the revenue generated from it.

10.7.1 IoT and Consumer experience enhancement

Customer relationship management is seeing new light of day with the integration IoT in the retail sector. The extensive data collection and presentation to the retail managers is enabling them to precisely understand the behaviour patterns of the customers.

Delivery updates to the customer:

Home delivery has exponentially grown both due to recent pandemic as well as the extensive utilization of internet shopping, reason be any, the handling of deliveries is a tedious task for the managers. What goes where, when, how, in what condition, etc. has an imperative role to play in the extensive online market system. IoT is being used as a tool of maintaining the track and order of the home deliverables with efficiency like never before. The IoT based tracking is enabling the companies to keep the customers promptly informed about their products' location which in turn is a bonus tip for increasing competitive advantage and increasing the customer loyalty.

Micro-targeting:

Data collected through the customer foot-fall or any kind of customer interaction with the retail store is closely monitored by the marketers to target customers as narrow as possible. The customer's experience enhancement is the key target to many marketers and IoT helps in fostering a superior customer connection through personalising.

In-store upgradation:

The design and atmosphere of the store is being enhanced with the implementation of IoT in better organizing the store layout, minimizing the human errors and even to an extent of providing artificial support at each aisle. Not just online markets, IoT is being used for transforming in-store/physical stores and is ex extremely impressive. An 1800 square foot store located in Seattle, USA – Amazon Go has integrated futuristic IoT handled physical stores. It uses technology like computer vision, machine learning, deep learning and sensor fusion to conduct business with minimum to no human interaction to give seamless no-wait-in-line concept in its store.

Personalized communication:

IoT can help managers to communicate with the customers with much accurate and specific information. IoT has the ability to identify and analyse the customer's movement in the store/website so that such data can be utilized by the managers to interact with customers in a much-personalized manner.

Smart shelves:

Stock management is one of the most important focus point for most for any retailer. Traditionally, the stock arrangements at retail stores was handled by human resources at the store and probability of errors is high in such practice. Recently with the integration of IoT, many retail outlets are able to easily handle the stocking problems by practicing concepts like Smart Shelves.

Smart shelves is a popular IoT integration in retail sector is. Composed of three components – an RFID Tag, a RIFD reader and an antenna, a simple smart shelve can solve many complications in the organising of retail store's shelves. For example, the reader reads the tag of a particular product and transmit the information through the antenna and when the stocking employee passes through a particular shelf or scans the relevant QR code, the status of shelves' stock and related details pop up in his/her device making their life easy. The information regarding the inventory management, over stocking, under stocking, etc. can be easily handled by using IoT and supervision on critical stock running out cases can also be done well in advance.

Incentives:

Incentives such as offers, discounts, coupons, etc. has always proven to be very influential for retailers and has proven to be agents to alter consumer buying behaviour. However, the incentives has traditionally been generic, meaning, the offers would be targeting every customer visiting the store irrespective of the buying behaviour and trend of the particular customer as there was no mechanism for very narrow segmentation of customers. With the integration of IoT devices in the retail outlets, there is a flow of humongous customer data which when analysed gives behaviours, trends, orientations, etc. of the customers at a very detailed level.

Using beacons is one such method of collecting data of customers. Beacons are tiny devices which when connected to a smartphone, send alerts to it based on the location and proximity. This technology is being used by some retailers by sending personalized or generic offers, discounts or information to the people who passes a particular store if their application is downloaded in that person's smart device. Macy's is a classic example which uses beacons to announce personalized offers and discounts depending of the customer's altered behaviour.

Optimizing Supply Chain Management:

The supply chain management's cruciality and demand varies from product to product. IoT has proven to be extremely beneficial when it comes to handling logistics and supply chain management. In the present online driven shopping environment, the tracking related issues are handled by extreme integration of IoT at various levels. Various crucial information such as shipment's location, shipment carrier's condition, the driver's details, the road map, delivery schedules, everything from the manufacturing to the product delivery can be easily supervised by using IoT.

Using beacons, RFID, GPS etc. IoT can increase information accuracy in supply chain. Such accurate information is imperative in perishable products like milk, fruits or vegetables, which needs appropriate temperature maintenance throughout the logistic channel. Such data can be used to regularising the transport activity, check the storage areas, and all of this in real time.

The global business fraternity, welcomed IoT with extended arms. A study conducted by Gartner, has showed that about 77% of the retailers had agreed that IoT has helped serve the customers better.

Products like beacons has helped retail stores extensively and the technology of beacon has proven to be highly efficient in two areas of retail – communication and store organising. Beacons are extensively used in the retail business as they are usually cost efficient and low energy consuming Bluetooth devices which can send push notifications to the customers based on their location in-store and also near to the store. The size of the beacon is the most loved characteristic of the device allowing the markets to install it anywhere in the store with minimum to no trouble of space utilization issues. Main functions of beacons are to communicate with the potential customers and incentivise them with best customized offers altered according to their frequency to the store, buying behaviour, likes and dislikes. A beacon can send an automated push message to the customer when he/she enters an aisle in the store with information of the products of sale, new arrivals, etc. The same if to be done without such technology would be just impossible with so many numbers of human resources going to multiple number of customers and explaining things in infinite ways. Implications of IoT ranges from tiny things like beacons to large manufacturing machineries, however, in retail sector the utilization of robots is gaining expected attention. Already some retailers have started to test robots for stocking shelves, and these robots are capable to of taking inventory count. Some restaurants in China are employing robots to serve food to customers in place of waiters. Retail giants like Walmart are have introduced robots which are free moving smart machines which mainly scans the shelves and prompts the information such as rearranging or restoring products to the concerned authority.

The struggle to attain operational efficiency has become a core objective of many retailer and IoT is assisting them to attain this competency and offering them minimum cost and maximum profits.

The thing is that, as to theory, it is excellent to spell, but, not so easy to deal with a multitude of device types, right from the point of sale to displays and beyond and, then consider a large retailer who operate on massive amount of data, with so many devices in each store and multiply that by hundreds or even thousands of locations it is huge by any means. All those data collected by retailer from every store every day, shows merchandise that triggered as sales conversions, through which one can identify peak sales of the period.

The management of human resource and other important resources of the business can be managed by the retail managers by using the Point Of Sale (POS) which helps the managers to understand the peak periods leveraging them to act accordingly.

In the early dawn of the IoT technology in retail arena, the major challenge in conducting IoT dependent business was that many times the data collected by the individual thing/devices as a part of IoT are designed to collect data individually and this enables the retail managers to understand the store's data in bits and pieces. However, the challenge is gradually being overcome by using newer sensor networks by which now the retail managers are able to connect multiple systems at same time and are able to extract a single view across a wide range of data sources and can even capture and organize data, access, where they are able to get rich actionable insights on the data.

Training of staff on identifying what the customers in the store really want is gaining extreme importance in the present business environment. The managers/retailers are focusing of training their staff in this direction.

Challenges with IoT in retail:

Retail has promising arena for IoT to flourish, it seems, neither software engineers nor businesses are letting the technology slip off, however, researchers and practitioners are many times sceptical about the down steep of the game – the challenges, the risks, the rough edges. The security and privacy of customers is a major question. Few pinching challenges what IoT has to offer for businesses are discussed below;

1. Competence: The technology comes with a cost. IoT is a sophisticated technology and many retailers lack the competence in the form of infrastructure, financial capabilities, network, etc. Complicated components, huge storage capacity, devices such as scanners, etc. are all need heavy investments.
2. Customer data security: IoT is still in the initial evolving stage with lot of security issues coming up frequently. Handling customer's sensitive data is a huge task in itself. Compliance with regulations and laws such as GDPR (General Data Protection regulation) is gaining high importance and aligning with such regulations might be challenging for marketers as the threat of cybercrimes can arise anytime resulting in deep trouble for the companies.
3. Data storage and management: collecting, storing and handling heavy datasets involves high costs and expertise, many retailers might find it difficult to handle resources for the job.

4. Threat to traditional retailers: Though currently, traditional retailers seems to be not extremely affected by the IoT and retailers using the technology, if the adaption of this technology catches hurtle the flow of customers towards these fascinating stores may exponentially grow resulting in heavy pressure on traditional retailers.

10.8 CONCLUSION

IoT adaption has proven high utility to both marketers and customers. The technology has definitely evolved over the years through combined efforts of many research and development wings to come out as a finished technology with ready usefulness.

IoT in retail industry has flourished in the recent times by ensuring the businesses are conducted with ease. Highly efficient information sharing, better communication, improved and informed supply chain are few most celebrated reaps of IoT in retail industry. Intensive research into this technology can further enhance the sophistication of the technology and usability of it in the retail industry. However, the technology is yet to evolve to its full potential with least risk of failure of fatigue. The risk of data breach, data storage and handling, etc. are still to be addressed efficiently. With more and more businesses adapting the technology, it is imperative that they are well informed about the risks associated to it so as to end up being an easy target.

Many companies like Amazon, Macy's, ZARA, etc. have already started to use IoT in their businesses and many success stories are floating from these company reports stating the utilization of IoT has bought positive trajectory in their growth graph.

In conclusion, the IoT in retail industry has high potential to growth and at the same time has high risk factor embedded into the execution of the technology. Bringing down the installation costs and securing the utilization patterns of the technology can assure a bright future to IoT in general as well as in the retail fraternity.

REFERENCES

1. Chui et al. (2017). Taking the pulse of enterprise IoT. McKinsey & Company.
2. "The Internet of Things" BCC Research, 2019. httpsi//www.bccresearch.com/market-research/information-technology/internet-of-things-iot-market.html
3. Khan, W. Z., Rehman, M. H., Zangoti, H. M., Afzal, M. K., Armi, N., & Salah, K. (2020). Industrial internet of things: Recent advances, enabling technologies and open challenges. *Computers & Electrical Engineering*, 81, 106522.

4. Molano, J. I. R., Lovelle, J. M. C., Montenegro, C. E., Granados, J., & Crespo, R. G. (2018). Metamodel for integration of internet of things, social networks, the cloud and industry 4.0. *Journal of Ambient Intelligence and Humanized Computing*, 9(3), 709–723.

5. Patel et al. (2017), What's new with the Internet of Things? McKinsey & Company. https://www.mckinsey.com/industries/semiconductors/our-insights/whats-new-with-the-internet-of-things

6. Atzori, L., Iera, A., & Morabito, G. (2011). Siot: Giving a social structure to the internet of things. *Communications Letters, IEEE*, 15(11), 1193–1195.

7. Pelino, M., Gillett, F.E. (2016). *ITIABD Tech, TT I&O - Forrester Research*.

8. Gubbi, J., et al. (2013). Internet of Things (IoT): A vision, architectural elements, and future directions. *Future Generation Computer Systems*, 29(7), 1645–1660.

9. Tripathy, B. K., & Anuradha, J. (Eds.). (2017). *Internet of things (IoT): technologies, applications, challenges and solutions*. CRC press.

10. Bench-Capon, T. J., & Dunne, P. E. (2007). Argumentation in artificial intelligence. *Artificial intelligence*, 171(10-15), 619-641.

11. Vermesan, O., & Friess, P. (Eds.). (2014). Internet of things-from research and innovation to market deployment (Vol. 29). Aalborg: River publishers.

12. Barnaghi, P., et al. (2012). Semantics for the Internet of Things: early progress and back to the future. *International Journal on Semantic Web and Information Systems (IJSWIS)*, 8(1), 1–21.

13. Carrez, F. (ed.) (2013). Converged architectural reference model for the IoT, available at: http://www.iot-a.eu/public/public-documents.

14. Gruschka, N., & Gessner, D. (2013). Concepts and Solutions for Privacy and Security in the Resolution Infrastructure. IoT-A Deliverable D, 4.

15. Lee, I., & Lee, K. (2015). The Internet of Things (IoT): Applications, investments, and challenges for enterprises. *Business Horizons*, 58(4), 431–440.

16. Caro, F., & Sadr, R. (2019). The Internet of Things (IoT) in retail: Bridging supply and demand. *Business Horizons*, 62(1), 47–54.

17. Tyo, R. A. (2006). Connecting the real-world environment to the digital backbone: RFID & wireless sensor networks. In meeting of Intel, 3rd Asia Academic Forum, Singapore.

18. Fortino, G., Guerrieri, A., Russo, W., & Savaglio, C. (2014, May). Integration of agent-based and cloud computing for the smart objects-oriented IoT. *In Proceedings of the 2014 IEEE 18th international conference on computer supported cooperative work in design* (CSCWD) (pp. 493-498). IEEE

19. Yu, H., Shen, Z., & Leung, C. (2013, August). From internet of things to internet of agents. *In 2013 IEEE international conference on green computing and communications and IEEE Internet of Things and IEEE cyber, physical and social computing* (pp. 1054-1057). IEEE.

20. Lee, I. (2019). The Internet of Things for enterprises: An ecosystem, architecture, and IoT service business model. *Internet of Things*, 7, 100078.

Chapter 11

Respiratory rate meter with the Internet of things

Efrain Villalvazo Laureano, Anmar S. Mora Martínez,
Ramón O. Jiménez Betancourt, Juan M. González López,
and Daniel A. Verde Romero
University of Colima

CONTENTS

ABSTRACT

More and more countries are increasing the infrastructure of their
Internet networks. In the same way, the speeds of communication networks have been growing; this has made it easier for most people to
have access to smartphones. On the other hand, health services are
being improved; hospitals have better technology for controlling,
detecting, monitoring, and treating diseases; however, not everyone has
access to these services. Also, the costs for hospital stays are high and
out of reach for most people. That is why the Internet of things is play-
ing a crucial role in improving this situation. This chapter presents a
respiratory rate meter with the Internet of things technology and all its
stages for its elaboration. First, it starts with the development of several
tests on a breadboard. It continues with the printed circuit (with cheap
elements and easy access); then, the programming code is made to be
implemented in the Particle Photon. Later, the program is presented to
upload the respiratory rate information to the cloud. Finally, the user
interface of the respiratory rate meter is displayed.

DOI: 10.1201/9781003304203-11

11.1   INTERNET OF THINGS IN HEALTHCARE PREAMBLE

Wireless technologies have greatly improved communication systems in the last 20 years. WiFi and the networks created for cell phones allow having a very good Internet connection, achieving a change in the use of people's technologies. In indoor spaces, WiFi is the ideal connection for users. In one study, it is said that in 2016, there were roughly five billion devices communicating over WiFi networks around the world. And for a few years now, WiFi has been creatively exploited for contactless human activity detection (Youwei zeng, 2019).

In recent years, mobile applications have increased and are supported by the Internet of things, which can be described in three stages: (1) The physical stage, which contains sensors of the physical environment. (2) The network stage connects to other intelligent elements, network devices, and servers; it also transmits and processes sensor data. (3) The application stage delivers application-specific services to the user (Sarangi, 2017). The stages of the Internet of things can be visualized in Figure 11.1.

Innovative rehabilitation based on IoT has emerged in recent years to mitigate the shortage of health-oriented resources due to the increasing population of older adults globally. An IoT-based healthcare system connects everyone to the resources available on a network to perform surgery, monitoring, and remote diagnostic health care using the Internet of things (Yuehong YIN, 2016).

The IoT infrastructure available in cities with features appropriate for smart devices is an excellent alternative to improving and expanding healthcare applications (Jaganathan Venkatesh, 2018).

Despite having excellent infrastructure and up-to-date technology, medical services are not available to everyone in the world. The purpose of intelligent medical services is to help users raise awareness about their medical condition and keep them updated on their health status. Smart device health care allows the management of some emergencies. Smart device health care

Figure 11.1 The stages of the Internet of things.

helps make most of the resources available and lowers the cost of treatment for users (P. Sundaravadivel, 2018).

In recent years, smartphones have become more specialized in different applications such as alarm clocks, notebooks, cameras, dictionaries, encyclopedias, fitness and wellness, and assistant; new functions are appearing that help make life easier for many people. Currently, we are working on the measurement and monitoring of biosignals for better management of physical well-being and health for the adoption of preventive measures. Health and wellness accessories are being created to help improve medical problems. Today, phones are equipped with thermometers, pulse monitors, pedometers, sleep trackers, calorie trackers, vein detectors, blood sugar monitors, and a host of other devices, either integrated as part of smartphones, or connected as external devices through an application (Shourjya Sanyal, 2018).

Clothing with soft, comfortable fabrics is increasingly essential for home health care. The demand for portable, quiet, and lightweight healthcare devices has gradually increased over the last decade. Many smart textile sensors have been developed and applied to automate environments for personalized user care. However, for many applications, multiple sensor measurements are needed for full sensory integration (Chien-Lung Shen, 2017).

Today, portable systems are becoming more popular in medical applications. Innovative fabrics have increased interest in being comfortable and allowing the free movement of patients. For that reason, an intelligent material for respiratory monitoring based on a piezoresistive sensor element has been created (N. Molinaro, 2018).

11.2 SOME APPLICATIONS OF THE INTERNET OF THINGS TO HEALTH CARE AND RESPIRATORY RATE

The main objective of monitoring the respiratory rate is that it is simple; in addition to that, it is carried out quickly with the devices that are available or within reach of the students. It is intuitive to use, with the sensors and elements that allow the execution of simple algorithms to perform a safe measurement of respiratory rate (Daniyal Liaqat, 2019).

Respiratory rate is a meaningful vital sign. It is an indicator that detects physiological deterioration promptly, in addition to being an anticipator of serious adverse events. Specifically, respiratory rate is a primary predictor of cardiac arrest and admission to the intensive care unit, and it is also useful for risk assessment after acute myocardial infarction (Carlo Massaroni, 2019).

The first thing to consider for any respiratory rate monitoring service, to be of good quality or reliable, is that the signal from the sensor must be of good quality. This is because the main objective is to detect the presence of respiration. If the signal source is of low quality, it can affect the possibility of distinguishing whether the user is breathing or not. However, this is compli-cated because the signals often carry noise submerged by numerous factors; these include sensors, electronic components, sensor locations, unwanted human movements, and environmental factors that impair the quality of the respiratory rate mini-monitoring system (Andrea Nicolò, 2020).

Home health and surveillance: Mobile health care is an area for patient monitoring that has been very important in recent years. Patients at home generally do not like to use adhesives and sensors such as electrodes for a long time. Instead, they prefer mobile health apps that often include pulse oximetry, whereby patients can easily insert their fingers into a pulse oxim-eter probe. Although the pulse oximeter provides excellent measurements, the precision challenges lie in estimating the respiratory rate on mobile health meters, primarily due to the effects or disturbances that are caused by movement (Marco A.F. Pimentel, 2017).

11.2.1 Measurement of respiratory frequency

The great interest in monitoring the respiratory rate is fundamental due to the increase in the development of a large number of sensors and the new techniques to measure the respiratory rate, which is classified into contact and without contact (C. Massaroni, 2021).

Respiratory rate (RR) is an essential physiological parameter that is a leading indicator of critical illness. Monitoring is easy to perform and effec-tive in helping to prevent sensitive events; several different, reliable, and accurate methods have been tried for this automatic tracking. With their different limitations, these are classified into three types: extraction of RR from other physiological signals, RR measurement based on respiratory movements, and RR measurement based on airflow (Haipeng Liu, 2019). The ways to measure respiratory rate are shown in Figure 11.2.

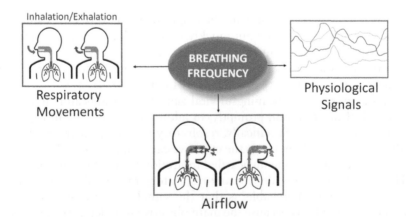

Figure 11.2 Ways to measure respiratory rate.

Predicting cardiorespiratory crises has been a challenge in patients with stable medical or surgical conditions when recovering on the general care floor. Events in hospitals can be prevented by early detection of deterioration of critical points by continuous electronic cardiorespiratory monitoring (Ashish K. Khanna, 2018).

The exact diagnosis of the respiratory rate is essential in environments or places that do not have the necessary resources to obtain other forms of measurement such as pulse oximetry or chest X-ray for the elaboration of diagnoses, and pneumonia is determined based only on the child's clinical signs. Given the high burden and infant mortality, better methods are required to measure respiratory rate as accurately as possible (Amy Sarah Ginsburg, 2018).

There are many parameters to determine the excellent state of health; one is the measurement of respiratory rate in a home setting because it significantly impacts the early detection of lung diseases. This variable is used as a physiological measure for disease monitoring in many areas, in particular continuous monitoring of respiration. Respiratory patterns associated with high stress levels can provide the user with relevant information about their psychological well-being over long periods. For them, it was developed. To that, a home system was designed that uses narrowband wireless signals to monitor a person's breathing anywhere in the house, even when behind walls, adapting to dynamically changing environments (Ruth Ravichandran, 2015).

Wireless breath rate verification without devices is a new technique for monitoring vital signs that can estimate non-contact respiratory rate using cycle analysis of human respiration on the surrounding wireless signals. The most modern methods have achieved excellent performance in tracking respiratory rates individually via WiFi, but they have their areas of opportunity with groups of more than three people (Qinghua Gao, 2020).

Monitoring patients' vital signs in different settings can be done using radar techniques, since the respiratory rate or the heart rate determines whether the person is alive or not, and this monitoring can be done through CMOS technology and the introduction of ultra-wideband radar (Cansu Eren, 2019).

Researchers designed a portable device without physical intervention to monitor the respiratory rate using capacitive sensors. The design and development foresee an electronic health platform based on the Internet. This system is housed in a vest suitable for comfortable, inexpensive, and unattached respiratory monitoring for chronic patients with lung disease during respiratory rehabilitation exercises outside the hospital (David Naranjo-Hernández, 2018).

In a respiratory rate meter, inkjet printing (IJP) was used to fabricate the sensors. It was easier to manufacture at a lower cost. The sensor was fabricated on a polydimethylsiloxane (PDMS) substrate using silver nanoparticle conductive ink. During the respiration, the sensor acts as a variable resistance (similar to a strain gauge) whose value changes with respiration, causing a resistive change, and using a Wheatstone bridge with three fixed resistors, and the fourth variable; plus an instrumentation amplifier, to finally provide the signal to an Arduino microcontroller to calculate the respiratory rate (Ala'aldeen Al-Halhouli, 2020).

11.3 RESPIRATORY RATE MONITOR WITH PARTICLE PHOTON

The IoT has become an everyday phenomenon because everything related to these technologies, such as hardware, software, accessories, and sensors, is within the reach of many people and is easy to use. Therefore, students, hobbyists, and non-programmers, even engineers from different disciplines, specialize in these areas.

In this project, it was decided to use Particle because it has hardware and software tools to facilitate prototyping, scaling, and managing IoT products. Additionally, cloud-connected IoT prototypes can be rapidly built. It allows going from a single prototype to many units with a cloud platform that grows as devices grow (Rashid Khan, 2016).

Other things that are considered when choosing this device are as follows: The Photon can be ordered with or without headers, which means it has the flexibility of being used as a prototype board. It is also compatible with Arduino, which is a device widely used by students.

The Photon has other features, such as an activation pin for waking up from low energy mode. The Photon is optimized to consume less energy, and this is possible, thanks to the new WiFi module it uses, which is very important when required in healthcare applications. Table 11.1 shows some of the main technical characteristics that were considered for choosing this device. After making the appropriate choice of the device for the respiratory rate meter, Figure 11.3 shows a general scheme that encompasses all the elements used to achieve the operation.

In the first place, a facemask is connected to the patient to detect the respiratory rate using a microphone type sensor; this signal is received through one of the analog inputs of the Photon; in this device, the necessary programming process is carried out to condition the signal based on the respiratory rate. Once the signal is conditioned, it is sent to the cloud through WiFi, and then the necessary programming is carried out to view

Table 11.1 Technical characteristics

Photon
1 MB flash memory
120 MHz ARM Cortex M3 processor
128 KB RAM
18 GPIO and peripheral pins
Real-time operating system (FreeRTOS)
Support for AP (access point) mode (SoftAP)
Open-source design

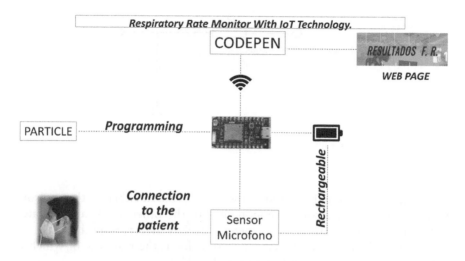

Figure 11.3 General diagram of the respiratory rate meter.

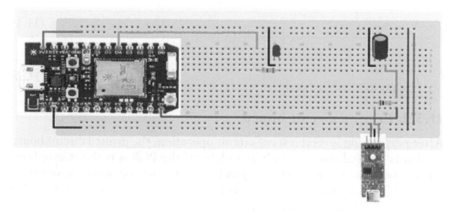

Figure 11.4 The electronic circuit in the protoboard.

it on a web page so that any user with Internet access and with the permissions can consult the information in real time (limited by Internet speed).

11.3.1 Electronic circuit

The first thing to do is to use a dashboard to perform various tests to ensure the correct operation of all components, as shown in Figure 11.4, which is recommended for anyone who wants to reproduce the meter design of respiratory rate before proceeding with the printing of circuit.

Analog input A0 of the Photon is used to receive the input signal from the microphone-type sensor; it is also necessary to use a passive RC filter

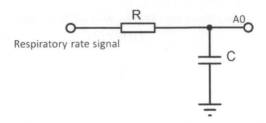

Figure 11.5 RC low-pass filter.

to attenuate the noise immersed in the signal, caused either by the environment, or by any electronic component. On the other hand, an indicator with an LED can ensure that the meter correctly detects respiration.

Figure 11.5 shows the RC-type low-pass filter, the response of which is calculated with the transfer function in Eq. 11.1.

Equation 11.2 was used to calculate the filter's cutoff frequency with the values of the resistance of 10 kΩ and the capacitor of 10 μf.

$$VA_0 = \frac{1}{RCS + 1} \tag{11.1}$$

$$f_c = \frac{1}{2\pi RC} \tag{11.2}$$

11.3.2 Printed circuit board

After performing several tests of circuit operation, the printed circuit board PCB was worked out. The only item left off the PCB was the microphone sensor, because it is necessary to place it on the person whose respiratory rate will be measured. A terminal with three connection points was added to the PCB to place the sensor wires.

In addition, the power supply of the circuit is carried out through a connector that can be easily attached to a cell phone charger or the USB port of any computer. Figure 11.6 shows the printed circuit with both sides.

11.4 PHOTON PROGRAMMING

For the Photon programming, the Particle platform was used because it makes it easy to integrate multiple Internet of things devices in the cloud. It also has the advantage of having a complete network infrastructure for these types of devices.

Programming it is recommended that the next instruction always be placed:

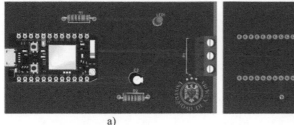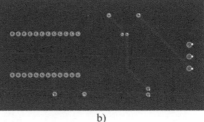

a)   b)

Figure 11.6 Printed circuit board.

SYSTEM_THREAD (ENABLED);

This code ensures that if the Photon runs out of Internet signal, keep receiving and executing the data from the microphone sensor.

Then the input variables of the microphone sensor were established.

```
int sensor=A0;
int lecturasensor=0;
```

Later, the variables were designated to create the frequency counter.

```
int intervaloEncendido=100; // Led on time.
int intervaloApagado=100; // Led off time.
int IntervaloBPM=10000; // Data sending time.
int IntervaloBPM2=1;
```

The last variable is the beats per minute (BMP), which was reduced to its equivalent in 10 seconds to not wait up to a minute to obtain the result.

```
int respiracion2=0; // Variable for respiratory rate.
void setup () // Program star.
pinMode(4, OUTPUT); // Led output.
Particle.variable("respiracion2", respiracion2); // Variable
that will be sent to the web page by wifi.
```

BPM calculations

```
señal=lecturaSensor; // Sensor reading (breath signal)
if ((señal) > (ultimamedicion+50)) { // This indicates that;
If the analog input signal is> 50, consider it as one
breath.

ultimamedicion=señal;
ciclo=1;
if (señal>=picodetension) {
picodetension=señal;
}
}
```

```
if ((señal)<(ultimamedicion-50)) {{ // This indicates that;
If the analog input signal is <-50, consider it as a breath.
ultimamedicion=señal;
ciclo=0;
if (señal<=valledetension) {
valledetension=señal;
}
}
```

The millis() function is similar to delay (), but the first one was selected for calculations because delay () has the disadvantage of trapping the micro-controller until the hold is executed. At the same time, millis () returns the number of milliseconds since the Arduino board starts running immediately after a reboot or power-up.

```
if(millis()-tiempoAnteriorBPM>=IntervaloBPM) {
  lecturaSensor=analogRead(sensor);
  estadoBPM=false;
  respiracion2=(pulsos*6);
  tiempoAnteriorBPM=millis ();
  pulsos=0;
}
if(millis()-tiempoAnteriorBPM2>IntervaloBPM2) {
  lecturaSensor=analogRead(sensor);
  estadoBPM=true;
  tiempoAnteriorBPM2=millis ();
}
if((millis()-tiempoAnteriorEncendido>=intervaloEncendido)
&&estadoLed==true && ciclo==0)
  {
  estadoLed=false;
  picodetension=señal;
  valledetension=señal;
digitalWrite (4, HIGH);
  tiempoAnteriorApagado=millis ();
}
```

With the above code, the Photon is instructed to perform the respiratory rate calculation every 10 seconds, and the result is sent to the web page.

The following line of code contains the variable for the web page, and it must be the one that includes the respiratory rate.

```
String respiracion2=String(respiracion2);
```

And with the following code, the data are published in Particle to verify if the information is correct.

```
Particle.publish("F. R", respiracion2, PRIVATE);
```

Like CodePen, it is a platform to share, update, view, comment on, design, and create web code, as well as being for rapid prototyping and testing of code snippets through a columnar interface for testing code of HTML, CSS, and JavaScript codes. That is why this platform was chosen to verify the results in real time.

Although the CodePen platform displays all three columns simultaneously, it was decided to separate them to place the comments of the lines of code more clearly. Table 11.2 is the HTML code.

Table 11.3 below shows and explains the CSS code.

With JavaScript, connections were established with Particle to enter the password and the email with which the Particle chip was registered and used for the application, to be able to access the variables. Table 11.4 contains all the JavaScript code and corresponding explanations.

Table 11.2 HTML code

HTML
<img id = "rectángulo"
This code indicates how the image will be called so that it can be moved in CSS.
src= "https://www.frases333.com/wp-content/uploads/2019/03/rectangulo.png"</img>
It is to enter the image of the rectangle shown in Figure 11.7.
<span id = "Frecuencia">???</span>
Name of the variable where the respiratory rate data will be displayed on the web page.

Table 11.3 CSS code

CSS
Positioning of variables and images with CSS.

```
#rectangulo {
  position: absolute;
  top:200px;
  left:300px;
  height:100px;
  width: 200px;
}
```

Code to place the variable in a position within the blue rectangle in Figure 11.7.

```
#Frecuencia {
  position: absolute;
  top:245px;
  left:375px;
}
```

Table 11.4 JavaScript code

JavaScript

```
var $lrms = $('#Frecuencia');
```

Assigning the frequency object to a new variable.

```
var irms=0;
```

This part of the code is required to obtain the variables published in the cloud.

Then it is necessary to give access to the PARTICLE account so that the variables can be seen on the web page with the following code.

```
var particle = new Particle ();
var token;
particle.login({username: '**********', password: '**********'}).then(
   function(data) {
     token = data.body.access_token; },
```

Next, you have to assign the ID of the PHOTON that is being used, for the data to be sent correctly, as shown in the following code:

```
setInterval(function() {
particle.getVariable({ deviceId: '**********',
```

Then the variable that contains the RESPIRATORY RATE is assigned to the variable:

respiracion2:

```
name: 'respiracion2', auth: token }).then(function(data) {
```

At the end of the code, the variable that will show the respiratory rate is assigned:

```
Irms = irms .toFixed(2);
$lrms.text(lrms+"R.M");
```

The previous line of code indicates that "irms" is where the breaths will be displayed and the "R.M" indicates that they are breaths per minute.

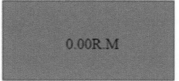

Figure 11.7 Respiration rate.

In CodePen, it was only used to visualize respiration rate, as seen in Figure 11.7.

Figure 11.8 Screen to create a web page.

Finally, the website was launched to the public through Google sites; this is a tool for creating web pages. This application is to create a website in a way as simple as editing a website.

Figure 11.8 shows the view to enter the code for creating the web page. It is worth mentioning that the application is in Spanish because it was created to be used in Mexico.

11.5 CONCLUSIONS

The Internet of things can help improve the situation of many patients who require constant monitoring of some medical parameters and who do not have enough resources to pay for their stay in hospitals.

This respiratory rate meter with IoT technology was achieved using the Photon device, which facilitated the development by having technology that connects directly to the WiFi network and is also compatible with Arduino.

The elements used for the project were inexpensive; however, the sensor calibration was challenging to adjust.

Although the Photon is readily incorporated into the Internet network, its response time depends on the WiFi speed and is not recommended for when it is required to monitor a variable in less than a second.

One of the areas of opportunity for this prototype is to improve the sensor, and another is to incorporate more medical parameters for health care.

REFERENCES

Ala'aldeen Al-Halhouli, L. A.-G. (2020). Clinical evaluation of stretchable and wearable inkjet-printed strain gauge sensor for respiratory rate monitoring at different body postures. *Applied Sciences*, vol. 10, no. 2, p. 480.

Amy Sarah Ginsburg, J. L. (2018). A systematic review of tools to measure respiratory rate to identify childhood pneumonia. *American Journal of Respiratory and Critical Care Medicine*, vol. 197, no. 9, pp. 1116–1127.

Andrea Nicolò, C. M. (2020). The Importance of respiratory rate monitoring: From healthcare to sport and exercise. *Sensors*, vol. 20, no. 21, p. 6396.

Ashish K. Khanna, F. J. (2018). Respiratory depression in low acuity hospital settings–Seeking answers. *Journal of Critical Care*, vol. 47, pp. 80–87.

C. Massaroni, A. N. (2021). Contactless methods for measuring respiratory rate: A review. *IEEE Sensors Journal*, vol. 21, no. 11, pp. 12821–12839.

Cansu Eren, S. K. (2019). The artifacts of human physical motions on vital signs monitoring. *Scientific Meeting on Electrical-Electronics & Biomedical Engineering and Computer Science (EBBT)*, pp. 1–5.

Carlo Massaroni, A. N. (2019). Contact-based methods for measuring respiratory rate. *Sensors*, vol. 19, no. 4, pp. 1–47.

Chien-Lung Shen, T.-H. H.-C.-C.-L.-C.-T. (2017). Respiratory rate estimation by using ECG, impedance, and motion sensing in smart clothing. *Journal of Medical and Biological Engineering*, vol. 37, no. 6, pp. 826–842.

Daniyal Liaqat, M. A.-E. (2019). WearBreathing: Real world respiratory rate monitoring using. *Association for Computing Machinery*, vol. 3, no. 2, pp. 1–22.

David Naranjo-Hernández, A. T.-B.-T.-R.-R.-M.-R. (2018). Smart vest for respiratory rate monitoring of COPD patients based on non-contact capacitive sensing. *Sensors*, vol. 18, no. 7, pp. 1–24.

Haipeng Liu, J. D. (2019). Recent development of respiratory rate measurement technologies. *Physiological Measurement*, vol. 40, no. 7, pp. 1–27.

Jaganathan Venkatesh, B. A. (2018). Modular and personalized smart health application design in a smart city environment. *IEEE Internet of Things Journal*, vol. 5, no. 2, pp. 614–623.

Marco A.F. Pimentel, A. E. (2017). Towards a Robust Estimation of Respiratory Rate from Pulse Oximeters. *IEEE Transactions on Biomedical Engineering*, vol. 64, no. 8, pp. 1914–1923.

N. Molinaro, M. D. (2018). Wearable textile based on silver plated knitted sensor for respiratory rate monitoring. *Annual International Conference of the IEEE Engineering in Medicine and Biology Society (EMBC)*, pp. 2865–2868.

P. Sundaravadivel, E. K. (2018). Everything you wanted to know about smart health care: Evaluating the different technologies and components of the internet of things for better health. *IEEE Consumer Electronics Magazine*, vol. 7, no. 1, pp. 18–28.

Qinghua Gao, J. T. (2020). Device-free multi-person respiration monitoring using WiFi. *IEEE Transactions on Vehicular Technology*, vol. 69, no. 11, pp. 1–5.

Rashid Khan, K. G. (2016). *Learning IoT with Particle Photon and Electron*. Birmingham: Packt Publishing Ltd.

Ruth Ravichandran, E. S.-Y. (2015). WiBreathe: Estimating Respiration Rate Using Wireless Signals in Natural Settings in the Home. *IEEE International Conference on Pervasive Computing and Communications*, pp. 131–139.

Sarangi, P. S. (2017). Internet of Things: Architectures, protocols, and applications. *Hindawi Journal of Electrical and Computer Engineering*, pp. 1–25.

Shourjya Sanyal, K. K. (2018). Algorithms for monitoring heart rate and respiratory rate from the video of a user's face. *IEEE Journal of Translational Engineering in Health and Medicine*, vol. 2017, pp. 1–11.

Youwei zeng, D. W. (2019). FarSense: Pushing the range limit of wifi-based respiration sensing with csi ratio of two antennas. *Proceedings of the ACM on Interactive, Mobile, Wearable and Ubiquitous Technologies*, vol. 3, no. 3, pp. 1–26.

Yuehong YIN, Y. Z. (2016). The internet of things in healthcare: An overview. *Journal of Industrial Information Integration*, vol. 1, pp. 3–13.

Chapter 12

Artificial intelligence with IoT for energy efficiency in buildings

Aya Sayed, Yassine Himeur and Faycal Bensaali
Qatar University

Abbes Amira
University of Sharjah
De Montfort University

CONTENTS

ABSTRACT

Observing the electricity consumption nowadays may be extremely daunting; therefore, optimizing the consumers' usage is critical to ensuring the sustainability of energy resources. The employment of innovative technologies (e.g., artificial intelligence (AI) and Internet of things (IoT)) to boost energy efficiency in houses or buildings is becoming more and more vital to support the sustainability and preservation

DOI: 10.1201/9781003304203-12

of resources. This chapter sheds light on the application of AI and IoT in improving residential energy efficiency by advancing state-of-the-art, evidence-based, AI-enabled energy efficiency recommendation systems (RSs). The framework makes use of AI and micro-moments concept and utilizes a variety of IoT sensors strategically positioned throughout the house to transform any habit according to the habit loop, where the end-user has to go through a cue, a routine and a reward. A RS is adopted in this change cycle since it relates the action to the reward and, hence, reinforces the new routine, where notifications are sent to users via the Home-Assistant[1] app with the energy-saving advice. In order to evaluate our energy-saving framework, a mini-pilot is initiated with a number of users with distinct electrical perspectives (up to 10 users) in various locations. The study's findings determine the impact of AI, IoT and RSs on energy efficiency.

12.1 INTRODUCTION

The Internet of things (IoT) is becoming a promising technology that many other cutting-edge technologies are relying on, such as artificial intelligence (AI) and machine learning (ML), health care, energy and smart city. Typically, data collected from a plethora of IoT devices connected to the Internet are of crucial importance for developing new services, improving productivity and efficiency, enhancing real-time decision making, resolving challenging problems and creating innovative experiences [20,28]. In the energy industry, the IoT technology has considerably helped in creating the intelligent networks, also named smart grids, by collecting, transmitting and preprocessing huge amounts of data, and hence opens the way for a new research area called big data analytics [27]. This area is booming due to the use of advanced deep learning models, e.g., convolutional neural networks (CNNs), recurrent neural networks (RNNs) and deep autoencoders (DAEs), which have the ability of executing feature engineering by themselves in an incremental manner. In this context, IoT aims at gathering and integrating data in a smart way from all of the assets attached to the energy network, increasing the flexibility of the energy systems and optimizing operation [12,38].

For the energy sector, the IoT technologies offer greater availability of information throughout the chain of value, allowing for amortization of better tools for decision making, such as AI or automatic learning [26]. They also permit remote control and automated execution of these decisions. These technologies constitute a control loop that consists of four functions: (1) physical process which includes the generation, transmission or consumption of electricity; (2) measurement process in which the sensors measure the statuses and outputs of the physical process; (3) decision

---

[1] https://www.home-assistant.io/.

making process that can be independent and decentralized or in coordination with other components; and (4) action process where the decisions are sent back to the actuators positioned on the smart grid for implementation [21]. Given the connectivity between the functions of this control loop, successful implementation requires architectures and standards that ensure interoperability between IoT technologies [6].

The majority of the IoT projects in the energy sector focus on applications oriented toward demand. However, correctly used IoT brings infinite benefits for the optimization of the entire chain of value, optimizing all of the phases and the communication between them, including the generation, transmission, distribution and consumption of energy. As the energy systems become increasingly complex and decentralized, the IoT applications improve the visibility and response capacity of the devices connected to the network [46]. Moreover, with the actual advances of AI, the algorithms can benefit from the capability of IoT devices to collect and preprocess high-quality data in real time to develop robust and accurate AI-based solutions that cover different energy aspects. In this regard, because the building energy sector is responsible for up to 40% of the worldwide energy usage, it has been of utmost importance to investigate the potential of IoT and AI together for reducing wasted energy in buildings and promoting energy-efficient behaviors [29].

This has been possible by combining the capability of IoT to collect accurate data with the analysis power of ML. Accordingly, this helps in developing effective building energy-saving solutions that are based on (1) detecting abnormal energy consumption behaviors; (2) forecasting energy demand; (3) preventing non-technical loss (NTL), i.e., power theft; (4) detecting or predicting power failures; and (5) managing the balance between offer and demand [13,18]. Moreover, the advent of RSs, which are another category of ML tools that can promote behavioral change and correction of users' practices, has opened new perspectives toward developing a new generation of energy efficiency systems. Accordingly, RSs can help end-users in correcting their energy consumption habits according to the habit loop, where the end-users have to go through a cue, a routine and a reward. Put differently, RSs promote energy consumption behavioral change by supporting end-users with in-time, tailored and engaging recommendations. This research area is attracting significant research and development in which several frameworks have recently been proposed to target current challenges and issues [14,39]. Additionally, the emergence of the explainability concept in RSs has helped in designing energy-saving recommendation frameworks that generate not only high-quality recommendations, but also intuitive explanations [36]. A typical example in this context is the DeepMind platform[2] developed by Google using AI and IoT for promoting

---

[2] https://internetofbusiness.com/google-using-deepmind-ai-to-reduce-energy-consumption-by-30/.

energy efficiency in its data centers and monitoring cooling independently in the facilities, where an AI-powered RS is designed.

Moving forward, as smartphones are becoming an indispensable part of individuals' lives, it is rational to include them in the energy-saving process. Indeed, they can play the role of visualization dashboards to showcase energy usage footprints, as well as they can hold tailored mobile apps for providing individuals with energy-saving notifications, recommendations and explanations [22]. In this line, smartphones can also be considered as a key element for altering end-users' behaviors. From another perspective, to analyze the manner end-users consume energy, it is significant to look at their intent-driven moments that have an impact on load usage [4,31]. This means the moments when end-users decide to act to turn on/off a device, adjust the indoor temperature using an AC or a thermostat, open the windows to have more luminosity, etc. These are named micro-moments, and they are game changers for both end-users and utilities companies because of their role in manipulating energy usage [37]. Put differently, they represent intent-rich moments when indoor environmental preferences are shaped and energy consumption decisions are made [5].

In this paper, we present an energy-saving framework that mixes together the concepts of AI, RSs, micro-moments as well as a range of IoT sensors strategically placed around an academic space to (1) detect and correct abnormal energy consumption habits and (2) promote energy-saving through providing end-users with personalized recommendations. Specifically, according to the habit loop, a person must go through a cue, a routine and a reward. Therefore, the RS is used in this change cycle because it associates the action with the reward, thus reinforcing the new habit, in which alerts with energy-saving advice are delivered to users via the Home-Assistant app. To evaluate our energy-saving framework, a mini-pilot is launched with numerous users from diverse regions who have different electrical views (up to 10 users). The outcomes of the study indicate the positive effects of implementing AI, IoT and RSs to facilitate energy efficiency.

The rest of this paper is organized as follows: Section 12.2 discusses the related works. Section 12.3 describes the proposed energy-saving solution based on IoT, AI, micro-moments and RSs. Section 12.4 presents the experimental results obtained on a real-world scenario. Finally, Section 12.5 derives the important findings and highlights future work.

12.2 RELATED WORKS: AI AND IoT FOR ENERGY MANAGEMENT

With the advent of AI, ML and IoT, it becomes possible to offer better energy efficiency opportunities in buildings. The term of smart buildings has been coined to define the buildings adopting these kinds of technologies for enabling end-users managing the rhythms of their lifestyle, increasing their comfort and optimizing their energy consumption [13]. In this context, a plethora of research works have been conducted to develop different types of energy efficiency systems and several industrial players have entered the promising market of building energy saving [47]. Generally, building energy-saving methods can be split into different categories based on methodology; however, in this section, we focus on overviewing three main types, which are based on behavioral change, thermal comfort optimization and load forecasting.

12.2.1 Energy-saving based on behavioral change

In [43], Tomazzoli et al. deployed an IoT and ML-based approach for (1) defining a centralized energy-saving architecture in distributed sub-networks of electric devices and (2) extracting behavioral energy consumption rules for identifying best consumption habits with reference to each device using rule-based algorithm and an ML clustering technique. In [17], the authors introduced an energy-saving scheme using a deep learning-based micro-moments scheme, called DeepM2, which helps in automatically detecting abnormal energy consumption behaviors. This was possible through analyzing appliance-level energy consumption footprints using a hybrid edge-cloud computing architecture. In [32], an energy management system was proposed to promote energy efficiency in IoT-based networks deployed in buildings. Genetic algorithms have been used to optimize energy usage during the operation of data sensing, processing and communication. In [49], the authors investigated a new methodology for incorporating big data analytics and ML into an intelligent platform that enables a smart building energy management. Accordingly, three different ML models have been deployed, i.e., random forest (RF), Rpart regression and deep neural networks (DNNs), along with dimensionality reduction strategies for creating an energy optimization method. Similarly, in [25], Machorro et al. introduced an AI-big data analytics framework, which has been integrated into the smart home energy management system to support energy efficiency, safety and building comfort. Typically, J48 ML model and Weka API have been used for (1) learning users' behaviors and load usage data and (2) classifying households with reference to their power consumption. Moreover, RuleML and Apache Mahout have been utilized for (1) generating energy-saving recommendations with reference to users' preferences and (2) preserving the buildings' comfort and safety.

Moving on, in [45], a smart energy consumption supervision platform is developed, which includes tree principal components for (1) data acquisition using IoT devices; (2) data integration using cloud data centers; and (3) big data analytics using energy consumption forecasting, anomaly and fault detection and differential management. This framework has been validated in a public building (at the South China University of Technology). Following a 3-year monitoring and application, the annual load usage of the pilot building has decreased by 35%. In [44], energy saving is achieved following four steps, which are summarized as follows: (1) Provide energy footprint visualizations and design smart suggestion models for assisting buildings' end-users and managers to analyze and develop demand plans based on electric equipment space occupancy; (2) use IoT for minimizing differences between predicted and real energy consumption; (3) accurately evaluate indoor environment comfort and improve equipment operation efficiency using quantized comfort rates; and (4) establish a persuasive energy efficiency workflow through providing personalized recommendations.

In [31], the authors developed an IoT-based smartphone energy-saving solution for endorsing end-users' energy-aware behaviors, namely IoT-based smartphone energy assistant (iSEA). Accordingly, this solution relies on tracking end-users' smartphones in a commercial building using deep learning model for identifying their energy consumption and delivering tailored and engaging advice to impact energy usage habits. It also employs an energy use efficiency index (EEI) for understanding end-users' behavior and categorizing it into efficient and energy-wasting activities. The iSEA architecture includes four layers: physical, cloud, service and communication. In [3], an AI-based energy-saving platform for residential buildings is developed, in which the micro-moment concept is used for providing an accurate comprehension of end-user energy consumption behaviors. This was made by (1) collecting energy micro-moments and ambient data using a set of IoT devices, (2) detecting abnormal profiles using an ensemble bagging tree (EBT) model and (3) formulating an ensemble of energy-efficient recommendations using a mobile app.

12.2.2 Energy saving based on thermal comfort optimization

It has been observed in different studies that building end-users are generally responsible for wasting a huge amount of energy, i.e., more than 50% in some cases, because of unnecessary heating, ventilation and air conditioning (HVAC) operation and sub-optimal thermal settings. Thus, there has been a move to develop energy-saving solutions based on optimizing thermal comfort. For instance, in [33], a non-intrusive energy-saving solution that can determine end-user behavior-based energy wastage related to the operation of the HVAC system in a typical building is developed. In this line, environmental patterns recorded from humidity and temperature sensors are fed into the ML models to infer energy-saving consumer behavior. In [48], an open IoT cloud-based platform is developed to promote energy efficiency of buildings' HVAC systems by using AI-big data analytics of different kinds of environmental data collected and aggregated using a fusion mechanism.

12.2.3 Energy saving using ML-based load forecasting

This kind of methods is receiving an increasing attention, especially with the appearance of deep learning, e.g., RNN, long short-term memory (LSTM) and bidirectional LSTM (Bi-LSTM) although they are usually complex [9,24]. In [7], Bedi at al. used IoT devices and ML models for promoting a sustainable and energy-efficient building environment. In this context, an energy prediction framework is developed using an exponential model and Elman recurrent neural network (RNN) model in an IoT-driven building. This technique forecasts load usage via (1) using different parameters, i.e., the historical energy consumption, ambient temperature and end-users occupancy states, and (2) detecting the relation between these parameters and utilizing it as an input for the developed techniques to improve the prediction accuracy. In the same way, in [46], the authors introduced a thermal energy forecasting approach using IoT devices and ensemble classifier. An online learning methodology has been adopted to train the predictive model using collected real sensor observations and hence has resulted in an optimized thermal energy consumption. In [30], a RF-based energy forecasting method is proposed, which is implemented on an hourly sampling rate. Similarly, energy forecasting in hotel buildings is conducted using a support vector machine (SVM)-based approach in [42]. In [10], an improved CNN model is used to design an energy prediction method based on cross-feature analysis, namely CNN-CF.

Moreover, in building automation systems (BASs), forecasting energy consumption is of significant importance to enable an effective management of energy, in which AI-big data analytics techniques play an essential role. In doing so, load patterns (and ambient conditions) are constantly collected from diverse building smart meters and then fed into the AI models to predict energy usage. Because of the real-time characteristic of short-term forecasting, it has been more challenging than generic forecasting. Thus, various AI-big data analytics models have been proposed [1,8,9,23,40]. In [30], a RF model is introduced to perform a short-term energy load prediction at an hourly sampling rate in various buildings by using different energy consumption datasets. In [41], the authors investigated the performance of diverse popular ML algorithms to predict buildings' heating and cooling energy usage. Accordingly, specific tuning has been carried out for every ML algorithm using two building energy consumption datasets generated in EnergyPlus and Ecotect. In [34], a transfer learning-based load prediction scheme is introduced, where energy consumption data of different buildings are used to forecast the load of a new building. This approach is able to work with various ML algorithms with pre- and post-processing phases.

Overall, developing robust and reliable energy-saving solutions has become simpler than ever before; however, it necessitates the complementarity of various technologies, i.e., IoT, AI and ML, ICT and smartphones. The latter help in modeling and predicting the operating efficiency of buildings and enabling end-users to promote energy-saving actions at the possibly lowest

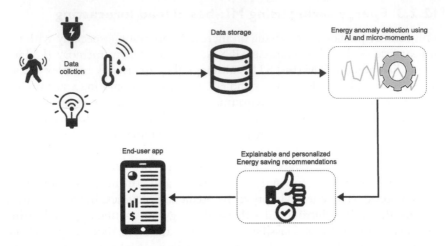

Figure 12.1 Overview of the proposed framework.

cost (with simple physical experiment). In what follows, we will present an effective energy-saving solution that employs AI and the micro-moments concepts, as well as a range of IoT sensors strategically placed around the space, to alter the abnormal energy consumption habits of end-users.

12.3 PROPOSED METHODOLOGY

The proposed framework was created to encourage consumers to modify their behavior by increasing their awareness of energy usage in private households and buildings [11,15]. It consists of four key steps: (1) data collection (i.e., consumption footprints and atmospheric conditions) from various appliances in academic buildings, (2) data processing (i.e., consumption footprints and atmospheric conditions) to extract energy micro-moments that help identify anomalies [19,35], (3) energy-saving-based recommendation generation [17] and (4) data visualization of the consumed power [2]. An illustration of the framework overview is shown in Figure 12.1.

12.3.1 Micro-moments concept

The notion of micro-moment was reintroduced by Google in 2015 as an adverting solution. Google defines a micro-moment as an intent-rich moment where decisions are made and preferences are established. These moments occur when a smart device users, for instance, turn to their phones to fulfill a need to learn something, explore something, purchase something or watch something[3]. These moments are critical for companies to under-

---

[3] https://www.thinkwithgoogle.com/.

stand since the appropriate intervention at the right micro-moment can increase user acceptance of a suggestion or recommendation. In the context of energy efficiency, micro-moments are described as brief periods of time during which a consumer can conduct an energy-related activity. Utilizing the micro-moment paradigm can be very beneficial in allocating the most suitable time to deliver energy-saving recommendations to the consumer and thus increasing the acceptance probability of such suggestions [16].

In this regard, aiming at identifying normal or abnormal consumption, a micro-moment analysis is conducted on the collected time series power consumption data. Therefore, the micro-moment classes are identified to describe power consumption observations of each appliance; they have been drawn using the occupancy profile analysis (O) and power consumption (P) of every domestic appliance with regard to device operation time (DOT), device standby power consumption (DSPC) and device active consumption range (DACR). In doing so, the micro-moment classes are defined as follows: class 0: Good usage refers to the case when power consumption is less than 95% of the maximum active consumption rate; class 1: Turning on the appliance refers to the micro-moment when the end-user turns an appliance on; and class 2: Turning off the appliance represents the micro-moment of switching off an appliance. These two classes are very important as they describe the intent-driven moments of decision making, i.e., starting a consumption or stopping it. Class 3: Excessive consumption is an abnormal consumption that is related to the case of having an excessive consumption, either by exceeding 95% of the maximum active consumption rate or by exceeding the DOT; and class 4: Consumption while outside refers to the case of consuming energy while the end-user is absent. This is considered as an abnormal consumption for an ensemble of device categories, including the air conditioner (A/C), television, light lamp, desktop/laptop and fan. Accordingly, for these kinds of appliances, the presence of the end-user during their operation is a must in order to not consider their energy consumption as abnormal. Table 12.1 summarizes the micro-moment classes defined and detected in this framework to analyze end-users' power consumption behavior.

Table 12.1 Micro-moment classes definition and description for anomaly detection

Label	Class	Micro-moment description
0	Good consumption	<95% of appliance's maximum active power consumption rate
1	Turn on	Switch on an appliance
2	Turn off	Switch off an appliance
3	Excessive consumption	>95% of appliance's maximum active power consumption rate
4	Consumption while outside	Appliance consumption if on while occupants are not present

---

Algorithm 12.1: Proposed rule-based algorithm for extracting power consumption micro-moment features

---

Result: M^2F: micro-moment feature vector
Read p, O, $DACR$, DOT, $DSPC$ and O_T: operation time;
Initialization: $M^2F=\varnothing$ **while** $t \leq l$ (with l is the length of the power signal) **do**
Rule 1: Non-excessive usage
if $p(t) \geq min(DACR)$ and $p(t) \leq 95\% \times max(DACR)$
    $M^2F(t)=0$ (Good usage);
Rule 2: Switching on a device
if $p(t) \geq min(DACR)$ and $p(t-1) \leq max(DSP\ C)$
    $M^2F(t)=1$ (Turn on device);
Rule 3: Switching off a device
if $p(t) \leq max(DSP\ C)$ and $p(t-1) \geq min\ (DACR)$
    $M^2F(t)=2$ (Turn off device);
Rule 4: Consumption exceeds 95% of DACR or DOT
if $p(t) \geq 95\% \times max(DACR)$ or $O_T\ (t) \geq DOT$
    $M^2F(t) = 3$ (Excessive consumption);
Rule 5: Consumption without presence of the end-user
if $O(t)=0$ and $p(t) \geq 0.95 \times DSPC$
    $M^2F(t)=4$ (consumption while outside);
end

The last two categories result in losing a huge amount of energy. Therefore, it is of paramount importance to detect this kind of anomalous consumption and thereby correct end-users' behavior. This is achieved via promoting end-users with personalized advice via the $(EM)^3$ mobile app, which notifies to take energy-saving actions when an anomalous consumption behavior is detected.

Moving on, Algorithm 12.1 describes the rule-based algorithm used to annotate energy consumption observations into the five micro-moment classes defined above, while Table 12.2 presents an example of the different appliance parameter specifications that are used in the rule-based algorithm to extract power consumption micro-moments.

12.3.2 Recommender system

The main objective of the RS is to gradually alter the consumer's routine, to elaborate, reducing the energy footprint of repetitive action. To do so, the energy-saving tips must be delivered at the right moment. In the recommendation message, a portion is devoted to explaining the rationale behind the triggering of each recommendation. Two main causes are accountable for triggering a recommendation, including the following:

Table 12.2 Power consumption specifications for different home appliances

Appliance	DOT	DACR (watts)	DSPC (watts)
Air conditioner	15 h 30 min	1,000	4
Microwave	1 h	1,200	7
Oven	3 h	2,400	6
Dishwasher	1 h 45 min	1,800	3
Laptop	12 h 42 min	100	20
Washing machine	1 h	500	6
Light	8 h	60	0
Television	12 h 42 min	65	6
Refrigerator	17 h 30 min	180	0
Desktop	12 h 42 min	250	12

- The knowledge that the user has left the room and left an appliance on, hence abusing electricity without need, and
- The user is occupying the room; however, the outside condition allows for turning off particular appliances and makes it possible to prevent dispensable usage.

12.3.3 Home-Assistant app

The majority of devices on the market today are cloud-enabled, making life easier for the average consumer. However, a paradigm shift will be brought about by the need to reduce transmission costs, avoid network latency and improve security and privacy, among other things. Home-Assistant is an open-source platform that helps to centralize all the sensors and gadgets available at home. The platform utilizes Message Queuing Telemetry Transport (MQTT), to communicate with other devices. Moreover, it encompasses an energy dashboard for making the visualization of energy consumption footprints super-easy for end-users. Therefore, it allows them to visualize at a quick glance how they are consuming energy every day, with other options, e.g., breaking down energy consumption per hour to have more in-depth and accurate insights.

12.3.4 Pilot installation

Multiple environmental modules are distributed among the different pilot locations, to measure different parameters (i.e., temperature, humidity and luminosity). Additionally, the room presence is detected using the supporting Home-Assistant app (i.e., Home-Assistant is the automation platform used for data management, visualization and analysis) includes a location tracking feature. In order to measure the power consumption of a variety of home appliances (e.g., monitor, laptop charger and kettle), our own designed and off-the-shelf smart plug solutions are utilized. The energy-saving tips are delivered to the supporting Home-Assistant app in the form of notifications. The participants of the study are asked to:

- Respond to the notifications by either accepting, rejecting or ignoring them.
- Solve a two-part survey to collect their views on energy saving before and after the study initiation.

The study questionnaire is undertaken with the goal of recognizing the energy-saving characteristics of consumers and offers foresight in order to predict how consumers can conserve energy on a daily basis.

12.4 EXPERIMENTAL RESULTS

In order to evaluate our energy-saving framework, a mini-pilot is initiated with a number of users having distinct electrical perspectives (up to 10 users) in various locations. The general setup in most locations is similar to the one shown in Figure 12.2. Participants were fairly distributed among

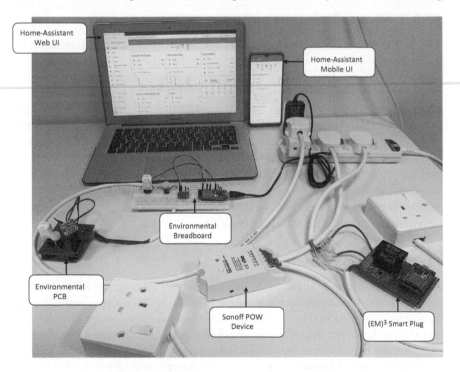

Figure 12.2 Overview of the testbed.

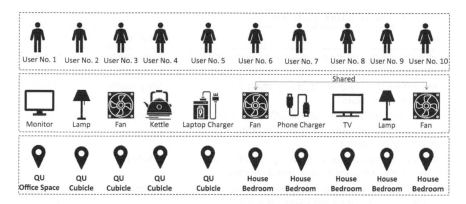

Figure 12.3 Visual map of the study sample size and characteristics.

the Qatar University (QU) buildings and various residential locations, as indicated in Figure 12.3.

12.4.1 Sample size and characteristics

To conduct the study, data were gathered from a total of ten participants, all of whom reside in Doha, Qatar. In terms of age groups, 60%, 20%, 10% and 10% of the participants are in 18–24, 25–34, 35–44 and 45–55 range, respectively. Additionally, 70% of the participants are females and 30% are males. Table 12.3 numerates the study demographics.

12.4.2 Survey overview

The distributed surveys are split into two sections, the first of which is delivered at the start of the study. The researchers will have an early sense of the participants' energy habits in the first section. The second section of the survey is provided at the end of the study to see whether there has been any behavior change as a result of participating in the pilot.

Aside from the questions given to determine the participant's gender, location, age group or occupation, we have prepared a list of questions to help

Table 12.3 Study demographics

Gender		Age		Profession	
Group	*Number*	*Group*	*Number*	*Group*	*Number*
Female	7	18–24	6	Student	2
Male	3	25–34	2	Researcher	6
		35–44	1	Academic staff	2
		45–54	1		

Table 12.4 Questionnaire questions

Questions	Max range	Min range
1 How much do you care about saving electricity in your home?	Very much	Not at all
2 How does the price of electricity affect your consumption habits?	Very much	Not at all
3 How often do you turn off the AC when you temporarily leave your living area at home (e.g. your bedroom)?	Always	Rarely
4 How often do you turn off the lights when you temporarily leave your living area at home?	Always	Rarely
5 How often do you disconnect power of your computer/tablet when you temporarily leave your living area at home?	Always	Rarely
6 What is the role of technology in changing energy consumption behavior?	Significant	Minor

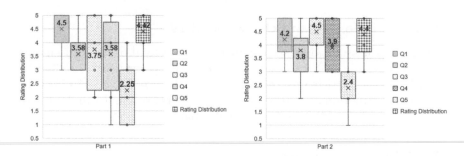

Figure 12.4 Visualization of the results of the questionnaire: (a) beginning and (b) end of the pilot.

us in recognizing the participants' behavior or habits toward energy saving. The list of questions is demonstrated in Table 12.4.

12.4.3 Results and discussion

12.4.3.1 Response analysis

To analyze the participants' responses, we employed the use of box and whisker plots since they are effective and easy to study. As in Figure 12.4, a clear increase is observed in the mean values of the questionnaire questions in Table 12.4, from the beginning and the end of the study period. This might indicate that the participants have gained a better grasp of how to preserve energy and are now aware of the economic and environmental consequences of their excessive consumption throughout the day.

Table 12.5 Part 2 questionnaire questions

Questions	Max range	Min range
1 How much would the provided data analytics through the mobile app impact your energy consumption in the future?	Very much	Not at all
2 How often did you receive energy-saving recommendations through the mobile app?	Always	Never
3 How often did you interact to the received recommendation notifications via the mobile app?	Always	Never
4 How often would you use the mobile application to visualize power consumption and/or other collected data?	Always	Never
5 How would you describe the change in your attitude towards energy conservation as a result of your involvement in the study?	Major	Minor

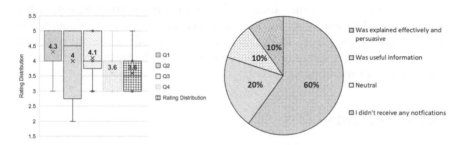

Figure 12.5 Visualization of the participants' evaluation of the framework: (a) questions and answers found in Table 12.5; (b) assessment of the recommendations.

12.4.3.2 Usefulness evaluation

In order to establish a viewpoint on the usefulness of the different components of the framework, a list of questions were included in the final questionnaire. The questions are shown in Table 12.5. The participants' answers are demonstrated in Figure 12.5. Most of the questions are answered with a mean of above 3.6. Furthermore, when asked to describe the energy-saving advice they got during the course of the study, 80% of the participants gave a positive response.

12.5 CONCLUSIONS

In this paper, we presented an energy-saving solution that is based on the complementarity of different technologies. The proposed framework employs AI and the micro-moments concepts, as well as a range of IoT sensors strategically placed around the space, to alter particular habit patterns.

According to the habit loop, a person must go through a cue, a routine and a reward. A RS is used in this change cycle because it associates the action with the reward, thereby reinforcing the new habit, in which alerts with energy-saving advice are delivered to users via the Home-Assistant app. To evaluate our energy-saving framework, a mini-pilot is launched with numerous users from diverse regions who have different electrical views (up to 10 users). The outcomes of the study indicate the positive effects of implementing AI, IoT and RSs to facilitate energy efficiency.

Nevertheless, the current implementation has a number of limitations, as the current sensing can be enhanced by using more accurate measuring chips (e.g., HLW8012). In addition, in terms of cybersecurity, the current implementation lacks the defense mechanisms against different cyber-attacks as it mainly relies on the edge computing security, which is not enough in some situations. To that end, it will be part of our future work to investigate the use of the cutting-edge cybersecurity techniques, such as the blockchain to reinforce the security on the edge devices and address users' privacy concerns and other security issues in some scenarios, e.g., when there is a need to send data to cloud data centers for further complex processing. Moreover, future work could include expanding the study sample size to involve more views and opinion to observe the framework response with a wider range of participants.

ACKNOWLEDGMENTS

This paper was made possible by National Priorities Research Program (NPRP) Grant No. 10-0130-170288 from the Qatar National Research Fund (a member of Qatar Foundation). Additionally, this study was made possible by the Graduate Assistantship (GA) program provided by Qatar University (QU). The authors are thankful to Mr. Adullah Alsalemi for his help in preparing the questionnaire. The statements made herein are solely the responsibility of the authors.

ETHICAL APPROVAL

The study was reviewed and approved by Qatar University Institutional Review Board (QU-IRB) with approval reference number: QU-IRB 1616-EA/21.

BIBLIOGRAPHY

1. T. Ahmad and H. Chen. Utility companies strategy for short-term energy demand forecasting using machine learning based models. *Sustainable Cities and Society*, 39:401–417, 2018.

2. A. Al-Kababji, A. Alsalemi, Y. Himeur, F. Bensaali, A. Amira, R. Fernandez, and N. Fetais. Interactive visual analytics for residential energy big data. *Inform. Vis*, pages 1–20, 2020.

3. A. Alsalemi, Y. Himeur, F. Bensaali, A. Amira, C. Sardianos, I. Varlamis, and G. Dimitrakopoulos. Achieving domestic energy efficiency using micro-moments and intelligent recommendations. *IEEE Access*, 8: 15047–15055, 2020.

4. A. Alsalemi, Y. Himeur, F. Bensaali, and A. Amira. Smart sensing and end-user behavioral change in residential buildings: An edge internet of energy perspective. *IEEE Sensors Journal*, 21(24): 27623–27631, 2021.

5. A. Alsalemi, Y. Himeur, F. Bensaali, A. Amira, C. Sardianos, C. Chronis, I. Varlamis, and G. Dimitrakopoulos. A micro-moment system for domestic energy efficiency analysis. *IEEE Systems Journal*, 15(1): 1256–1263, 2020.

6. N. Bansal. Iot applications in energy. In *Designing Internet of Things Solutions with Microsoft Azure*, pages 115–134. Springer. Apress Berkeley, CA, 2020.

7. G. Bedi, G. K. Venayagamoorthy, and R. Singh. Development of an iot-driven building environment for prediction of electric energy consumption. *IEEE Internet of Things Journal*, 7(6): 4912–4921, 2020.

8. J.-S. Chou and D.-S. Tran. Forecasting energy consumption time series using machine learning techniques based on usage patterns of residential householders. *Energy*, 165: 709–726, 2018.

9. S. Fathi, R. Srinivasan, A. Fenner, and S. Fathi. Machine learning applications in urban building energy performance forecasting: A systematic review. *Renewable and Sustainable Energy Reviews*, 133: 110287, 2020.

10. Z. Geng, Y. Zhang, C. Li, Y. Han, Y. Cui, and B. Yu. Energy optimization and prediction modeling of petrochemical industries: An improved convolutional neural network based on cross-feature. *Energy*, 194: 116851, 2020.

11. Y. Himeur, A. Elsalemi, F. Bensaali, and A. Amira. Recent trends of smart non-intrusive load monitoring in buildings: A review, open challenges and future directions. *International Journal of Intelligent Systems*, pages 1–28, 2020. doi.org/10.1002/int.22876

12. Y. Himeur, A. Elsalemi, F. Bensaali, and A. Amira. Detection of appliance-level abnormal energy consumption in buildings using autoencoders and micro-moments. In *The fifth International Conference on Big Data and Internet of Things (BDIoT)*, pages 1–13, 2021.

13. Y. Himeur, A. Alsalemi, A. Al-Kababji, F. Bensaali, and A. Amira. Data fusion strategies for energy efficiency in buildings: Overview, challenges and novel orientations. Information Fusion, 64: 99–120, 2020.

14. Y. Himeur, A. Alsalemi, A. Al-Kababji, F. Bensaali, A. Amira, C. Sardianos, G. Dimitrakopoulos, and I. Varlamis. A survey of recommender systems for energy efficiency in buildings: Principles, challenges and prospects. *Information Fusion*, 72: 1–21, 2021.

15. Y. Himeur, A. Alsalemi, F. Bensaali, and A. Amira. Effective non-intrusive load monitoring of buildings based on a novel multi-descriptor fusion with dimensionality reduction. *Applied Energy*, 279: 115872, 2020.

16. Y. Himeur, A. Alsalemi, F. Bensaali, and A. Amira. A novel approach for detecting anomalous energy consumption based on micro-moments and deep neural networks. *Cognitive Computation*, 12(6): 1381–1401, 2020.

17. Y. Himeur, A. Alsalemi, F. Bensaali, and A. Amira. The emergence of hybrid edge-cloud computing for energy efficiency in buildings. In *Proceedings of SAI Intelligent Systems Conference*, pages 70–83. Springer, 2021.

18. Y. Himeur, A. Alsalemi, F. Bensaali, and A. Amira. Smart power consumption abnormality detection in buildings using micromoments and improved k-nearest neighbors. *International Journal of Intelligent Systems*, 36(6): 2865–2894, 2021.

19. Y. Himeur, A. Alsalemi, F. Bensaali, A. Amira, I. Varlamis, G. Bravos, C. Sardianos, and G. Dimitrakopoulos. Marketability of building energy efficiency systems based on behavioral change: A case study of a novel micromoments based solution. *arXiv preprint arXiv*, 2020.

20. Y. Himeur, K. Ghanem, A. Alsalemi, F. Bensaali, and A. Amira. Artificial intelligence based anomaly detection of energy consumption in buildings: A review, current trends and new perspectives. *Applied Energy*, 287: 116601, 2021.

21. N. Hossein Motlagh, M. Mohammadrezaei, J. Hunt, and B. Zakeri. Internet of things (iot) and the energy sector. *Energies*, 13(2): 494, 2020.

22. P. Inyim, M. Batouli, M. Presa Reyes, T. Carmenate, L. Bobadilla, and A. Mostafavi. A smartphone application for personalized and multi-method interventions toward energy saving in buildings. *Sustainability*, 10(6): 1744, 2018.

23. S. Li, P. Wang, and L. Goel. A novel wavelet-based ensemble method for short-term load forecasting with hybrid neural networks and feature selection. *IEEE Transactions on Power Systems*, 31(3): 1788–1798, 2015.

24. X.J. Luo, L. O. Oyedele, A. O. Ajayi, and O. O. Akinade. Comparative study of machine learning-based multi-objective prediction framework for multiple building energy loads. *Sustainable Cities and Society*, 61: 102283, 2020.

25. I. Machorro-Cano, G. Alor-Hernández, M. Andrés Paredes-Valverde, L. Rodríguez-Mazahua, J. Luis Sánchez-Cervantes, and J. Oscar Olmedo-Aguirre. Hems-iot: A big data and machine learning-based smart home system for energy saving. *Energies*, 13(5): 1097, 2020.

26. M. M. Martín-Lopo, J. Boal, and Á. Sánchez-Miralles. A literature review of iot energy platforms aimed at end users. *Computer Networks*, 171: 107101, 2020.

27. G. H. Merabet, M. Essaaidi, M. B. Haddou, B. Qolomany, J. Qadir, M. Anan, A. Al-Fuqaha, M. R. Abid, and D. Benhaddou. Intelligent building control systems for thermal comfort and energy-efficiency: A systematic review of artificial intelligence-assisted techniques. *Renewable and Sustainable Energy Reviews*, 144: 110969, 2021.

28. C. K. Metallidou, K. E. Psannis, and E. Alexandropoulou Egyptiadou. Energy efficiency in smart buildings: Iot approaches. *IEEE Access*, 8: 63679–63699, 2020.

29. P. Pawar, M. TarunKumar, et al. An iot based intelligent smart energy management system with accurate forecasting and load strategy for renewable generation. *Measurement*, 152: 107187, 2020.

30. A.-D. Pham, N.-T. Ngo, T. T. Ha Truong, N.-T. Huynh, and N.-S. Truong. Predicting energy consumption in multiple buildings using machine learning for improving energy efficiency and sustainability. *Journal of Cleaner Production*, 260: 121082, 2020.

31. H. N. Rafsanjani, A. Ghahramani, and A. Hossein Nabizadeh. ISEA: Iot-based smartphone energy assistant for prompting energy-aware behaviors in commercial buildings. *Applied Energy*, 266: 114892, 2020.

32. M. Raval, S. Bhardwaj, A. Aravelli, J. Dofe, and H. Gohel. Smart energy optimization for massive iot using artificial intelligence. *Internet of Things*, 13: 100354, 2021.

33. R. Raza, N. U. L Hassan, and C. Yuen. Determination of consumer behavior based energy wastage using iot and machine learning. *Energy and Buildings*, 220: 110060, 2020.

34. M. Ribeiro, K. Grolinger, H. F. ElYamany, W. A. Higashino, and M. A. M. Capretz. Transfer learning with seasonal and trend adjustment for cross-building energy forecasting. *Energy and Buildings*, 165: 352–363, 2018.

35. C. Sardianos, C. Chronis, I. Varlamis, G. Dimitrakopoulos, Y. Himeur, A. Alsalemi, F. Bensaali, and A. Amira. Smart fusion of sensor data and human feedback for personalised energy-saving recommendations. *International Journal of Intelligent Systems*, pages 1–20, 2021.

36. C. Sardianos, I. Varlamis, C. Chronis, G. Dimitrakopoulos, A. Alsalemi, Y. Himeur, F. Bensaali, and A. Amira. The emergence of explainability of intelligent systems: Delivering explainable and personalized recommendations for energy efficiency. *International Journal of Intelligent Systems*, 36(2): 656–680, 2021.

37. C. Sardianos, I. Varlamis, C. Chronis, G. Dimitrakopoulos, Y. Himeur, A. Alsalemi, F. Bensaali, and A. Amira. Data analytics, automations, and micro-moment based recommendations for energy efficiency. In *2020 IEEE Sixth International Conference on Big Data Computing Service and Applications (BigDataService)*, pages 96–103. IEEE, 2020.

38. C. Sardianos, I. Varlamis, C. Chronis, G. Dimitrakopoulos, Y. Himeur, A. Alsalemi, F. Bensaali, and A. Amira. A model for predicting room occupancy based on motion sensor data. In *2020 IEEE International Conference on Informatics, IoT, and Enabling Technologies (ICIoT)*, pages 394–399. IEEE, 2020.

39. C. Sardianos, I. Varlamis, G. Dimitrakopoulos, D. Anagnostopoulos, A. Alsalemi, F. Bensaali, Y. Himeur, and A. Amira. Rehab-c: Recommendations for energy habits change. *Future Generation Computer Systems*, 112: 394–407, 2020.

40. S. Seyedzadeh, F. P. Rahimian, I. Glesk, and M. Roper. Machine learning for estimation of building energy consumption and performance: A review. *Visualization in Engineering*, 6(1): 1–20, 2018.

41. S. Seyedzadeh, F. P. Rahimian, P. Rastogi, and I. Glesk. Tuning machine learning models for prediction of building energy loads. *Sustainable Cities and Society*, 47:101484, 2019.

42. M. Shao, X. Wang, Z. Bu, X. Chen, and Y. Wang. Prediction of energy consumption in hotel buildings via support vector machines. *Sustainable Cities and Society*, 57: 102128, 2020.

43. C. Tomazzoli, S. Scannapieco, and M. Cristani. Internet of things and artificial intelligence enable energy efficiency. *Journal of Ambient Intelligence and Humanized Computing*, pages 1–22, 2020.

44. I. Wu, C.-C. Liu, et al. A visual and persuasive energy conservation system based on bim and iot technology. *Sensors*, 20(1):139, 2020.

45. L. Xing, B. Jiao, Y. Du, X. Tan, and R. Wang. Intelligent energy-saving supervision system of urban buildings based on the internet of things: A case study. *IEEE Systems Journal*, 14(3): 4252–4261, 2020.

46. H. Xu, Y. He, X. Sun, J. He, and Q. Xu. Prediction of thermal energy inside smart homes using iot and classifier ensemble techniques. *Computer Communications*, 151: 581–589, 2020.

47. B. Yan, F. Hao, and X. Meng. When artificial intelligence meets building energy efficiency, a review focusing on zero energy building. *Artificial Intelligence Review*, 54(3): 2193–2220, 2021.

48. Y. Yu. Ai chiller: An open IoT cloud based machine learning framework for the energy saving of building hvac system via big data analytics on the fusion of bms and environmental data. *arXiv preprint arXiv:2011.01047*, 2020.
49. M. Zekić-Sušac, S. Mitrović, and A. Has. Machine learning based system for managing energy efficiency of public sector as an approach towards smart cities. *International Journal of Information Management*, 58: 102074, 2021.

Index

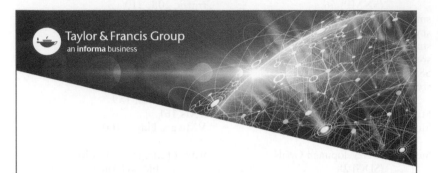